SEASONS
to taste

LAURIE STOVALL BABCOCK

© 2009 by Robert D. Babcock

All rights reserved. Published 2009.

ISBN: 9780977952366

Printed in China

Published by Blackwell Press, Lynchburg, Virginia
www.BlackwellPress.net

To order:
Send $35 plus $5 shipping
(Virginia residents add $1.75) to:
Seasons to Taste
1300 Court Street
Lynchburg, VA 24504

Proceeds from the sale of *Seasons to Taste* will benefit Daily Bread, Lynchburg Grows, and the Lynchburg Humane Society.

This book is dedicated to the many people in my life who have shared their love of cooking with me. Many of the recipes have been adapted from old family favorites or have been graciously given for me to include in this collection. A special thanks goes to my mother and two grandmothers who inspired me with their love of cooking and hospitality.

Writing this book has been a major effort for me because of the challenge —the overwhelming number of cookbooks available. I persevered, however, because I felt I had such an incredible collection of recipes, compiled over my fifteen years in the catering business. Many of the recipes became favorites at our parties and it is for this reason that I wanted to share them with you.

For many years people have shared their favorite recipes with me. Because I was in the catering business, it gave me the opportunity to not only try them once or twice, but many times. Each recipe became individualized through adjustments in ingredients, seasonings and directions. I encouraged and received much feedback both in my kitchen and from guests at the various events.

In designing my cookbook, I decided to divide it into sections around the four seasons, as if each section were a party held at a certain time of the year. You will find that most of my recipes include fresh ingredients because I like to use things that are at their peak flavor. Each season will include appetizers, salads, entrees, breads, soups and desserts. Some will have extra sections, such as a canning section for the summer harvest. The seasonal theme though is only a guideline and many of the recipes can and should cross over to all the seasons.

—Laurie Stovall Babcock,
1952–2005

I do not like to use prepackaged or convenience foods in my cooking. Most of my recipes will instruct you on canning your own sauces, seasonings and marinades. There are no short cuts to good cooking, but the result is well worth the effort. The title of the book was a fitting summary of how I cook, *Seasons To Taste*. All food should be tasted and adjusted for just the right amount of seasoning, no matter how carefully you follow a recipe.

Laurie's Gift

Seasons To Taste is a parting tribute—not only to Laurie but to those of you who knew her. As you read this cookbook, enjoy the recipes with family and friends, remember that creating this book was Laurie's parting gift. She wanted to leave something to remember her by—and what would be more fitting than a cookbook full of delicious seasonal recipes selected by her personally for you to enjoy.

Laurie took great pleasure in finishing *Seasons To Taste* before her death. She worked hard to introduce menus inspired by each season's special foods. She loved the thought of sharing the recipes that she had cooked so often to bring pleasure to friends and patrons. *Seasons To Taste* is Laurie's legacy. It is hoped that a special familiar recipe, a notation, or maybe a hand drawing by her daughter, Tucker, will jog a fond memory of Laurie with you.

Laurie was blessed with a large family of relatives and friends. She was wife to husband Bobby; mother to daughter Tucker; sister to Meg, Brack, and Bill; and friend to many. Born in Lynchburg in 1952 to Margaret and Brack Stovall, Laurie remained a Lynchburg resident until her death from complications from Scleroderma in 2005. She was the granddaughter of noted folk artist Queena Stovall and the Rev. Graham Gilmer who served as pastor of Rivermont Presbyterian Church for 30 years.

Laurie started cooking with her mother and grandmothers, Queena and Ma Gilmer, at an early age. She loved to cook and entertain and was expert at both in her career as a professional caterer. Laurie's hospitality was far-reaching.

One thank you note, in particular from the hundreds she received from patrons, is worth mentioning because it expresses the essence of Laurie's catering skills. It was written on November 6, 1988 by Jane White of Lynchburg:

Those of us involved in the production of *Seasons To Taste* share our sincerest thanks to Laurie for enriching our lives, our homes, and for sharing her favorite seasonal recipes for us to enjoy.

Dear Laurie,

This is my unsolicited testimonial—just in case you need a boost!

We were totally pleased, and thrilled even, with every aspect of your catering for the wedding reception. It was a colossal undertaking—at least for me—but perhaps not for you because you handled every detail with the greatest efficiency and serenity and the end result was perfect. The menu, but more importantly the taste of all the food, was delicious and its display festive, memorable and appealing.

I would be delighted to endorse you for any project you might undertake and we feel very fortunate to have been the beneficiary of your services for one most special event.

With thanks,

Jane

Contents

FOREWORD
A Tradition of Family Hospitality
   By Meg Stovall Laughon
      In loving memory of my sister, Laurie. xix

PREFACE
To Everything There Is a Season xxi

ACKNOWLEDGEMENTS xxii

SPRING

Appetizers

Marinated Shrimp and Artichokes 3
Indian Chicken Spread 4
Smoked Salmon Canapés 5
Cheese Canape Shells 5
Eggplant Caponata 6
Spinach Phyllo Triangles 7
Fresh Herb Dip 8
Vegetable Crudités 9
Mediterranean Cheese Spread 11
Mushroom Tarts 12
Lamb Sausage Meatballs 13
Hummus Spread 14
Hummus with Roasted Red Pepper 15

Beverages

The Cocktail Bar 16
Minted Whiskey Sour 17
Mimosa 18
Wedding Punch 18
Dandelion Wine 19
Lu's Iced Tea 20

Soups

Creamy Vidalia Soup 21
Hot and Sour Soup 22
Lentil and Mushroom Stew 23
Cannellini and Vegetable Soup 24
Cucumber Gazpacho 25

Salads

Creamy Lemon Dijon Vinaigrette 26
Curried Shrimp Salad 26
Spring Salad with Buttermilk Dressing 27
Lamb Salad with Yogurt Dressing 28
Sally's Cucumber Aspic with Mint Mayonnaise 29

Spring

Entrees

Mediterranean Shrimp Pasta	30
Salmon Moutard	31
Roasted Leg of Lamb	32
Louise's Mint Sauce	32
Corned Beef and Oven Steamed Vegetables	33
Deep-Fried Soft Shell Crabs	34
Mushroom and Chicken Crêpes	35
Duck Breast with Porcini Wine Sauce	36
Fancy Baked Chicken	37
Margaret's Funeral Casserole	38
Country Chicken Salad	39
Southern Fried Chicken	40
Spicy Chicken Milk Gravy	41

Side Dishes

Baked Herb Pasta	42
Mississippi Green Beans	43
Black Beans and Saffron Rice	44

Desserts

Chocolate Mousse	45
Irresistible Brownies with variations	46
Raspberry Shortbread	48
Chocolate Mousse Tarts	49
Carrot Wedding Cake	50
Lemon Poppy Seed Pound Cake	51
Frozen Lemon Soufflé	52
Lemon Butter	53
Reese's Gateau Ganache	54
Little Bits	55
Chocolate Buttermilk Cake	56
Butter Cream Frosting	57
Ma's Strawberry Shortcake	58
Agnes's Pound Cake	60

Spring

Breads
Irish Soda Bread 61
Four Cheeses Focaccia 62
Cousin Martha Grune's Sally Lunn. 63
Helen's Sally Lunn Bread 64
Buttermilk Biscuits 65
Challah 66
Cinnamon Raisin Bread 67

Brunches
Holden Beach Eggs Benedict 68
Mushroom Quiche 69
Date Nut Breakfast Muffins 70
Cheese Fondue Casserole 71
Spring Shad Roe 72

SUMMER

Appetizers
Crabmeat Tarts 75
Cream Cheese Tart Shells 75
Tomato Pies 76
Garden Quesadillas 77
Goat Cheese Quesadillas 78
Greek Dolmades 79
Yogurt Dressing 80
Shrimp and Cilantro Rollups 81
Oriental Crab Salad 82

Beverages
Rum Painkiller 83
Caribbean Delight 83
Café Margarita 84
Bahama Mama 84
Wine Punch 85
Dave's Whiskey Sour 85
Chilly Irishman 85

Soups
Creamed Zucchini Soup 86
Fresh Peach Soup 87
Chloknik 88
Gazpacho 89
Toni's Chilled Beet Borscht 90

Salads
Black Bean and Rice Salad 91
Roasted Corn Salad with Lime Vinaigrette ... 92
Tomato Aspic 93
Coleslaw Dressing 94
Broccoli Picnic Salad 95
Cobb Salad 96
Cucumbers in Sour Cream Sauce 97
Summer Rice Salad 98

Summer

Entrees

Shrimp and Cannellini Beans.....................100
Chesapeake Bay Crab Cakes....................101
Suck Mountain Barbeque Sauce..................102
Becca's Burgers.................................103
Daddy's Barbequed Chicken....................104
Grilled Chuck Steak............................105
Pork Barbeque Sauce for Ribs..................106
Peach Barbeque Rib Sauce.....................107
Grilled Beef Tenderloin........................108
Deviled Crab Meat.............................109
Chicken Salad.................................110
Inglewood Road Barbeque Sauce for Chicken.......111
Crispy Baby Back Ribs.........................112
Grilled Tandori Chicken........................113

Side Dishes

Grilled Yams..................................114
Chinese Noodles..............................115
Easy No-Fail Corn on the Cob..................116
Uncle William's Corn Pudding..................117
Grilled Eggplant Pasta.........................118
Three Baked Bean Pot.........................119
Yellow Squash Casserole......................120
Grilled Chipotle Corn on the Cob...............121
Curry Stuffed Potatoes........................122
Indian Green Beans...........................123
Catherine's Tomato Casserole..................124

Summer

Desserts

- Kathie's Amaretti Nut Crunch Pie 125
- Butter Layer Cake. 126
- Raspberry Almond Cake............................. 127
- Chocolate Mocha Cake............................. 128
- Fresh Peach Cake................................. 129
- Chocolate Pound Cake 130
- Cissa's Almond Squares........................... 131
- Romanov Fruit Sauce.............................. 132
- Momma's Banana Split Pie 133
- Peach Ice Cream.................................. 134
- Strawberry Banana Nut Ice Cream 135
- Nana's Mile High Birthday Cake................... 136

Canning

- Bread and Butter Pickle 139
- Green Tomato Pickle 140
- Cucumber Relish 141
- Pickled Dilly Beans 142
- Pickled Eggplant 143
- Dill Pickles..................................... 144
- Pickled Jalapeño Peppers.......................... 145
- Tomato Marmalade 146
- Ginger Preserves 147
- Strawberry Preserves 148
- Tomato Juice..................................... 149
- Peach and Habanero Salsa 150
- Summer Marinara Sauce 151
- Summer Pesto..................................... 152
- Tomato Chutney................................... 153
- Peach Chutney 154
- Picking Cherries Jubilee 155
- Figs in Wine Sauce 156

xi

FALL

Appetizers
Roasted Garlic Spread.......................... 159
Spicy Crab and Artichoke Dip 160
Sausage Swirl Canapés.......................... 161
Mushroom Pate 162
Fresh Tomato Bruschetta........................ 163
Party Crab Mold................................ 164
Beer Cheese 165
Smoked Trout Spread............................ 166
Lucy-and-Her Shrimp............................ 167
Oven Fried Oysters............................. 168
Smoked Salmon Lox 169

Soups
Corn Chowder................................... 170
White Chili 171
Virginia's Brunswick Stew 172
Brunswick Stew For A Crowd 173
Potato Leek Soup with Truffle Oil 174
Sweet Potato and Jalapeño Soup................. 175
Beans and Greens Soup 176
Westport Fish Chowder.......................... 177
Shrimp Bisque.................................. 178
Mulligatawny Soup 179

Salads
Fresh Pear Salad 180
French Vinaigrette Dressing.................... 181
Nutty Oriental Slaw............................ 182
Jellied Seafood Salad.......................... 183
Indian Salad................................... 184
Apple and Fennel Salad......................... 185
Congealed Cranberry Salad 186

Fall

Entrees

- Muffulettas 187
- Aged Standing Rib Roast 188
- Pork Chops with Creamy Chipotle Sauce 189
- Pork Roast with Apple Cider Sauce 190
- Spicy Baby Back Ribs with Salsa Verde 191
- Southwest Seared Tuna 192
- Elegant Shrimp Crêpes 193
- Rosemary Chicken Thighs 195
- Easy Chicken Divan 196
- Chicken Enchiladas 197
- Roasted Turkey and Gravy 198
- Venison 199
- Doves 200
- Quail 201
- Pheasant Breast 202
- Flossie's Turkey Pot Pie 203
- Picnic Chicken Strips 204

Side Dishes

- Potatoes Au Gratin 205
- Rosalie's Deviled Eggs 206
- Green Bean and Potato Salad 207
- Stuffed Banana Peppers 208
- Spicy Chiles and Grits 209
- Creamy Herb Risotto 210
- Curry Butter Bean Casserole 211
- Apricot Kugel 212
- Thanksgiving Dressing for Turkey 213
- Southwest Sweet Potato Casserole 214

Desserts

- Estelle's Oatmeal Lace Cookies 215
- Mrs. Jones' Fried Pies 216
- Pecan Pie 217
- Easy Apple Crisp 218
- Cranberry Dessert Cheese 219
- Black Forest Cake 220
- Caramel Cake 221
- Toffee Ice Cream Torte 222

Fall

Fresh Apple Cake 223
Cider Sorbet 224
Greg's Best Chocolate Chip Cookies 225
Mississippi Mud Squares 226
Date Nut Filled Cookies 227

Breads

Cheese Biscuits 228
Jalapeño Hush Puppies 229
Refrigerated Blueberry Muffins 230
Risen Muffins 231
Honey Sweet Wheat Bread 232
Black Russian Yeast Bread 233
Onion Dill Bread 234

Brunches

Jammin' Muffins 235
Swiss Apple Quiche 236
Sante Fe Granola 237
David Hugh's Blueberry Pancakes 238
Cornmeal Waffles 239
Cornbatter Cakes 240
Hot Fruit Compote 241
Smoked Salmon Hash with Poached Egg 242
Open Faced Crab Sandwich 244
Bran Raisin Muffins 245
Orange Swirl Sweet Rolls 246
Rhonda's Banana Bread 247
Fresh Peach Coffee Cake 248

WINTER

Appetizers

Mississippi Cheese 251
Cheese Straws 252
Holiday Stuffed Mushrooms 253
Country Layered Pâté 254
Christmas Pâté 255
Smoked Oyster Spread 256
Shrimp Mousse 257
Creamed Mushrooms and Peppers 258
Meatballs in Chutney Sauce 259
Baked Crab Dip 260
Hot Chile Chicken Dip 261
Piccadillo Dip 262

Beverages

Hot Mulled Cider 263
Kate's Eggnog Punch 264
Hot Buttered Rum 265
Russian Tea Mix 266
Hot Cocoa Mix 267

Soups

Lamb and Navy Bean Soup 268
Hearty Green Soup 269
Chili 270
Tucker's Soup for Supper 271
Black Bean Soup 272
Cheddar Cheese Chowder 274
Cream of Broccoli and Stilton Soup 275
Oyster Stew 276
Manhattan Seafood Chowder 277
Marge's Split Pea Soup 278
Carrot and Parsnip Soup with Orange 279
Southwest Chicken and Hominy Stew 280

Winter

Winter

Salads
Warmed Tuscan Bean Salad 281
Cherry Fruit Salad 282
Winter Salad 283
John Tucker Percy's Dressing 284
Grapefruit Aspic 285

Entrees
Boeuf Au Pot 286
Orla's Chicken and Shrimp Spaghetti 287
Sausage and Rice Casserole 288
Polly's Pot Luck 288
Sea Scallops in Saffron Sauce 289
Cajun Seafood Gumbo 290
Chicken Curry with Seven Boys 292
Garlic Roasted Chicken 293
Chinese Glazed Chicken Wings 294
Pork Tenderloin with Apples and Mustard Glaze 295
Wild Duck 296
Braised Pheasant with Sour Cream and Grapes 297
Pizza or Focaccia Dough 298
Lemon Thyme Stuffed Chicken Breast 300
Caribbean Chicken Sandwich 301

Side Dishes
Shredded Potato Casserole 302
Country Snaps with Cucumber Garnish 303
Wild Rice and Mushroom Casserole 304
Caramelized Onions with Pasta 305
Spinach and Artichoke Casserole 306
Baked Herb Tomatoes 307
Meg's Company Beans 308

Desserts
Virginia Jefferson's Chocolate Tarts 309
Brown Sugar Ginger Crisps 310
Gum Drop Cookies 311
Winnie's Three Layer Candy 312
Danish Pudding Cake 313
Kakkie's Christmas Cookies 314

Winter

Christmas Gingerbread Boys................... 315
English Trifle............................... 316
Cherry Cobbler Jubilee....................... 317
Caramel Pound Cake........................... 318
Caramel Glaze................................ 319
Fresh Ginger Pound Cake...................... 320
Rum Cake..................................... 321
Chocolate Yule Log........................... 322
Rich Fudge Frosting.......................... 323
Mushroom Meringues........................... 324
Christmas Cookies For Man's Best Friend...... 325

Breads

Sopaipillas.................................. 326
Ro's Oatmeal Bread........................... 327
Cheese Bread with Jalapeño................... 328
Judy's Corn Sticks........................... 329
Country Spoon Bread.......................... 330

Brunches

Creamed Eggs................................. 331
Huevos Rancheros............................. 332
Christmas Morning Buckwheat Cakes............ 333
Melissa's Sour Cream Coffee Cake............. 334
Fresh Blueberry Coffee Cake.................. 335
Caramel Sticky Buns.......................... 336
Orange Poppy Seed Muffins.................... 337

All Seasons

FOR ALL SEASONS

Sauces

Ginger Dipping Sauce 341
Sesame Sauce 342
Plum Sauce 343
Horseradish Sauce for Tenderloin 343
No Fail Bearnaise 344
Spicy Steak Sauce 345
Chipotle Mayonnaise 345
Caper Sauce 346
Seafood Cocktail Sauce 346
Ginger Sauce 347
Garden Dill Sauce 348
Hollandaise 348
Chocolate Fondue Sauce 349
Raspberry Sauce 350

Mom's Biscuits 351

Foreword

A Tradition of Family Hospitality
By Meg Stovall Laughon

IN LOVING MEMORY OF MY SISTER, LAURIE

Laurie took great pleasure in finishing this cookbook. In spite of her illness, she worked hard to introduce menus inspired by each season's special foods. She loved the thought of sharing the recipes that she had cooked so often to bring pleasure to her family, friends and customers.

In the last weeks of her life, Laurie was putting the finishing touches on writing this cookbook. She had jotted down notes on fall and winter but her strength failed before she was able to write the introductions to the last two seasons. I believe that if Laurie had been able, she would have concluded her introduction by sharing some familiar remembrances we both have of our mother and grandmothers and their love for cooking.

Laurie's summertime kitchen always resonated with recollections of the busy, sociable kitchens of our grandmothers. Our grandmother Gilmer (Ma) and grandmother Stovall (Grandma) had kitchens running full steam to deal with the abundant produce of their gardens and to prepare meals for family and friends.

Laurie's kitchen, where so much good food was prepared for good friends and happy occasions, was a natural extension of the kitchens of our mother and grandmothers. For her, as for all of them, hospitality was a huge part of life.

Even though modern kitchen conveniences had taken the place of the churns, wood stoves and slop cans for the pigs of our grandmothers' kitchens, the generous spirit of earlier generations still existed in Laurie's kitchen.

In the fall, the kitchens of our grandmothers became busy hives filled with people making the most of late summer produce and preparing for the cold months ahead. The last of summer's tomatoes, just by themselves, would have meant much happy activity in the kitchen. There were friends and relatives involved in canning tomatoes, pickling green tomatoes, making tomato marmalade, homemade ketchup and tomato juice. Many other vegetables would have been put away for the time of the dormant garden. Grandma, by this time in the year, would have stowed dandelion wine, corn whiskey and damson liqueur under her bed for fermenting—treats to take the chill off of the short days of winter along with country ham sandwiches.

Since neither of our grandmothers knew how to drive, planning ahead for

> *"I've had a happy life. I've never been blue or lonesome. The Lord has been good to this household—good to this family."*
>
> —Queena Stovall, 1977
> *Amherst New-Era Progress*

the winter months of dormant gardens was essential. So right alongside the preparation of food for the night's guests, there would be those engaged in canning and pickling and preserving for wintertime company. In Grandma's kitchen there was a wood stove as well as an electric stove. I remember that ovens were active producing breads, cakes, cobblers and pies. At the same time kettles and jars and all the paraphernalia of putting up and canning food covered the stove top.

Both of our grandmothers loved the land and they loved people—and their big bustling kitchens were the merging points for these two loves. The meal preparations were social events themselves. In those kitchens, many busy hands transformed the produce from the garden into occasions to gather friends and family. I remember that at Grandma's it was not uncommon to have ten or twelve people at the table several times a week. Ma also had frequent guests at her table. Her generous and hospitable inclinations served well in her role as a preacher's wife. Laurie fashioned her own cooking style and sense of hospitality after her able and loving role models—Ma, Grandma and Momma.

Laurie died in February of 2005 at the age of 52 before she was able to complete *Seasons To Taste*. Before her death, we discussed dedicating this cookbook in memory of Momma, Ma and Grandma, Laurie's cooking mentors. It is indeed a fitting tribute, one for which they would be pleased. But since I now have the honor of writing the final chapter for Laurie, I think an equally fitting dedication would be to dedicate *Seasons To Taste* to Laurie, my sister and best friend whom I miss deeply each and every day. Her cookbook is a tribute to her life, to her daughter, Tucker, and husband, Bobby, to her family, and many, many friends. It is my privilege to honor her in my closing remarks and dedicate this cookbook in loving memory of Laurie.

Preface

To everything there is a season
And a time to every purpose
Under heaven

Ecclesiastes 3:1

The world we live in is carefully ordered and controlled by nature and its changing seasons. With each season, we move through a new cycle of change that stimulates all of our senses; we know spring is near because we feel the added warmth in the air. Whether consciously or not we, too, adjust to each season by the clothes we wear, what we do, and the foods we eat, which are dependent on the availability of fresh meats and produce. I have organized this cookbook around the four seasons with each section containing a full complement of foods. Although you can use many of these recipes year-round, I have put them in a particular season as part of a menu or party idea based on the freshness of the ingredients available.

When I was catering and would often book parties months in advance, the time of year and the time of day were my first thoughts in planning a menu. Our taste for certain foods changes as the weather changes with the seasons. Springtime evokes thoughts of baby vegetables, fresh greens and lighter foods. Color is very important in spring and it is the first time in the year that fresh flowers can be incorporated in the meal. Springtime in Virginia often shows itself with yellow and purple crocus pushing their flower heads up through a little dusting of snow. With these first flowers also come thoughts of entertaining after the long months of winter.

> "When I was catering and would often book parties months in advance, the time of year and the time of day were my first thoughts. Not only do foods, but our taste for certain foods, change as the weather changes with the seasons."

Acknowledgments

Thank You

So many times, we find ourselves rushing through life to get it all done that we rarely have time to reflect and just be still. This cookbook is a testament to the fruits of just being still. Early each morning, Laurie spent quiet hours typing and reworking these recipes. And, it was in those sacred moments that she found herself most at peace in her last days. Sharing her legacy of food, family and faith became a labor of love that brought joy, purpose and stillness to her heart.

From Laurie's quiet moments, this cookbook grew with the help of her loyal friends and family whom she entrusted to finish that which she had begun, *Seasons to Taste*. It is with sincere gratitude that we thank the following people for their time, effort and dedication in seeing the project come to fruition.

Like Laurie's welcoming hospitality, this cookbook is a family affair. Most noticeably, the illustrations in *Seasons to Taste* are by her talented daughter, Tucker Adamson of Richmond. Aunt Catherine Stovall, was responsible for reading and rereading each recipe for accuracy and order. As a fabulous cook herself with a library of hundreds of cookbooks, who better than she to lead this cookbook to publication! Her involvement was invaluable, and with her death in 2007 we lost a key ingredient of our family.

Blessing the meal is an important Stovall family tradition and no one upheld this more than Laurie. Her brother, Brack, has composed the blessings for each season. We hope that they will be a blessing to your family as well. Husband Bobby, knowing Laurie's cooking so well, provided intimate advice, moral encouragement, and sustenance (wine, chips and dip) to keep the team on track. Special thanks go to Laurie's sister, Meg Laughon, who spearheaded the publication process and added the sidebars and seasonal floral ideas.

Publishing a cookbook takes not only expert cooks but also good friends. Clarkie Patterson, with her creativity and editorial expertise, was instrumental in consolidating many facts and thoughts into text. Ghost writers included Mary Abrams, Kate Hearne, Elizabeth (Lele) Heathwole, and Jessica Ward. Rhonda Clower and Melissa Johnson organized the seasonal foods table from a myriad of notes, conversations and interviews Meg had conducted with local farmers and artisans. Proofreaders and recipe editors included Cathy Capps, Helen Gilmer, Betty Jo Hamner, Ailene Jenkins, Beverley Laughon, Becky O'Brian, Toni Piggot, Betty Smiley, Patty Webb, and Susan Wright. Many thanks to Nancy Marion for her design expertise and unwavering patience. To all who have provided encouragement to see this project through, we thank you.

Laurie's faith was manifest in a living, breathing, doing kind of faith. As such, proceeds from the sale of *Seasons to Taste* will benefit Daily Bread, Lynchburg Grows, and the Lynchburg Humane Society—the non-profit organizations most dear to her. The italicized comments at the end of many recipes are Laurie's, providing loving advice and reflections. Her faith was in such words. And it continues on as others gather around the table with loved ones each season to break bread and give thanks.

Enjoy!

He makes grass grow for the cattle,
and plants for man to cultivate—
bringing forth food from the earth:
wine that gladdens the heart of man,
oil to make his face shine, and bread
that sustains his heart.

Psalm 104: 14-15

The seasons begin with spring. It is the awakening of the world around us that calls for a celebration. I begin looking for signs of renewed life in my perennial and herb beds; signs of fresh chives, sprigs of new mint and parsley. After a long, cold winter I am ready to throw open the windows and have a party. Spring offers a variety of opportunities to entertain including St. Patrick's Day Supper, an Easter Brunch, a May wedding or bridesmaid luncheon. Food you serve in the spring deserves an extra garnish of fresh flowers and herbs; rose petals, Johnny jump-ups, nasturtiums and violets are just a few of the edible flowers that can be minced and sprinkled over soups and salads in spring.

SPRING BLESSING:

As we prepare this table for friends, surrounded by the evidence of Your promise of life from the dark and frozen earth, let us be mindful of the promise of Your bounty in the coming of Your Kingdom. Bless this food we are about to receive. Let our hearts embrace Your presence and open the doors to all that is possible, so the assurance of Your love is known by all we encounter.

APPETIZERS

Smoked Salmon Canapés
SERVES 8

> 1 tablespoon Dijon mustard
> 1 tablespoon red onion, minced
> 1 tablespoon capers, drained
> 2 teaspoons fresh dill, snipped
> 4 ounces goat cheese
> 1 loaf French bread, sliced
> 3 ounces smoked salmon, sliced

Combine first four ingredients and set aside. Slice bread in 1/4-inch slices and brush lightly with olive oil. Bake on a cookie sheet at 300° for 30 minutes or until completely dried out.

Spread each crostini with goat cheese and a small dollop of the mustard sauce. Top with a slice of salmon and garnish with fresh dill or parsley, cracked black pepper and a few capers. Serve immediately.

Cheese Canapé Shells
MAKES 24 TARTLET SHELLS

> 4 tablespoons margarine, chilled
> 3 ounces cream cheese
> 1 cup cheddar cheese, shredded
> 1 cup flour
> 1/4 teaspoon cayenne pepper
> 1/2 teaspoon salt

Sift together flour, cayenne and salt. Cut in margarine, cheddar cheese and cream cheese until the mixture resembles cornmeal and holds together when pressed. Divide dough into 24 walnut size balls and press in small tartlet pans. Bake in a 350° oven for 10–12 minutes until browned. Place pans on cooling rack for 5 minutes and then remove shells carefully.

These shells may be used in a variety of ways; filling them with chicken or crab salad, diced fresh or grilled vegetables or a spoonful of spicy chili.

Spring

Spring

Seasonal Plant Material

Lilac

Azalea

Camellia

Witch Hazel

Crabapple

Viburnum

Lenten Rose

Hellebore

Arum

Rhododendron

Scotch Broom

Beech

Jasmine

APPETIZERS

Eggplant Caponata
SERVES 8

- 1 medium eggplant, cubed
- 2 medium onions, diced
- 4 stalks celery, finely chopped
- 3 tablespoons olive oil
- 16 ounce can plum tomatoes, undrained
- 1 tablespoon capers
- 1/2 cup red wine vinegar
- 1 heaping tablespoon sugar
- 1 teaspoon fresh oregano, minced
- 1/2 teaspoon fresh basil, minced
- 16 ounce jar Greek olives, pitted
- 1 anchovy, mashed thoroughly

Toss cubed eggplant with a sprinkle of kosher salt and let stand until it beads with water. Squeeze dry between paper towels to remove excess moisture.

Sauté eggplant, onions and celery in olive oil for 10 minutes, until soft. Remove from heat and add tomatoes, capers, 1/4 cup wine vinegar, sugar, oregano, basil and salt and pepper to taste. Coarsely chop olives and add to above mixture with the anchovy. Place in a casserole dish and bake uncovered at 325° for 2 1/2 hours. About half way through cooking, add the remaining vinegar. Remove from oven, cool and refrigerate until ready to serve.

Serve the caponata at room temperature with grilled toast or fresh pita bread.

APPETIZERS

Spinach Phyllo Triangles
SERVES 18

1 pound phyllo dough, thawed in refrigerator
1 pound butter, clarified
2 bunches green onions, minced
2 tablespoons olive oil
3 (10 ounce) boxes frozen chopped spinach
3 cups Swiss cheese, grated
1/4 cup pesto sauce
2 tablespoons fresh dill, snipped
1 cup feta cheese, crumbled
1 tablespoon lemon pepper
2 teaspoon salt
4 eggs, beaten slightly

Sauté green onions in olive oil. Prepare spinach according to directions, draining well. In large bowl, combine onions, spinach, Swiss cheese, pesto, dill, feta cheese, lemon pepper, salt and eggs. Cover and refrigerate overnight.

On a clean, dry surface, place one sheet phyllo, short side nearest to you. Lightly brush with butter and add 2 more sheets of phyllo, buttering each layer. With pizza cutter, cut sheet in half horizontally, then in half vertically. Cut each vertical section in thirds, making a total of 12 strips. Place one heaping teaspoon of spinach mixture at end of each strip. Fold as you would a flag, making first a triangle fold across the filling and continuing to fold up the strip to the end. Butter the outside of the triangle and place in a container, separating each layer with wax paper. Triangles may be frozen up to 6 weeks.

To cook, place frozen triangles on a cookie sheet. Bake at 425° 12–15 minutes, turning once until golden brown. Serve in a shallow basket, lined with fresh greens and flowers if desired.

Spring

Spring

APPETIZERS

Fresh Herb Dip
SERVES 15

    1 cup mayonnaise
    1 tablespoon lemon juice, freshly squeezed
    ¼ teaspoon salt
    ¼ teaspoon paprika
    1 tablespoon fresh basil, minced
    1 tablespoon fresh parsley, minced
    1 tablespoon fresh oregano, minced
    1 tablespoon onion, grated
    1 clove garlic, crushed
    1 tablespoon chives, snipped
    1 teaspoon curry powder
    1 teaspoon Worcestershire sauce
    ½ cup sour cream

Combine all ingredients and refrigerate overnight to allow flavors to blend. Serve with a mixture of fresh spring vegetables, blanched asparagus, steamed whole artichokes, baby carrots, steamed haricot vert, oven roasted new potatoes, snow peas and radish roses.

Spring

APPETIZERS

Vegetable Crudités
SERVES 50

- 1 pound green beans, stem end cut
- 1 bunch carrots, peeled and cut in julienne strips
- 1 head broccoli, cut in florets
- ½ head cauliflower, cut in florets
- 1 red bell pepper, cut in thin strips
- 6 red potatoes, peeling left on and cut in wedges
- 1 pound asparagus, ends broken off
- ½ pound brussel sprouts, washed and cut in half
- 1 bunch green onions, ends trimmed
- 2 turnips, peeled and sliced ¼-inch thick
- 1 pound okra, tip of stem trimmed
- 1 pint cherry tomatoes, washed
- 1 jicama, peeled and cut in julienne strips
- ½ pound snow peas, stem end trimmed
- 1 bunch radish, stems trimmed
- FRESH HERB DIP (P. 8)

Choose any six of the vegetables above for a platter serving 50 people. Choices should be made based on the freshness and availability of the produce. Cut vegetables in 2–3 bite size pieces and keep in separate zip lock bags until ready to serve.

Vegetables may be prepared up to one day in advance of a party and kept in the refrigerator. The following are the methods we used to prepare the crudités.

Potato wedges—place on a baking sheet and toss with 2 tablespoons of olive oil, salt, pepper and pasta herbs. Roast in a 350° oven for 25–30 minutes until browned and crispy. The potatoes are best if they are not refrigerated. They may be done an hour or so in advance, and left on the counter until ready to serve.

After blanching the vegetables, drain them immediately and spread them on a cooling rack covered with a towel, to air dry and cool. Store each vegetable separately in plastic bags or bowls in the refrigerator.

CONTINUED NEXT PAGE

Spring

May Day Baskets

This spring, revive an old tradition. Surprise good friends and neighbors by affixing a May Day basket to their front door handles.

Select a small basket or create your own container (cone shapes work well). Fill it with an assortment of fresh-picked spring flowers and other treats. Fasten the basket to the door handle with ribbon.

APPETIZERS

Vegetable Crudités continued

Green beans—blanch 4 minutes

Brussel sprouts—blanch 5 minutes

Okra—blanch one minute

Snow peas—blanch one minute

Asparagus—lay flat in a roasting pan fitted with a wire rack. A pound of finger-thin asparagus will take between 4–5 minutes. The asparagus should be bright green, firm and hot to the touch.

Immediately transfer the asparagus to a cooling rack to air dry. Lay flat in a plastic container when cool and refrigerate.

Broccoli, cauliflower, red bell pepper and cherry tomatoes need only be washed, trimmed or cut and refrigerated.

Turnips and jicama—best if purchased in the fall when they are at the height of their season. Both root vegetables should feel firm to the touch and the peeling smooth and unblemished. We often cut the slices of turnips with cookie cutters to add a unique garnish to the platter. You may, however, cut both the turnips and jicama in strips and place in a plastic bag in the refrigerator.

Carrots—place strips in ice water for one hour to curl strips.

Green onions—to make fans, trim the green ends to within 2 inches of the white bulb. With a sharp paring knife, cut several 1-inch deep slices at both ends of the onion. Place in ice water until the ends curl, remove and place in a plastic bag in the refrigerator.

Radishes—to make "roses," use a very sharp paring knife. Beginning at the stem end, cut a $1/2$-inch slice just along the red peeling to within $1/4$ inch of the bottom of the radish. Each radish should have 5–6 slits around the root. Place the radishes in ice water in the refrigerator overnight to open the "rose petals."

You will need a fairly large platter to display your vegetables effectively. Arrange them according to the color, shape and size. A pint of HERB DIP or one of your choice should be sufficient for 50 people, although you may need more, depending on how many vegetables you prepare.

APPETIZERS

Mediterranean Cheese Spread
SERVES 15

- 1/2 cup sun-dried tomatoes, packed in oil
- 8 ounces cream cheese, softened
- 8 ounces goat cheese, room temperature
- 1/2 teaspoon salt
- 1 tablespoon fresh basil, minced
- 3 cloves garlic, minced
- 1/4 teaspoon black pepper, freshly ground

Combine all ingredients in bowl of processor and process just until smooth and blended. Pack in a small crock or bowl and refrigerate until ready to serve. Remove cheese 30 minutes before serving to soften. Serve with wheat crackers or fresh vegetables.

Spring

Spring

APPETIZERS

Mushroom Tarts
SERVES 24

24 slices white bread, very fresh
3 tablespoons shallots, finely chopped
4 tablespoons butter
1/2 pound mushrooms, minced
3 tablespoons flour
1 cup cream
1/2 teaspoon salt
1 dash cayenne pepper
1 1/2 tablespoons chives, snipped
1 teaspoon lemon juice, freshly squeezed
2 tablespoons Parmesan cheese, freshly grated

Remove crusts from bread and flatten slightly with a rolling pin. Cut each slice in a 3-inch round and press into a greased 2-inch individual tartlet tin. Bake 10–15 minutes at 350° until crisp but not browned. Set on rack to cool.

Melt butter in a pan and sauté shallots 3–4 minutes. Add mushrooms and cook 5–7 minutes, stirring constantly, until most of the liquid is evaporated. Sprinkle flour on top of the mushrooms and whisk in the cream. Bring to a boil, stirring and cooking 2 minutes until mixture thickens. Add salt, cayenne, chives and lemon juice. Taste for seasoning.

At this point the mushroom mixture may be held in the refrigerator for 1–2 days. Just before serving, place tart shells on a cookie sheet and mound filling (approximately 1 1/2 tablespoons) in each. Sprinkle with Parmesan cheese and bake at 350° for 10 minutes until lightly browned. Garnish with a sprig of parsley or a sprinkle of chives and serve immediately.

APPETIZERS

Lamb Sausage Meatballs
SERVES 18

>   3 pounds lamb shoulder, trimmed and ground
>   ½ pound pork fatback, ground
>   2 teaspoons kosher salt
>   ½ teaspoon black pepper, freshly ground
>   3 cloves garlic, minced
>   1 tablespoons cumin seed, roasted and ground
>   2 tablespoons olive oil
>   1 tablespoon dried oregano, toasted lightly

Have the butcher grind the lamb and fatback together. In a medium mixing bowl, combine the lamb meat and the rest of the ingredients, mixing lightly to combine thoroughly. Form into 1-inch meatballs and place on a cookie sheet. Bake in a 400° oven for 15 minutes and remove to paper towels to cool. At this point the meatballs may be frozen or refrigerated overnight.

When ready to serve, place in a shallow baking dish and pour one cup of Louise's Mint Sauce (see page 32) over the lamb balls. Toss to coat, cover and heat 20 minutes at 350° until hot. Place in a chafing dish with additional sauce in which to dip.

Spring

Spring

APPETIZERS

Hummus Spread
SERVES 12

1 1/3 cups chickpeas, dried
4 cloves garlic, crushed
1 1/2 teaspoons kosher salt
5 tablespoons lemon juice, freshly squeezed
3/4 cup tahini
1/4 cup fresh parsley, minced
1/2 teaspoon black pepper, freshly ground
1/8 teaspoon cayenne pepper
1/4 teaspoon ground cumin
2 tablespoons good quality olive oil

Soak chickpeas in 2 quarts of water overnight. Drain and add water to cover by 3 inches. Bring to a boil and cook on low boil 2 hours until very soft. Add more water if necessary to keep peas covered by 1 inch of water. Drain when done and immediately put through a ricer or mash thoroughly by hand. Add the remaining ingredients and taste for seasoning. Refrigerate several hours to blend flavors.

Serve hummus with fresh pita bread or use as a spread on fresh vegetable sandwiches.

APPETIZERS

Hummus with Roasted Red Pepper
SERVES 12–15

> 2 16 ounce cans garbanzo beans, drained
> 1 cup tahini
> 2 garlic cloves, minced
> 2 teaspoons soy sauce
> 1 teaspoon ginger paste, available in Indian markets
> 2 teaspoons sea salt
> fresh ground pepper
> 4–5 tablespoons lemon juice
> 1 red pepper, roasted and coarsely chopped
> extra virgin olive oil

Place all ingredients except the olive oil in the bowl of a food processor. With the machine running, gradually drizzle in the olive oil until the hummus is a smooth consistency. Taste for seasoning, adding additional salt or lemon juice as needed. Refrigerate until ready to serve with fresh pita bread or pita chips.

Spring

BEVERAGES

The Cocktail Bar

    1.75 liters vodka
    1.75 liters bourbon
    1.75 liters scotch
    1 liter gin
    3 liters red wine
    1.50 liters white wine
    2 cases beer
    4 liters tonic water
    2 liters club soda
    2 liters ginger ale
    2 liters cola
    2 liters diet cola
    1 liter orange juice
    2 liters bottled water
    3 limes, cut in wedges
    1 lemon, cut in wedges
    75 pounds ice

Over the years I have probably received more calls asking for a formula to determine the quantities necessary for a cocktail party. Although the guest list may influence whether you buy more or less of the above, this will give you a general idea for what is needed.

Most people tend to overbuy and there is a lot to be said for not running to the store in the middle of a party. The rule of thumb is that you can make 36 (1 1/2 ounce) drinks from a 1.75 bottle of liquor. A bottle of wine (.75 liters) will serve 2 people and a case of beer will serve 6 people.

I also recommend that you have on hand 50 (12 ounce) glasses, one dozen wine glasses and 150 cocktail napkins. Although a bartender is always a help, a party of 50 or less may be set up as self service. A 3–5 gallon crock makes a great ice bucket because it will hold much more than a store-bought ice bucket. Place extra mixers under the table, but convenient to reach. You will also need 2 pitchers (water and orange juice), a 2-ounce jigger, an ice tea spoon, a cork screw, 2 bowls for fruit, a scoop for the ice and a beer cooler.

At today's prices and depending on what specific brands you buy, you can expect the bar to cost between 5 and 6 dollars per person.

BEVERAGES

Minted Whiskey Sour
SERVES 16

2 1/2 cups water
2 cups sugar
8 large lemons
2 oranges
2 cups fresh mint leaves
32 ounces Bourbon
12 fresh mint sprigs, for garnish

Combine water and sugar in a 2-quart saucepan and boil for 10 minutes. Juice the lemons and oranges, reserving the fruit halves. Place the fruit halves and mint leaves in a large heat proof bowl. Pour hot syrup over the fruit and allow to steep until completely cooled. Strain through a fine sieve, stir in fruit juices and pour into glass jars. Refrigerate several hours. May be made several days in advance.

When ready to serve, pour 2 ounces of bourbon and one ounce of syrup over a 9 ounce glass filled with crushed ice. Stir well and garnish with a mint sprig.

This syrup may be used to make a very nontraditional Kentucky Mint Julep on race day. I have found that many people prefer the additional flavor of the fruit juices to the more familiar recipe of mint and sugar.

Spring

Spring

Cookie-Sheet Grass

It takes two weeks to grow real grass for use in Easter baskets and spring centerpieces.

Line the bottom of a cookie sheet with plastic and fill it with a layer of moistened potting soil. Sprinkle with wheatgrass seeds (found in health food stores). Press the seeds gently into the soil, adding a little more potting soil if needed. Cover with a plastic bag or wrap.

When sprouts appear in 3–5 days, move to a sunny spot and mist regularly. In a week or so, you'll be able to cut sections of grass to fit the shape of your containers.

BEVERAGES

Mimosa
SERVES ONE

Fill a champagne flute ¼ full with fresh orange juice. Add 2 dashes of Grand Marnier and fill to the top with a good quality sparkling wine. Serve immediately, garnished with a fresh orange slice.

Wedding Punch
SERVES 15

    2 quarts tea, freshly brewed
    12 ounces frozen, concentrated lemonade
    12 ounces frozen, concentrated limeade
    1½ cups cranberry juice
    2 liters ginger ale

Combine tea, lemonade, limeade and cranberry juice in large non-corrosive container. Chill several hours or overnight. Add ginger ale just before serving. Garnish punch by floating fresh strawberries, lemon slices or fresh mint leaves.

This recipe is also a delicious base to use with Bourbon. Omit the ginger ale and add Bourbon to taste.

BEVERAGES

Dandelion Wine
SERVES 30

    1 quart Dandelion blooms, packed tightly
    1 gallon water, boiling
    1 lemon, sliced
    3 oranges, sliced
    1 box golden seedless raisins
    3½ pounds sugar
    1 tablespoon dry yeast

Gather your blooms in the early morning, before the hot sun has hit them. Spread them out on newspaper in the shade for 30 minutes, to give the ants time to crawl off. Put the blooms in a 3 gallon crock and pour the boiling water over them. Let stand 36 hours and strain the blooms through a couple of thicknesses of cheese cloth. Wash out the crock and add the liquid back to it. Add the lemons, oranges, raisins, sugar and yeast. Stir well and cover the crock with a damp double thickness of cheesecloth. Let stand in a warm place for 10 days, stirring daily.

Strain mixture again through several layers of cheesecloth and bottle. Do not cap too tightly and store in a cool, dry place. Wine will be cloudy for the first few months, but will clear as it ages.

This recipe brings back fond memories of sitting on the front porch of my grandmother's house, sipping some of her vintage wine. Dandelion wine is very similar in taste to a sweet sherry. Its clear amber color sparkles in a cut glass decanter and its flavor will mellow after 1–2 years.

Spring

Spring

BEVERAGES

Lu's Iced Tea
SERVES 4

> 2 family sized tea bags
> 12 sprigs fresh mint, washed
> 1 1/2 cups sugar
> 6 tablespoons lemon juice, freshly squeezed
> 1/8 teaspoon salt

Bring one quart of water to a boil. Pour over tea bags and mint sprigs in a small crock or pitcher. Let stand 5 to 10 minutes. Remove tea bags and mint. Stir in sugar, lemon juice and salt. Add one quart of cold water and stir well. Store in refrigerator until ready to serve. Garnish each glass with lemon slices and sprigs of fresh mint.

Lu's Tea comes from a friend's grandmother who lived on the Mississippi bayou. She always kept a pitcher of chilled tea ready to refresh us on those hot summer afternoons. Nothing else can do the trick!

SOUPS

Creamy Vidalia Soup
SERVES 8

- 8 slices bacon, coarsely chopped
- 4 tablespoons butter
- 3 pounds Vidalia onions, chopped
- 8 cloves garlic, crushed
- 2 cups white wine
- 4 cups chicken broth
- 1 tablespoon fresh thyme, minced
- 2 teaspoons salt
- 1/2 teaspoon white pepper
- 1 cup half and half
- 1 cup sour cream
- 3 tablespoons lemon juice, freshly squeezed
- 1 teaspoon Tabasco® sauce
- 1 pinch nutmeg, freshly grated
- 2 cups homemade croutons
- 1 bunch green onions, chopped

Sauté bacon in pan until it begins to foam and crispen. Reserve bacon grease and drain bacon bits on paper towels.

In a large pot, combine 4 tablespoons of bacon grease and 4 tablespoons of butter. When sizzling, add onions and garlic. Cook until translucent and golden in color. Add the wine, broth and thyme. Season to taste with salt and pepper. Bring to a boil and simmer one hour.

Strain soup, reserving broth, and process onions until smooth. Stir back into the broth (soup may be frozen at this point) and chill overnight.

One hour before serving, whisk in the cream and sour cream. Season with lemon juice, Tabasco® and fresh nutmeg. Serve soup in chilled bowls, garnishing with reserved bacon, croutons and minced green onions.

For a pretty springtime garnish, dollop sour cream on soup and sprinkle with edible flowers, such as Johnny jump-ups, violets, lilacs or redbud blossoms.

Spring

Spring

SOUPS

Hot and Sour Soup
SERVES 10–12

4 quarts chicken stock
2 stalks lemon grass, outer leaves removed, cut in 2-inch pieces
3 dried lime leaves
3 cloves garlic, minced
6 ounces shitake mushrooms, cut in 1-inch slices
3 serrano peppers, seeded and diced
2 jalapeño peppers, seeded and diced
2 medium carrots, cut in 1-inch slivers
1 pound extra firm tofu, cut in $1/2$-inch cubes
3 tablespoons cornstarch
$1/2$ cup rice wine vinegar
$1/2$ cup apple cider vinegar
3 tablespoons sesame oil
2 teaspoons chili oil
3 tablespoons soy sauce
3 eggs, beaten
2 bunches green onions, minced
fried wonton strips for garnish

Bring the chicken stock to a boil and stir in lemon grass, lime leaves and garlic. Reduce heat and simmer one hour. Stir in the mushrooms, peppers, carrots and tofu. Continue to simmer for 30 minutes until vegetables are cooked through. In a small bowl, combine the cornstarch with a little vinegar, whisking until smooth.

Add rest of vinegars, sesame oil, chili oil and soy sauce. Bring soup to a boil, stirring constantly until it thickens slightly. Taste for seasoning. Slowly swirl eggs in soup, stirring continuously and serve immediately in heated soup bowls. Garnish the top with minced green onions and serve the crispy wonton strips on the side.

SOUPS

Lentil and Mushroom Stew
SERVES 6

- 2 quarts chicken broth
- 2 cups dried lentils
- 2 tablespoons olive oil
- 1 medium onion, chopped
- 1/2 pound mushrooms, sliced
- 1 teaspoon dried basil
- 2 ribs celery, chopped
- 2 carrots, thinly sliced
- 16 ounce can diced tomatoes
- 1 teaspoon kosher salt
- 2 tablespoons balsamic vinegar
- 1 pinch sugar
- 1/2 teaspoon black pepper, freshly ground

Bring the chicken broth to a boil in an 8-quart stock pot. Slowly stir in the lentils and simmer one hour. Heat the olive oil in a medium skillet and sauté the onions, mushrooms and basil. Stir this mixture into the undrained lentils, along with the celery, carrots and tomatoes. Continue to simmer one additional hour or until the lentils are soft. Stir in the salt, pepper, sugar and vinegar. Taste for seasoning.

The stew may be served in a large soup bowl with crusty bread on the side, or over steaming brown rice as a heartier main dish.

Spring

Spring

Edible Flowers A–M

Anise Hyssop

Apple

Arugula

Basil

Bee Balm

Borage

Broccoli

Chamomile

Chicory

Chives

Chrysanthemum

Coriander

Dandelion

Daylily

Dill

Elderberry

English Daisy

Fennel

Garlic Chives

Greek Oregano

Hibiscus

Honeysuckle

Hyssop

Jasmine

Johnny-Jump-Up

Lavender

Lemon

Lilac

Linden

Marjoram

Mint

Mustard

SOUPS

Cannellini and Vegetable Soup
SERVES 8

2 cups cannellini beans, dried
2 bay leaves
2 tablespoons olive oil
1 medium onion, finely chopped
1 rib celery, finely chopped
1 medium parsnip, finely chopped
2 cloves garlic, minced
3 medium tomatoes, finely chopped
3 cups chicken broth
1 1/2 tablespoons kosher salt
1 teaspoon black pepper, freshly ground
1 tablespoon fresh thyme, minced

Wash cannellini beans and place in a large 4-quart pan. Add water to cover by 3 inches and allow beans to soak at least 8 hours. Drain water and add fresh water. Bring to a boil and add bay leaves. Continue to boil slowly, adding water as necessary, until beans are thoroughly cooked and soft. Drain beans, reserving 1–2 cups of bean liquid. Partially mash half of the beans, leaving half of the beans whole. Set aside.

In medium skillet, heat olive oil and add onions, sautéing until translucent. Stir in celery and parsnip and continue to cook 5–6 minutes. Add garlic and tomatoes and simmer until mixture is thick and tomatoes have cooked down a bit.

Return beans, bean liquor, chicken broth and vegetables to the 4-quart pot. Add 2–3 cups of water if necessary to thin soup. Bring soup to a boil and reduce to simmer. Season with salt, pepper and fresh thyme and cook 20–30 minutes, stirring often.

Serve soup in heated bowls, garnishing with additional fresh thyme or fresh black pepper. If desired, drizzle slices of a coarse, country bread with olive oil and thin slices of parmesan cheese and run under the broiler until cheese is just melted. Serve immediately.

SOUPS

Cucumber Gazpacho
SERVES 8

> 3 medium cucumbers, peeled, seeded and cut in chunks
> 2 cloves garlic, mashed
> 3 cups chicken broth
> 3 cups sour cream
> 3 tablespoons white vinegar
> 2 teaspoons kosher salt
> 1/2 cup green onion, minced
> 1/4 cup fresh mint leaves, minced
> 1/4 cup edible flowers, julienne strips

Place cucumber chunks in the bowl of a food processor or blender. Add some chicken broth and process until smooth. Add the rest of the chicken broth, garlic, sour cream, vinegar and salt. Pulse a few times to incorporate the ingredients. Transfer to a glass or plastic container and refrigerate several hours or overnight.

To serve, pour into chilled bowls and garnish with green onions, mint leaves and flowers. Serve immediately.

A fresh flower garnish is a lovely way to present a special dish. There are many edible flowers that can be used, but one should only serve flowers that you know to be nonpoisonous. In the spring time, violets, lilacs, redbud flowers, Johnny jump-ups, rose petals and pansies can be used. Day lilies, nasturtiums, calendulas, bee balm and honeysuckle blossoms will add color and interest to your summertime platters. You should take care to use only flowers that have been grown organically and are thoroughly washed. Dry the individual flowers well and wrap in a damp paper towel in a plastic bag for 1–2 days. Hosta leaves can be used as the lining for a platter or basket, but are not good to eat. Try snipping a few handfuls of flower blossoms into your favorite pound cake to give it a colorful confetti look.

Spring

Edible Flowers N–Y

Nasturtium
Nodding Onion
Okra
Orange
Pansy
Pea
Pineapple Guava
Pineapple Sage
Radish
Red Clover
Redbud
Rose
Rose of Sharon
Roselle
Rosemary
Runner Bean
Safflower
Sage
Scented Geranium
Signet Marigold
Society Garlic
Squash Blossom
Sunflower
Sweet Woodruff
Thyme
Tuberous Begonia
Tulip
Violet
Winter Savory
Yucca

Spring

SALADS

Creamy Lemon Dijon Vinaigrette

2 lemons, juice and zest, zest finely chopped
1 1/2 cups white wine vinegar
5/8 cup sugar
1 cup Dijon mustard
1 1/2 cups canola or salad oil

Combine all ingredients, except oil, in a mixing bowl, incorporate well. Slowly add the oil while blending the mixture to reach smooth, emulsified consistency.

Curried Shrimp Salad

SERVES 6

2 pounds shrimp, cooked, tail removed
1 cup water chestnuts
1/4 cup onions, diced
1/4 cup celery, diced
3/4 cup mayonnaise
2 teaspoons curry powder
2 tablespoons soy sauce
1/2 cup toasted almonds

Mix shrimp, water chestnuts, onions and celery. In a small bowl mix mayonaise, curry powder and soy sauce; pour over shrimp mixture. Top with almonds. Garnish with mandarin oranges.

This is a wonderful luncheon salad.

SALADS

Spring Salad with Buttermilk Dressing
SERVES 8

- 1/2 pound spring greens mix
- 1 head Bibb lettuce
- 1 16 ounce can artichokes
- 1 8 ounce can black olives, pitted

- 1/2 cup sour cream
- 1/2 cup buttermilk
- 1/4 cup fresh parsley, minced
- 1/2 teaspoon dried tarragon
- 1/4 teaspoon white pepper, freshly ground
- 1/2 cup mayonnaise
- 1/4 cup green onion, minced
- 2 tablespoons white wine vinegar
- 1/2 teaspoon salt
- 1 small purple onion, thinly sliced
- 1/2 pint cherry tomatoes, halved

Wash and spin dry greens. Break into bite size pieces and chill. Cut artichokes into quarters and slice black olives into thirds. Chill until ready to assemble.

Combine remaining ingredients, except tomatoes and onions, in food processor. Mix until smooth and refrigerate.

To assemble salad, place assorted greens on each salad plate. Arrange artichokes, black olives, onions and tomatoes on top. Spoon 1–2 tablespoons of dressing over salad and serve immediately.

Spring

Spring

SALADS

Lamb Salad with Yogurt Dressing
SERVES 4

 1 pound fresh baby spinach, washed and spun dry
 1 pound cooked lamb, cut into julienne strips
 1 medium cucumber, peeled and thinly sliced
 1/2 bunch radishes, thinly sliced
 1 small Vidalia onion, thinly sliced
 4 eggs, hard cooked and sliced
 1/4 pound bacon, cooked and crumbled
 2/3 cup plain yogurt
 1 tablespoon lemon juice, freshly squeezed
 3 cloves garlic, crushed
 1/4 teaspoon white pepper
 1/2 teaspoon salt
 2 tablespoons fresh dill, minced
 3 tablespoons olive oil

In a large wooden bowl or on separate luncheon-size plates, arrange spinach leaves, then lamb strips, cucumber, radish, Vidalia onion and eggs. In a small bowl, combine yogurt, lemon juice, garlic, pepper, salt and fresh dill. Whisk in olive oil and spoon over salad. Sprinkle with crumbled bacon bits and serve immediately with crusty French baguette.

A wonderful way to use up leftover leg of lamb for a light Sunday supper.

SALADS

Sally's Cucumber Aspic with Mint Mayonnaise
SERVES 10

    2 large cucumbers, peeled, seeded and grated
    2 envelopes gelatin
    1/2 cup white vinegar
    1/2 cup sugar
    2 tablespoons lemon juice, freshly squeezed
    1 teaspoon salt
    1 small can crushed pineapple

Place grated cucumber in a colander and allow to drain 15 minutes over a bowl, reserving the liquid. Measure 1/2 cup of the liquid into a measuring cup, adding water if necessary to make 1/2 cup. Sprinkle the gelatin over the top and mix well. Allow to soften for 5 minutes. Bring 2 cups of water to a boil and pour over gelatin, stirring until it is thoroughly dissolved.

Transfer cucumbers to a medium bowl and stir in the vinegar, sugar, lemon juice, salt and drained pineapple. Add gelatin and stir well. Pour into an oiled 5–6 cup gelatin mold and allow to congeal several hours or overnight.

To serve, unmold on a lettuce or hosta lined platter. Serve with Mint Mayonnaise on the side.

Mint Mayonnaise
SERVES 10

    1 cup mayonnaise
    1 tablespoon rice vinegar
    1 tablespoon sugar
    1/2 teaspoon salt
    1/4 cup fresh mint leaves, minced

Heat vinegar for a few seconds in the microwave until it is hot. Stir in the sugar until it is dissolved. Add the remaining ingredients and taste for seasoning. Store up to 3 days in the refrigerator.

Use Mint Mayonnaise on cucumber tea sandwiches, lamb rolls, or as a light dressing on fresh cooked green peas.

Spring

Coloring Eggs with Natural Dyes

Fruits and vegetables will color Easter eggs the natural way. Boil and refrigerate eggs as usual, then cook up a batch of your favorite plant-based colors:

4 cups fresh or frozen fruits and vegetables or 1–3 Tbsp. spices

4 cups water

2 tablespoons of vinegar

Bring dye mixture to a boil and simmer for 15–30 minutes. Strain and cool until warm. Soak hardboiled eggs in the natural dye for at least 5–15 minutes. For darker hues, let the eggs soak longer in the refrigerator.

See next page for natural dyes.

ENTREES

Mediterranean Shrimp Pasta
SERVES 12

1 pound angel hair pasta
1 pound medium shrimp, cooked and peeled
1 bunch green onion, minced
8 ounces feta cheese, crumbled
1/4 cup red wine vinegar
1 teaspoon Dijon mustard
1 tablespoon lemon juice, freshly squeezed
1/4 teaspoon sugar
1 tablespoon fresh oregano, minced
1 1/2 teaspoons Greek season salt
1/2 teaspoon black pepper, freshly ground
1/3 cup vegetable oil
1/2 cup olive oil
1 pint cherry tomatoes, cut in half

Break up angel hair pasta in 2–3 pieces. Cook al dente and drain well. Combine shrimp with pasta, green onions and feta cheese. Make a vinaigrette with the vinegar, mustard, lemon juice, sugar, oregano, pepper and Greek seasoning. Slowly whisk in oils until creamy. Pour over shrimp mixture and refrigerate one hour or overnight. At the last minute garnish with cherry tomato halves and fresh sprigs of oregano.

ENTREES

Salmon Moutard
SERVES 6–8

3 pound salmon filet cut in 6–8 serving size pieces
4 tablespoons butter
1/4 cup flour
1 1/2 cups milk
1 1/2 cups grated extra sharp cheddar cheese, divided
1 large shallot, minced and sautéed in 1 Tbsp. butter
1/2 cup white wine
1 1/2 tablespoons Dijon style mustard
1/4 cup capers, drained
2 tablespoons of lemon juice
salt to taste
1/4 teaspoon black pepper
1/4 teaspoon red pepper
1/4 cup fresh parsley, minced

Melt butter in medium saucepan and whisk in flour. Cook 4–5 minutes, stirring constantly, but do not brown. Slowly whisk in milk and cook until thickens. Sauce will be thicker than the usual béchamel sauce. Stir in 1/2 cup cheddar cheese and set aside.

In small sauté pan, cook shallots until translucent and stir in wine. Bring to a boil and cook until reduced by half. Stir in mustard, capers, lemon juice, salt, peppers and parsley. Add béchamel sauce and taste for seasonings. Thin a scant 1/4 cup of sauce with 2–3 tablespoons of cream and spoon a thin layer of this sauce into a flat casserole. Place the salmon filets on top of the sauce and carefully top each filet with the thicker caper sauce. Sprinkle each with the remaining cheddar cheese and a sprinkle of paprika. Place in a 350° oven for 30 minutes until fish is baked through. Serve immediately.

Spring

Natural Dyes

Green: spinach leaves

Yellow: orange or lemon peel, paprika, carrots, golden apple peels

Orange yellow: onion skins

Gold: ground turmeric (3-4 Tbsp.)

Blue/Lavender: red cabbage, blueberries, blackberries, red grape juice

Red-Pink: raspberries, cranberries, fresh or pickled beets, radishes

Color intensifies with more concentrated fruit/vegetable/spice

Spring

ENTREES

Roasted Leg of Lamb
SERVES 10

- 6 pound leg of lamb
- 6 cloves garlic, slivered
- 2 tablespoons fresh rosemary, snipped
- 1 teaspoon kosher salt
- 1 teaspoon black pepper, freshly ground

Insert garlic slivers across top of lamb. Sprinkle with rosemary, salt and pepper. Place in roasting pan and bake at 500° for 15 minutes. Turn oven down to 350° and continue to bake 15 minutes per pound or until a thermometer registers 130° for medium rare. Allow roast to sit 15 minutes before slicing, cutting perpendicular to the bone. Serve with Louise's Mint Sauce.

Louise's Mint Sauce
SERVES 12

- 1 cup brown sugar
- 1 teaspoon dry mustard powder
- 1 tablespoon cornstarch
    (maybe more if needs additional thickening)
- 1 teaspoon salt
- 1/2 teaspoon turmeric
- 1 cup apple cider vinegar
- 2 handfuls fresh mint leaves

Combine brown sugar, mustard powder, cornstarch, salt and turmeric in medium saucepan. Gradually whisk in vinegar until smooth. Heat slowly, stirring constantly until thickens. Pour over mint in non-corrosive bowl. Allow to cool and store in refrigerator until ready to use. This sauce will keep for up to 4 weeks.

A wonderful minty sauce. You will never settle for mint jelly again.

ENTREES

Corned Beef and Oven Steamed Vegetables
SERVES 6

- 3 pounds corned beef brisket
- 1/4 cup water
- 4 cloves garlic, sliced
- 1 tablespoon pickling spices
- 2 bay leaves
- 6 small onions, cut in half
- 1 pound carrots, peeled and cut in 2-inch sections
- 3 pounds small red potatoes
- 1 small head of cabbage, cut in wedges

Wash packaging spices off the corned beef and place in a roasting pan. Add the water, garlic, pickling spices and bay leaves. Cover tightly with a lid or aluminum foil and place in a 300° oven for 3 hours (or 1 1/4 hours per pound). Remove corned beef from oven and add onions, carrots and potatoes. Cover and return to oven at 325° for 45 minutes or until potatoes test fork tender. Add cabbage, cover, return to oven and allow cabbage to steam for 15–20 minutes. Remove corned beef and cover vegetables to keep warm. Thinly slice beef across the grain. Serve corned beef and vegetables with horseradish and Irish soda bread if desired.

An easy meal to fix, just time consuming in the cooking. If desired cook the beef, onions, carrots and potatoes the day before. Refrigerate in the pan with the juices. Reheat for 15 minutes before adding the cabbage and cook an additional 20–30 minutes.

Spring

Spring

ENTREES

Deep-Fried Soft Shell Crabs
SERVES 6

    12 medium sized soft shell crabs, cleaned, dredged in flour
    2 egg whites, slightly beaten
    2 tablespoons olive oil
    1 tablespoon white wine vinegar
    1 scant cup flour
    2 teaspoons baking soda
    1/3 cup cornstarch
    1 teaspoon salt
    1/2 teaspoon cayenne pepper
    1 cup water
    vegetable oil

In a large bowl, beat together the egg whites, olive oil and vinegar. Mix together one scant cup flour, baking soda, cornstarch, salt and cayenne pepper. Beat into the egg mixture until smooth and beat the water in a little at a time. Cover and allow to stand 15 minutes until it thickens slightly.

Heat 3 inches of oil in a large, deep frying pot to 360°. Use a small cube of bread to test for temperature—it should sizzle when it hits the oil. Pierce each crab claw in several places to reduce spattering and fry in small batches until golden brown. Serve immediately with lemon wedges and seasoned vinegar if desired.

This tempura batter is also excellent for shrimp, calamari and fresh vegetables.

ENTREES

Mushroom and Chicken Crêpes
SERVES 6

    6 tablespoons butter
    9 tablespoons flour
    2 cups chicken stock
    1 2/3 cups heavy cream, divided
    3 tablespoons white wine
    1 teaspoon salt
    pepper to taste
    3 egg yolks, beaten
    1 tablespoon fresh lemon juice
    5 green onions, minced
    1 pound sliced mushrooms
    2 tablespoons butter
    1 teaspoon herbes de provence
    2 1/4 cups cooked and chopped chicken
    1 1/2 cup grated Gruyere cheese
    1/2 cup fresh breadcrumbs (see note page 37)
    paprika
    12 CRÊPES (p. 193)

Melt the butter in a four-quart saucepan. Whisk in the flour and cook, stirring constantly for 3–4 minutes. Gradually whisk in the chicken stock and 2/3 cup of cream and cook until sauce thickens. Stir in the white wine, salt and pepper and taste for seasoning. Temper the eggs by adding some of the hot sauce to the yolks, whisking constantly. Stir the eggs back into the sauce and cook on low heat for 4–5 minutes. Do not allow sauce to boil. Stir in the lemon juice and green onions. Taste for seasoning again. Cool slightly.

Sauté mushrooms in 2 tablespoons of butter until just cooked through. Season with a little salt, pepper and the herbes de provence. Drain excess liquid and transfer to a large bowl. Stir in chicken. Add 1 1/2–2 cups of sauce to chicken and mushrooms, reserving remaining sauce. Filling should be thick enough to hold in the crêpes, but not too much sauce.

Stir in 1 cup of cream to reserved sauce to thin it. Pour a little in the bottom of the baking dish. Place 1/4 cup of filling in the center of a crepe and roll gently. Place the crepe in the baking dish, seam side down. Repeat with the rest of the crêpes. Sprinkle the tops with the grated cheese, bread crumbs and paprika to color. Bake uncovered in a 350° oven for 30–45 minutes until piping hot and browned on top. Serve immediately.

Spring

Spring

ENTREES

Duck Breast with Porcini Wine Sauce
SERVES 4

    4 boneless duck breasts, approximately 8 ounces each
    Kosher salt
    Freshly ground black pepper
    ¼ cup olive oil
    1 cup Madeira wine
    4 tablespoons softened butter, divided
    4 ounces Porcini mushrooms
    ½ cup light cream

Sprinkle both sides of each duck breast with salt and pepper. Cover lightly and allow to sit at room temperature for 30 minutes. Heat a grilling pan until medium hot. Pour in ¼ cup of olive oil and when sizzling add duck breast, skin side down. Cook about 6–8 minutes until skin is crispy and well browned. Turn and cook an additional 8 minutes for medium rare. Remove to warm platter and cover with foil to rest. Pour off excess oil and add Madeira wine. Swirl to remove any bits from pan. In small saucepan melt 2 tablespoons of butter. Sauté porcini mushrooms for 3–4 minutes until beginning to wilt. Stir in wine and reduce to 2 tablespoons. Whisk in remaining 2 tablespoons of softened butter and the light cream. Heat without boiling just until hot. Serve immediately over sliced duck breast medallions.

ENTREES

Fancy Baked Chicken
SERVES 4

½ cup butter, melted
¾ cup Parmesan cheese, grated
1 clove garlic, minced
½ teaspoon kosher salt
4 chicken breast halves, skinned and boneless
¼ cup flour
1 ½ cups fresh breadcrumbs
Paprika

Combine butter, Parmesan, garlic and salt in a shallow bowl. Dredge each chicken breast in flour, shaking to remove any excess flour and then in butter mixture. Roll in breadcrumbs and place in a well-greased casserole. Spoon any remaining butter over top of breasts and bake in a 350° oven for 45 minutes or until breasts reach 160°.

To make fresh breadcrumbs, use day old bread with a firm crumb. Break into pieces and place in the bowl of a processor. Pulse on and off until you have fine crumbs. They may be frozen up to one month. Thaw completely before trying to use.

Spring

37

Spring

ENTREES

Margaret's Funeral Casserole
SERVES 6

    6 chicken breast halves, skin on and bone in
    2 8-ounce cans water chestnuts, sliced
    4 ounces pimientos, diced
    1/2 teaspoon Greek seasoning salt
    1/2 teaspoon salt
    1/4 teaspoon cayenne pepper
    1 teaspoon lemon juice
    1 1/2 cups mayonnaise
    1 cup grated cheddar cheese
    1 small can French fried onion rings

Place chicken breasts in a large 6–8-quart pot and add cold water to cover. Bring to a boil over medium heat, stirring occasionally to rotate chicken. When the water comes to a full boil, cut off the heat and cover. Allow the chicken to sit in the water until it is totally cool, or refrigerate overnight. Cooking chicken by this method will prevent it from being tough and dried out. Remove skin and bones from meat and either pull or cut into large bite size pieces. Set aside.

In a large bowl, combine the water chestnuts, pimientos, salts, pepper, lemon juice and mayonnaise. Adjust seasonings if necessary and then add the chicken. Stir carefully, so as not to break up the chicken. Place in a 2-quart casserole and sprinkle the cheese over the top. Bake in a 350° oven for 20–30 minutes, until thoroughly heated. Sprinkle the onion rings over the top and return to the oven for an additional 5 minutes. Be careful not to overheat the casserole as it will separate. Serve immediately.

This casserole will not freeze, but the chicken can be done in advance and frozen, so that it is ready at a moment's notice. Momma was often seen bringing this casserole to someone in need and it was always a welcomed sight.

I usually save any chicken water and add the bones back to the pot. Bring this to a boil and add a bay leaf, a few onions, black pepper corns and a little salt. Simmer 1–2 hour and cool. Strain through a fine sieve and freeze in pint size bags for a wonderful stock.

ENTREES

Country Chicken Salad
SERVES 6

    1 1/2 pounds boneless chicken breasts, poached
    1/2 pound country ham, thinly sliced and cut in julienne strips
    1/4 pound Swiss cheese, grated
    6 sun-dried tomatoes in oil, diced
    1 bunch green onions, minced
    1/2 pound white mushrooms, chopped
    2 tablespoons olive oil
    2 tablespoons lemon juice, freshly squeezed
    1 1/2 cups mayonnaise
    1 tablespoon basil pesto

Cut chicken breasts in julienne strips and combine with ham, Swiss cheese, tomatoes, green onions and mushrooms. Sprinkle with olive oil and lemon juice, tossing lightly to combine.

Mix together the mayonnaise and pesto, adding more or less pesto to taste. Stir this into the chicken mixture, combining well. Taste for seasonings and add salt and pepper to taste. Refrigerate until ready to serve.

Country Chicken Salad may be served as an entree on a bed of fresh greens or in a Cheese Tart Shell as an appetizer.

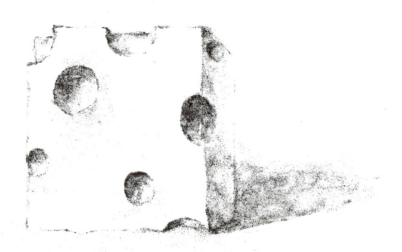

Spring

Spring

Prolonging Peonies

- **Enjoy fresh peonies in arrangements through the end of June. Here's how:**

- **Cut long, leafy stems in May when buds are open just enough to show a hint of color and feel like a marshmallow to the touch. Be careful, cutting too many stems will starve the plant.**

- **Place the peonies in a vase full of cold water. After a few hours remove the flowers from the vase and wrap in plastic. Refrigerate the stems, laying them wrapped on their sides on the shelf.**

- **The stems will start to look dead after awhile. Don't be fooled! Give the stems a fresh cut and place in hot water. Watch the flower start to pop open several hours later. You can keep peonies going this way weeks after the blossoms outside have disappeared.**

ENTREES

Southern Fried Chicken
SERVES 8

2 whole chickens, 3 pounds each
3 cups apple cider vinegar
1 cup buttermilk
1 tablespoon kosher salt
2 teaspoons cayenne pepper
1 tablespoon whole thyme leaves
1 teaspoon garlic powder
1 teaspoon onion powder
Peanut Oil
3 cups flour
1 teaspoon salt
1 teaspoon cayenne pepper
1/2 teaspoon sugar
1/4 teaspoon baking powder

Cut each chicken into 8 pieces and reserve the back and giblets for stock if desired. Place chicken pieces in plastic bowl with a cover.

Combine vinegar, buttermilk, kosher salt, 1 teaspoon cayenne pepper, thyme leaves, garlic powder and onion powder. Pour over chicken and allow to marinate in refrigerator at least 2 hours. Remove chicken from refrigerator, drain well and place in colander at room temperature for 30 minutes before frying.

Heat 2 inches of peanut oil in large cast iron skillet until it reaches 350°.

Combine flour, salt, one teaspoon cayenne, sugar and baking powder in large bowl. Dredge each chicken piece in flour until it is well coated. Shake off any excess flour.

Carefully place chicken in hot oil, being sure not to crowd. Turn chicken after 3–4 minutes, and continue to turn frequently to brown each piece evenly. The chicken will cook in approximately 20–30 minutes, depending upon the size of each piece. To prevent overcooking the chicken, maintain an even oil temperature and turn often. Chicken is done when the internal temperature is 160° or the juices are clear when pierced. Remove to paper towels to drain. If not serving immediately, cover with a kitchen towel and place in a barely warm oven.

I like to buy very small whole chickens and cut them up myself. You can ask the butcher to do this for you. If you buy chickens already cut up, they will typically weigh 4–5 pounds each and will not be as sweet or tender as the young chickens.

ENTREES

Spicy Chicken Milk Gravy
SERVES 6

    2 tablespoons drippings
        (oil used to fry chicken with brown bits)
    2 tablespoons flour
    1 cup chicken stock
    ½ cup cream
    1 teaspoon kosher salt
    ½ teaspoon cayenne pepper
    ½ teaspoon hot sauce
    1 teaspoon cumin, ground

After frying chicken, remove all but 2 tablespoons of the oil and any browned bits in the bottom of the pan. Whisk in the flour and cook over medium heat for 2–3 minutes. Slowly whisk in the chicken stock and cream, stirring constantly until the gravy just begins to boil and thickens. Season with salt, pepper, hot sauce and cumin, adjusting to individual taste. Serve immediately over fried chicken pieces.

Spring

Spring

SIDE DISHES

Baked Herb Pasta
SERVES 8

8 ounces angel hair pasta, broken into pieces
½ cup butter, melted
½ cup Parmesan cheese, grated
1 cup sour cream
1 tablespoon fresh basil, minced
1 tablespoon chives, snipped
1 tablespoon fresh parsley, minced
1 teaspoon fresh lemon thyme, snipped
1 teaspoon salt
½ teaspoon black pepper, freshly ground

Cook pasta according to directions, rinse in cool water and set aside.

In medium bowl, mix together the butter, 6 tablespoons of Parmesan cheese, sour cream, herbs, salt and pepper. Gently stir in the pasta and mix well. Turn into a greased 1½-quart casserole. Top with the remaining 2 tablespoons of Parmesan cheese and a sprinkle of paprika. Cover tightly with aluminum foil and bake at 350° for 20–30 minutes. Serve immediately.

This pasta recipe may be baked in individual ramekins. Grease or butter ½ cup ramekins. Sprinkle Parmesan cheese evenly in the bottom and sides of each dish. Pack pasta mixture in the ramekins and cover tightly with aluminum foil. Place the dishes in a 9 x 13-inch pan with ½ inch of water in the bottom. Bake in a 350° oven for 20 minutes. To serve, turn out the pasta onto a heated platter and garnish with additional fresh herbs.

SIDE DISHES

Mississippi Green Beans
SERVES 8

    1 tablespoon vegetable oil
    6 slices turkey bacon, cut into ½-inch pieces
    2 pounds frozen, cut up green beans
    ½ cup water
    1 teaspoon salt
    1 teaspoon black pepper, freshly ground

Heat oil in a 12-inch cast iron skillet until hot. Stir in the turkey bacon and cook until crisp and browned. Remove bacon from skillet and set aside. Add water to skillet with any drippings that are left and stir to loosen browned bits in the bottom of the pan. Add the green beans, salt and pepper. Bring to a boil and return the bacon to the skillet. Cover and reduce the heat. Simmer for 20 minutes, remove top and continue to cook, stirring occasionally, until all the liquid boils away. Serve immediately.

Spring

SIDE DISHES

Black Beans and Saffron Rice
SERVES 6

2 cups black beans, soaked overnight
2 bay leaves
6 cloves garlic, minced
1 1/2 teaspoons kosher salt
1/2 teaspoon black pepper, freshly ground
1/2 teaspoon red pepper flakes
1 teaspoon cumin, ground
3 cups chicken stock
1 tablespoon butter
1/2 teaspoon salt
1/4 teaspoon saffron threads, crumbled
1 1/2 cups rice

Drain black beans, place in a 4-quart pot and add fresh water to cover by 3 inches. Add bay leaves and garlic and bring beans to a boil. Cook one hour or longer at a low boil, until beans are cooked through and soft. Stir in kosher salt, black pepper, red pepper flakes and cumin. Reduce heat to a simmer and continue to cook beans an additional 30 minutes until most of the liquid is boiled out and thickened slightly.

While beans are simmering, bring the chicken stock to a boil. Add the butter, salt and saffron, stirring to melt the butter. Stir in the rice, cover and simmer 18–20 minutes until all the liquid is absorbed and the rice is cooked.

To serve, spoon the rice on the plate and the black beans on top. If desired serve a habanero hot sauce on the side.

DESSERTS

Chocolate Mousse
MAKES 36 MINIATURE TARTS: 6–8 INDIVIDUAL SERVINGS

8 ounces semi-sweet chocolate, broken into pieces
4 ounces unsweetened chocolate
¾ cup butter
5 eggs, separated
3 tablespoons Cointreau
½ cup powdered sugar
1 cup heavy whipping cream

Melt chocolate and butter in medium pan over barely simmering water. Stir constantly until smooth. Set aside.

Beat egg yolks in large bowl. Slowly add chocolate mixture, beating until smooth. Stir in Cointreau. Beat egg whites with a pinch of cream of tartar or salt until shiny and stiff. Fold one third of the whites at a time into the chocolate mousse, until all of it has been incorporated. Beat the whipping cream, add sugar until stiff, and fold into the mousse. Cover and chill several hours in the refrigerator. Serve the mousse in individual dessert cups with fresh fruit or as a filling in pie or tart shells.

This mousse freezes very well and is nice to have on hand for a last minute dessert. Divide into pint containers and place in refrigerator to thaw.

Spring

DESSERTS

Irresistible Brownies with variations
MAKES 24 SQUARES

- 4 ounces chocolate, unsweetened
- 1 cup butter
- 4 eggs, room temperature
- 2 cups sugar
- 1 teaspoon vanilla extract
- 1 cup flour
- 1/4 teaspoon salt
- 3/4 cup pecans, toasted and broken in pieces, optional

Melt chocolate and butter over hot, not boiling, water. Set aside and cool slightly.

In mixing bowl, beat eggs until foamy. Gradually beat in sugar and continue to beat 8–10 minutes, until it is thick and pale lemon in color. Stir in vanilla and chocolate mixture. Combine flour and salt and fold into batter. Stir in pecans, if desired, and spread in a greased and floured 9 x 13-inch pan. Bake in a 350° oven for 25 minutes, until brownies are shiny and firm on top. Do not overbake. Set on a rack to cool. If desired spread your choice of fillings on cooled brownies and glaze with 4 ounces of unsweetened chocolate and 4 tablespoons of margarine melted together. I usually leave out the pecans if I am using a filling.

DESSERTS

These fudge-like brownies can be layered with your choice of four different fillings to suit either your tastes or the occasion. After the brownies have been glazed be sure to place plastic wrap directly on the warm chocolate to give it a glossy finish when cooled. Use a very sharp knife to score the top before it hardens completely.

Variations

Mint Filling
2 cups powdered sugar, 4 tablespoons softened butter, 2 tablespoons milk, 3 drops peppermint oil and 2 drops green food coloring

Orange Filling
2 cups powdered sugar, 4 tablespoons softened butter, 2 tablespoons milk, 1/4 teaspoon orange oil and one tablespoon grated orange rind

Peanut Butter Filling
2 cups powdered sugar, 1/4 cup creamy peanut butter, 2 tablespoons milk and 1/2 teaspoon vanilla extract

Amaretto Filling
2 cups powdered sugar, 4 tablespoons softened butter, 2 tablespoons Amaretto and 1/4 cup toasted sliced almonds

Peppermint Candy Filling
2 cups powdered sugar, 4 tablespoons softened butter, 1/4 teaspoon peppermint flavoring and one cup crushed peppermint candies

Spring

DESSERTS

Raspberry Shortbread
MAKES 100 PIECES

6 cups flour, divided
2½ cups brown sugar, divided
2¼ cups butter, softened and divided
½ teaspoon salt
3 teaspoons almond extract, divided
2¼ cups raspberry jam
2¼ cups powdered sugar
3 tablespoons milk

Preheat oven to 350°. Grease and flour a 12 x 18-inch pan or two 9 x 13-inch pans. Combine 3 3/4 cups of flour, one cup brown sugar and 1½ cups softened butter in a large bowl. Cut with a pastry blender until it resembles coarse meal. Press firmly into the bottom of the prepared pan. Bake 10–15 minutes until lightly browned. While the shortbread is baking, combine 2¼ cups flour, 3/4 cup butter, 1½ cups brown sugar, salt and one teaspoon almond extract. Mix together until it resembles coarse crumbs.

Carefully spread the jam over the hot shortbread and sprinkle the second mixture evenly over the top. Bake an additional 20 minutes until lightly browned. While it is baking, combine the powdered sugar, milk and 2 teaspoons of almond extract in a small bowl. Beat until smooth. Drizzle over the surface of the hot shortbread and place on a rack to cool.

When the shortbread has completely cooled, cut into 2-inch squares. Turn on diagonal and cut across pan, forming 2 triangle shaped cookies out of each square. Store in airtight container for up to 2 weeks.

DESSERTS

Chocolate Mousse Tarts
MAKES 36 BITE SIZE TARTS

    1 recipe CHOCOLATE MOUSSE (P. 45)
    1 recipe CREAM CHEESE TART SHELLS (P. 75)
    1 jar raspberry jam
    1 pint fresh raspberries
    sprigs of fresh mint leaves

Carefully spread a thin layer of raspberry jam in the bottom of each tart shell. Spoon the chocolate mousse on top and garnish with a whole raspberry and a fresh mint leaf. Refrigerate if not serving immediately.

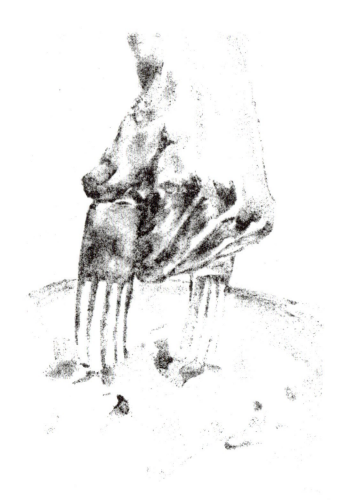

Spring

Spring

DESSERTS

Carrot Wedding Cake
SERVES 20

2 1/2 cups flour
2 cups sugar
1 teaspoon baking soda
1 teaspoon baking powder
1 teaspoon salt
1 1/2 cups safflower oil
4 eggs, beaten
3 cups carrots, grated
1/2 cup raisins
1/2 cup dates, chopped
1 banana, mashed
1/2 cup coconut, grated
1 cup pineapple, crushed
1 teaspoon vanilla extract
2 teaspoons cinnamon
1 recipe CREAM CHEESE ICING

Sift together flour, sugar, baking soda, baking powder and salt. Set aside. In large mixing bowl, beat together oil and eggs. Stir in dry ingredients and then add carrots, raisins, dates, banana, coconut, pineapple, vanilla and cinnamon. Spoon batter into well-greased and floured bundt pan or two 10-inch cake pans. Bake at 325° for 60–75 minutes or until the cake tests done. Let cake cool in pan for 10 minutes and then turn onto a rack. Cool completely before icing. Decorate top of cake with crushed pecans if desired.

Cream Cheese Icing

1 cup powdered sugar
8 ounces cream cheese, room temperature
8 tablespoons butter, room temperature
2 teaspoons vanilla extract

In medium bowl, combine all ingredients and mix until smooth and creamy. Spread on inside and outside of cake.

DESSERTS

Lemon Poppy Seed Pound Cake
SERVES 15

- 1 cup butter, softened
- 2 cups sugar
- 4 eggs
- 1 cup buttermilk
- 4 teaspoons grated lemon zest
- 1/2 teaspoon vanilla extract
- 3 cups flour
- 1/2 teaspoon baking soda
- 1/2 teaspoon baking powder
- 1/2 teaspoon salt
- 1/4 cup poppy seeds
- 1 cup powdered sugar
- 1 1/2 tablespoons lemon juice, freshly squeezed

In large mixing bowl, cream butter and sugar until light and fluffy. Beat in eggs one at a time. Stir in buttermilk, lemon zest and vanilla. Sift together flour, baking soda, baking powder and salt. Stir into batter and mix one minute. Add poppy seeds. Pour into greased and floured 12 cup bundt pan and bake at 350° for 55–65 minutes. Cool in pan for 10 minutes and turn out on cooling rack.

In small bowl, mix together powdered sugar and lemon juice. Carefully pour glaze over cake when completely cool.

Spring

Spring

DESSERTS

Frozen Lemon Soufflé
SERVES 12

> 2 recipes Lemon Butter, see next page
> 1 recipe Raspberry Sauce (p. 350)
> 1 cup heavy cream, whipped
> 8 egg whites
> 1 pinch cream of tartar
> 1/2 pound vanilla wafer cookies, crushed
> 3 tablespoons butter, melted
> 1 lemon, rind grated and juiced

Make Lemon Butter, up to 2 weeks in advance, reserving 8 egg whites for the soufflé. (freeze whites if not being used within 24 hours) Measure out 2 1/2 cups of the Lemon Butter and fold into the whipped cream. Beat the egg whites with a pinch of cream of tartar until it holds stiff peaks. Fold the whites into the lemon soufflé, cover and refrigerate until ready to use.

Mix together the vanilla wafers, melted butter, lemon juice and lemon rind. Press into the bottom of a 10-inch spring form pan. Pour the lemon soufflé mixture on top and place in the freezer for at least 6 hours or up to 36 hours. To serve, place 1–2 tablespoons of Raspberry Sauce on each dessert plate. Carefully place a wedge of lemon soufflé on top and garnish top with 3 whole raspberries. Place a twisted lemon slice and a sprig of mint on the side of each plate.

DESSERTS

Lemon Butter
SERVES 12

    6 egg yolks, beaten
    1 cup sugar
    2 lemons, rind grated and juiced
    2 tablespoons butter
    1 dash salt

Combine all ingredients in top of a double boiler. Place over simmering water and cook, stirring constantly until thickens and coats a wooden spoon. Place in a glass jar and refrigerate. The Lemon Butter will keep for several weeks. Serve over pound cake or as a filling for pies or cakes.

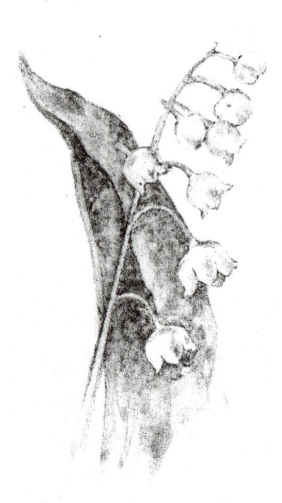

Spring

A New Leaf

The first leaves of spring are natural stencils. Try using them on dyed eggs to make a lasting impression. In addition to Easter egg dye, you'll need leaves, all-purpose glue, stencil paint, and a stencil brush.

1. **Color white hardboiled eggs using natural or store-bought dyes, rinse, and dry thoroughly.**

2. **Apply a thin layer of glue to the back of a leaf and gently adhere it to the shell. I recommend ferns or a small, delicate leaf.**

3. **Using a gentle dabbing motion, stipple on a light coat of paint.**

4. **When the paint is dry, peel away the leaf to reveal its pattern.**

5. **Make sure your stenciled eggs are completely dry before arranging them in a basket.**

DESSERTS

Reese's Gateau Ganache
SERVES 8

> 6 egg whites, room temperature
> 1 1/2 cups sugar
> 1 1/2 cups pecans, toasted lightly
> 1 1/2 teaspoons white vinegar
> 1/2 teaspoon vanilla extract
> 4 ounces semi-sweet chocolate, divided
> 1 cup heavy whipping cream

Line two 9-inch cake pans with wax paper. Grease and flour bottom and sides of pans. Line bottom with parchment paper and lightly grease. Set aside.

Beat egg whites until frothy. Gradually add sugar, a few tablespoons at a time, while continuing to beat the egg whites until they hold stiff peaks. Finely grind the pecans and fold into the egg whites. Add the vinegar and the vanilla and stir well to incorporate. Carefully spread the mixture evenly in the prepared pans. Bake in a preheated 375° oven for 35–40 minutes until the meringue is totally dry. Turn out on a rack to cool. Meringues may be made several days in advance. Keep tightly covered in a tin.

Melt 3 ounces of chocolate in a double boiler over hot water. Set aside, but keep chocolate warm.

Whip the cream until glossy and it holds stiff peaks. Remove 1/2 of the whipped cream to a bowl and fold in 1/2 of the melted chocolate. Place one of the meringues on a platter and spread with the chocolate and whipped cream mixture. Place the second meringue on top and spread with the remaining whipped cream. Dip a rubber spatula in the remaining melted chocolate and swirl the chocolate through the whipped cream to create a marbleized effect on top. Refrigerate until ready to serve.

Melt the reserved one ounce of chocolate in a double boiler over hot water. Use a waxy leaf, approximately 2 1/2–3-inches long, such as a camellia leaf. Wash and thoroughly dry 9–10 leaves and carefully paint only the back side of each leaf with the warm chocolate. Place on a rack to cool completely. When the chocolate has hardened, peel the leaf away and garnish the top of the gateau with the chocolate leaves.

DESSERTS

Little Bits
MAKES 48 PIECES

- 1 box graham cracker crumbs
- 3 eggs, separated
- 1 1/2 cups sugar, divided
- 16 ounces cream cheese, softened
- 8 ounces sour cream
- 1/2 teaspoon vanilla extract

Butter 48 1 1/2-inch muffin cups and coat generously with graham cracker crumbs. Set aside.

In a medium bowl, beat egg yolks, 3/4 cup of sugar and cream cheese until fluffy. In a separate bowl, beat the egg whites until they hold stiff peaks. Fold into the cream cheese mixture and spoon into the prepared muffin cups, filling to 3/4 full. Bake in a 350° oven for 20 minutes. Remove from the oven and place on a rack to cool.

While the cookies are cooling, turn the oven to 400°. Combine the sour cream, 3/4 cup sugar and vanilla in a 9-inch pie pan. Stir well and bake 5 minutes. Stir well and bake 2 more minutes. Remove from oven.

After cookies have cooled slightly (5–10 minutes), remove from pans. Spoon one teaspoon of sour cream filling in each cookie. Store in refrigerator after they have cooled completely.

Spring

Spring

Candied Violets

Decorate cakes, tarts, and cookies with delicate candied violets. The process is tedious, but the results are spectacular. Mint leaves, pansies, rose petals, and Johnny-jump-ups may also be used.

1 egg white

2 drops 100-proof vodka

1 cup superfine granulated sugar

1 bunch of freshly picked violets

Beat egg white in a small bowl until frothy. Add the vodka and set aside. Line a cake rack with a piece of parchment paper. Pick violets with a 2-inch stem (only 5 or 6 at a time to keep them from wilting). Using a fine arts paintbrush, carefully brush each violet with egg white, being sure to coat all surfaces. Gently sprinkle each one with sugar on the front and back. Place on the parchment paper and repeat the process until you have the desired amount of sugar. Place the rack and violets in a cool, dry, well-ventilated area overnight. Store dried candies in an air-tight container. They may be frozen for up to a year.

DESSERTS

Chocolate Buttermilk Cake with Butter Cream Frosting
SERVES 15

$2\frac{1}{2}$ cups all purpose flour
$\frac{1}{2}$ cup unsweetened cocoa powder
2 teaspoons baking soda
$\frac{3}{4}$ teaspoon salt
$2\frac{1}{4}$ cups sugar
1 cup unsalted butter, room temperature
2 large eggs
1 teaspoon vanilla extract
2 cups whole buttermilk

Preheat oven to 350°. Butter three 9-inch diameter cake pans. Line bottom with a cut out wax paper circle. Butter paper and lightly flour bottom and sides of pans. Set aside.

In small bowl, sift together flour, cocoa, baking soda and salt. Set aside. Cream together sugar and butter. Beat in eggs until creamy, scraping down sides of bowl. Stir in vanilla. Add flour and buttermilk alternately, beginning and ending with the flour. Stir only long enough to incorporate ingredients. Divide batter between the three pans and bang sharply on the counter to displace air bubbles. Place in center of oven and bake 30 minutes, or until tester comes out clean. Cool in pans 10 minutes, before turning out on racks. Peel off paper and cool completely.

Spread Butter Cream between layers and on outside. Keep cake in cool place or refrigerated until ready to serve.

DESSERTS

Butter Cream Frosting
ONE 9-INCH CAKE

    1 cup sugar
    6 large egg yolks
    1 1/2 tablespoons water
    1 1/2 cups butter, room temperature
    1 1/2 teaspoons vanilla extract

Beat sugar and egg yolks together until thick and light colored. Place over a pan of simmering water, being careful not to allow the bottom of the bowl to touch the hot water. Whisk constantly until mixture reaches 170°, approximately 12–15 minutes. Remove from heat and beat with electric mixer on high until completely cool. Gradually add softened butter, one tablespoon at a time, beating well after each addition. Stir in vanilla and continue to beat until thick and creamy. Spread on cake immediately.

Spring

Spring

Five Simple Rules for Planting a Produce Garden

1. Rich, well-drained soil is essential for helping plants resist insects, disease, and drought. Each year, build up your soil by working lots of organic matter into your beds. Composted leaves are an easy, inexpensive mulch for your beds, and can be tilled in to improve the soil.

2. To keep the soil loose, dig when the ground is dry. Digging when wet can result in compacted soil.

3. Change the placement of your plants each year to keep the soil from becoming depleted. Heavy feeders such as cabbage should be followed with a cover crop of buckwheat, clover, or annual rye. Till in the cover crop to replenish the soil.

Continued on next page

DESSERTS

Ma's Strawberry Shortcake
SERVES 12

    3 cups flour
    1/4 teaspoon salt
    14 tablespoons butter, chilled and divided
    1 cup chilled water
    1 1/2 cups sugar, divided
    2 cups water
    1/2 teaspoon almond extract
    2 quarts strawberries
    1 1/2 cups heavy whipping cream
    3 tablespoons powdered sugar

To make the shortcake biscuit, combine the flour, salt and 1/4 cup of sugar in the work bowl of a food processor. Add 12 tablespoons of butter, cut into pieces and pulse until it resembles coarse meal. Transfer to a bowl and sprinkle the iced water over the top, lightly incorporating the ingredients with a fork just until moistened. Press gently together to make a soft dough. Turn out on a lightly floured board and press to make a flat cylinder. Roll out to 1/4-inch thickness and cut out individual shortcakes with a 4-inch round cutter. Bake on an ungreased cookie sheet in a 425° oven for 12–15 minutes until light tan in color. Be careful not to overcook. Remove from oven and place on rack to cool.

Bring water to a boil in a small saucepan. Stir in the rest of the sugar and boil 5 minutes. Remove from heat and stir in 2 tablespoons of butter and almond extract. Set aside to cool.

Wash strawberries and reserve 6 absolutely perfect ones for a top garnish. Cut these strawberries in half lengthwise, leaving half the green top and stem. Cap the rest of the strawberries and cut into 1/4-inch slices. Sprinkle with just a bit of sugar, stir well and set aside.

DESSERTS

Whip the cream with the powdered sugar until it forms soft, glossy peaks. Refrigerate until ready to assemble.

To serve shortcakes, split each biscuit in half and place the bottom half on a dessert plate. Drizzle one tablespoon of almond syrup over the biscuit bottom. Place ½ cup of sliced strawberries on top and drizzle with syrup. Place the top half of the biscuit on the strawberries and dollop with 2 tablespoons of whipped cream. Garnish with the strawberry half and a sprig of mint. Serve immediately.

Shortcake biscuits and syrup may be made several weeks in advance if needed. Wrap biscuits well and freeze. Syrup may be kept in refrigerator in a glass jar. Surprise your guests one morning and serve these delicious shortcakes for breakfast.

Spring

4. Hand-water your plants or use a soaker hose instead of using sprinklers. This conserves water, and provides moisture directly to the base of the plants.

5. Different plants do well in different areas. Keep notes on how your plant selections perform, in order to choose the ones that are best-suited for your area.

DESSERTS

Agnes's Pound Cake
Serves 20

3 cups flour
1 teaspoon baking powder
1/2 cup shortening
1 cup butter, softened
3 cups sugar
5 eggs, room temperature
1 cup milk
1 teaspoon vanilla extract
1/2 teaspoon lemon extract

Preheat oven to 325°. Grease and flour large bundt pan. Combine flour and baking powder and set aside.

Cream together butter, shortening and sugar until light and fluffy. Add eggs, one at a time, beating well after each addition. Stir in dry ingredients, alternating with the milk. Stir in the extracts and spoon into the prepared pan. Bake in center of the oven for 1 1/2 hours or until cake tests done. Cool on a rack for 10 minutes before turning out to cool completely. Dust top of cake with powdered sugar.

This old fashioned pound cake has a rich buttery taste. Be careful not to over beat the batter and have all ingredients at room temperature. If desired a sugar glaze can be brushed on the cake after baking.

BREADS

Irish Soda Bread
SERVES 8

    4 cups flour
    1 teaspoon baking soda
    1/2 teaspoon baking powder
    1 1/2 teaspoon salt
    2 tablespoons sugar
    4 tablespoons margarine, cold
    1/2 cup raisins, soaked in 1/4 cup of Irish whiskey
    2 tablespoons caraway seeds
    2 cups buttermilk

Preheat oven to 375° and grease a round oven-proof pie pan.

In a large mixing bowl, combine flour, baking soda, baking powder, salt and sugar. Cut in margarine with a pastry blender, until it resembles coarse cornmeal. Mix in the raisins and caraway seeds. Make a well in the center and stir in the buttermilk all at once. Work quickly to incorporate all the ingredients, without overworking the dough. Turn out on a floured board and gently knead a couple of times, pressing into a round shape. Place in the pie pan and cut a 1/2-inch deep cross slash over the top. Bake in the oven for 50 minutes or until lightly browned. Remove from the oven and brush the top with melted margarine if desired. Serve immediately with plenty of butter or wrap tightly in foil and freeze.

Although traditional Irish Soda Bread does not have raisins, I prefer a bit of sweetness, especially when served with a St. Patrick's Day meal of corn beef, potatoes and cabbage.

Spring

Spring

BREADS

Four Cheeses Focaccia
MAKES ONE LOAF

- 1 tablespoon yeast
- 1/2 teaspoon sugar
- 1 cup water, heated to 110°
- 3 1/2 cups flour
- 1 teaspoon salt
- 5 tablespoons olive oil, divided
- 3/4 cups Parmesan cheese, grated, and divided
- 1 cup mozzarella cheese, grated
- 1/2 cup Gorgonzola cheese, crumbled
- 1 cup fontina cheese, grated
- 1 small onion, thinly sliced
- 1 teaspoon kosher salt
- 1 medium red bell pepper, roasted and peeled

Preheat oven to 400°. In a small bowl, combine water, sugar and yeast. Whisk until yeast dissolves and set in warm, draft-free place to proof.

In 4–5-quart mixing bowl, use dough hook to combine flour, salt, 3 tablespoons of olive oil and 1/2 cup Parmesan cheese. Add yeast mixture and mix thoroughly. Continue to knead dough 2–3 minutes with the machine running. Dough will be sticky. Form into a ball and place in oiled bowl to rise. Cover with plastic wrap and set in a warm place to rise, until doubled in size.

Punch down and press into a lightly greased jelly roll pan, 10 x 15-inch. Let rise one hour. In a small bowl, combine remaining 1/4 cup Parmesan, mozzarella, Gorgonzola, fontina, onion and pepper. Sprinkle over the focaccia dough and drizzle with the remaining oil. Sprinkle with kosher salt and bake in the bottom third of the oven for 35–45 minutes until lightly browned. Slice and serve immediately.

BREADS

Cousin Martha Grune's Sally Lunn
MAKES ONE BUNDT LOAF

1 tablespoon yeast
1 1/2 cups milk, heated to 110°
5 cups flour
1/3 cup sugar
2 teaspoons salt
1/2 cup margarine, cold
3 jumbo eggs, room temperature and beaten

Dissolve yeast and a pinch of sugar in the milk. Set aside to proof. Measure the flour into a large bowl and stir in the sugar and salt. Cut the margarine into the flour, until it resembles coarse cornmeal. Make a well in the center and pour in the eggs and yeast mixture. Stir quickly to thoroughly combine all ingredients. Dough will be very soft and slightly sticky.

Cover the bowl with plastic wrap and let rise in a warm, draft-free place for 4–5 hours. (I usually make the dough in the morning and let it sit all day, finishing it in time for supper). Punch down and spoon into one large well-greased bundt pan or 2 large loaf pans. Allow to rise again until double in size. Bake in a preheated oven for 400° for 60 minutes for the bundt pan or 30–40 minutes for loaf pans. Reduce the oven heat if the bread begins to brown too quickly.

Spring

Spring

Conditioning Hydrangeas

Cut hydrangeas in the morning, and put in a bucket of water immediately. Strip off all the leaves and slit the stems vertically to allow water to be absorbed more efficiently. You may want to immerse the stem and flower head in water for about an hour, as the bloom likes the moisture and will give you a longer vase life. After conditioning, place the stems in a vase of water with a preservative.

BREADS

Helen's Sally Lunn Bread
MAKES ONE BUNDT LOAF

1 tablespoon dry yeast
1/2 cup water, heated to 110°
1 teaspoon sugar
1 cup milk
1/2 cup sugar
2 teaspoon salt
4 tablespoons margarine
3 eggs, room temperature and beaten
5 cups unbleached flour, divided

In a small bowl, combine yeast, water and one teaspoon sugar. Whisk to dissolve and set in a warm, draft-free place to proof.

Heat milk until warm and place in a large bowl. Stir in 1/2 cup sugar, salt and margarine. Stir until margarine melts and cool slightly. Stir in the beaten eggs and 3 cups of flour. Add yeast mixture and stir in the remaining flour, combining well. Place batter in a well-greased bundt pan and bake in a 350° oven for 40–45 minutes until done. Turn out onto a rack to cool or serve immediately. Sally Lunn will slice better when cooled.

These two recipes for Sally Lunn are actually quite different. Cousin Martha Grune's (I never have known who she was, but her recipe was written out by my mother many years ago) recipe is more bread-like in texture and is less sweet. Helen's recipe has a delicate crumb and sweetness that complements any meal, including breakfast. Both loaves, if prepared ahead, should be buttered and wrapped in aluminum foil. Heat for 30 minutes in a preheated 350° oven.

BREADS

Buttermilk Biscuit
SERVES 8 OR MAKES 24 BISCUITS

1 3/4 cups flour
2 teaspoons baking powder
1 teaspoon sugar
1/2 teaspoon baking soda
1/2 teaspoon salt
4 tablespoons cold margarine
3/4 cup whole buttermilk

Pre-heat oven to 425°. In a medium bowl, combine all dry ingredients. Cut in margarine until it resembles coarse cornmeal. Make a well in the center of the bowl and pour the buttermilk in all at once. Stir quickly, pulling the dry sides into the wet center, turning the bowl as you stir until all ingredients are incorporated. Turn out onto a floured board and knead gently 2–3 times. Roll the dough with a light touch, turning and flouring to keep from sticking to the surface, to a 1/4-inch thickness. Cut out the biscuits with a 2 1/2-inch cutter, pressing straight into the dough, without twisting. Place the biscuits on an ungreased cookie sheet and pierce 2 or 3 times with a fork tine. Bake at 425° for 10–12 minutes or until lightly browned. Brush with melted margarine while hot, if desired and cool on a rack.

Making biscuits takes a very light touch. The dough should never be handled as one would a yeast bread. Keeping your hands, board and rolling pin well floured will prevent this soft dough from sticking and tearing. When rolling the dough out, lightly push from the center out to insure an even thickness.

Spring

Spring

"It is the simple things of life that make living worthwhile, the sweet fundamental things such as love and duty, work and rest and living close to nature."

Words by Laura Ingalls Wilder from *Souvenirs: Gifts from the Garden*

BREADS

Challah
MAKES 2 LOAVES

1 tablespoon dry yeast
1/2 cup water, heated to 110°
1/4 cup butter
1/4 cup sugar
1/2 cup boiling water
2 tablespoons honey
1 1/2 teaspoons salt
1 1/2 tablespoons oil
4 eggs, room temperature
5 cups flour
1 egg yolk, beaten with a little water
2 tablespoons sesame seeds, toasted

Combine the yeast, water and a pinch of sugar in a small bowl and set aside in a warm place to proof.

In a large bowl, combine the butter, sugar and boiling water. Stir until melted. Add the honey, salt and oil and cool slightly. Add the 4 whole eggs, one at a time, beating well after each addition. Add the yeast mixture and beat in the flour one cup at a time. After the flour has all been added, turn out onto a floured board and knead 10 minutes until smooth and pliable. Place in an oiled bowl, cover and let rise in a warm, draft-free place until doubled in size. Punch down and knead one minute. Divide dough in half and then into thirds. For each loaf, roll each piece into a long thin cylinder, approximately 18 inches in length. Pinch three "ropes" together at the top and braid dough to the bottom, pinching again to hold. Tuck ends under and place on a greased baking pan. Repeat with the other loaf. Cover with a clean kitchen towel and allow to rise until doubled. When the loaves are ready to bake, brush the loaf gently with the extra egg yolk. Sprinkle the top with the sesame seeds and bake at 350° for 25–35 minutes. Transfer to a cooling rack when done.

This traditional Jewish bread has just a hint of sweetness, with a rich egg and yeast flavor. It makes delicious sandwiches or is lovely as a gift to a special friend.

BREADS

Cinnamon Raisin Bread
MAKES 2 LOAVES

    2 tablespoons dry yeast
    2 1/4 cups water, heated to 110°, divided
    1 pinch sugar
    1/2 cup sugar, divided
    1 tablespoon salt
    2 tablespoons butter, softened
    6 1/2 cups flour, divided
    1 cup raisins
    2 teaspoons cinnamon
    2 tablespoons water
    Butter, softened

In a small bowl, whisk together the yeast, pinch of sugar and 1/2 cup of water. Set aside in a warm place to proof.

In a large mixing bowl, combine remaining 1 3/4 cup water, 4 tablespoons sugar, salt, 2 tablespoons of butter and 3 1/2 cups of flour. Beat until smooth and stir in raisins. Continue to add remaining flour until it forms a soft dough. Turn out onto a floured board and knead 8–10 minutes until smooth and elastic. Place in a large greased bowl and cover with plastic wrap. Set aside in a warm place to rise until doubled in size. Punch down and turn out onto a floured board. Divide dough in half and roll each half into an 18 x 9-inch rectangle. In a small bowl, mix together 1/4 cup sugar and cinnamon. Sprinkle each half with one tablespoon of water and half of the cinnamon sugar. Roll up tightly, beginning with the short side. Press edges together and fold ends under. Place in a 9 x 5-inch greased loaf pan. Brush top with softened butter and set aside to rise until doubled in size. Bake in pre-heated 425° oven for 25–30 minutes. Remove from pan and set on a rack to cool.

A delicious and unusual tea sandwich can be made with this bread. Slice the loaf thinly and then cut each into thirds. Butter lightly and top with very thinly sliced country ham. Top with another slice of buttered bread. Keep the sandwiches tightly covered until ready to serve. The slightly sweet taste of the bread is a perfect complement to the salted smoky flavor of the ham.

Spring

Spring

Decorating Eggs the "Natural" Way

Goose Eggs

Brown Eggs

Blue/Green (Aracana Chicken) Eggs

All of these eggs can be obtained at the Farmer's Market

Pierce each end of the egg with a small nail. Use a syringe to either suction or push the yolk/white from the egg.

To decorate the eggs, use a combination of the following seeds and/or grains. Place the seeds on the egg using Elmer's glue and a toothpick to spread the glue. Use your imagination!

Mustard Seeds

Peppercorns

Barley

Oatmeal

Rice, Wild Rice

Cantaloupe, Honeydew, Pumpkin, Watermelon Seeds

Sweet Anise

Lavender

Poppy Seeds

Fennel Seeds

Lentils

Spinach Seeds

Laurie and I, with friends, had a wonderful time sitting around the kitchen table, making these fun creations. The idea came from our mother who did this years before with some of her friends.

—Meg Laughon

BRUNCHES

Holden Beach Eggs Benedict
SERVES 6

>   4 qt. water
>   1/4 cup cider vinegar
>   12 large eggs
>   1 cup flour
>   1/2 teaspoon salt
>   1/4 teaspoon black pepper, freshly ground
>   12 medium, soft shell crabs, cleaned
>   1/2 cup butter
>   6 English muffins, split and buttered
>   HOLLANDAISE (P. 348)
>   2 lemons, cut in wedges

Prepare Hollandaise according to the recipe. This may be done in advance and refrigerated or prepared first and kept at room temperature.

Bring 4 quarts of water and vinegar to a boil in an 8-quart pot. Reduce to just below the boiling point and carefully slip each egg into the water. Do not crowd the eggs. Allow the eggs to poach, without boiling, about 3–4 minutes or just until the eggs begin to float to the surface. Remove the cooked eggs with a slotted spoon and place in a large bowl of <u>HOT</u> water. This will keep the eggs warm, but they will not continue to cook.

Combine in shallow dish, the flour, salt and pepper. Dredge each crab in the flour mixture, shaking off the excess. Melt the butter in a large 10–12-inch skillet over medium heat. When the butter begins to sizzle, add floured crabs and brown 5–6 minutes on each side, starting with the top side first. Remove from skillet and keep warm.

While crabs are cooking, toast the English muffins. To assemble, place one crab on each muffin half. Remove the poached egg from the hot water and dry carefully with a paper towel. Place on top of the crab and drizzle with 2 tablespoons of Hollandaise. Garnish with a lemon wedge and serve immediately.

BRUNCHES

Mushroom Quiche

SERVES 6

- 1 small onion, finely chopped
- 1/2 pound mushrooms, sliced
- 3 tablespoons olive oil
- 3 eggs, beaten
- 1/2 cup half and half
- 1 cup sour cream
- 1/2 teaspoon nutmeg, freshly ground
- 1/2 pound Swiss cheese, shredded
- 1 tablespoon flour
- salt & pepper
- 9-inch baked pie crust

In a medium skillet, heat olive oil until hot. Sauté onions and mushrooms until translucent and mushrooms give up their juices. Continue cooking until liquid is reduced by half, stirring often.

In a small bowl, combine eggs, half and half, sour cream, nutmeg, salt and pepper. Toss cheese and flour together and stir into egg mixture. Stir in onions and mushrooms. Pour into a prepared pie shell and bake 45 minutes at 350°. Remove from oven and allow to sit 5 minutes before slicing in wedges. Serve immediately.

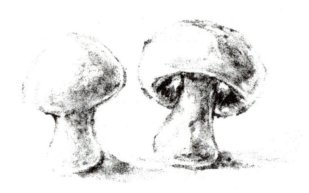

Spring

Spring

BRUNCHES

Date Nut Breakfast Muffins
MAKES 45 MUFFINS

1 cup butter, softened
1 3/4 cups sugar
3 eggs, beaten
3 cups flour
1 teaspoon salt
1 1/2 teaspoons baking soda
1 cup buttermilk
8 ounces dates, chopped
1 cup pecans, coarsely chopped
1 tablespoon orange juice
1 tablespoon orange zest, grated
2 cups orange juice
1/2 cup sugar

In large mixing bowl, cream butter and 1 3/4 cups sugar. Beat in the eggs. Sift together flour, salt and baking soda. Add to the butter mixture, alternating with buttermilk. Begin and end with the flour. Stir in the dates, pecans, orange zest and one tablespoon orange juice. Spoon into well-greased 1 1/2-inch muffin tins and bake at 375° for 15–20 minutes.

Mix together the 2 cups of orange juice and 1/2 cup sugar. While muffins are still warm in the pan, spoon one tablespoon of orange syrup over each. After juice is absorbed, remove from the pans and place on a cooling rack.

BRUNCHES

Cheese Fondue Casserole
SERVES 10

2/3 cup butter, softened and divided
1 clove garlic, minced
1 teaspoon mustard powder, divided
1 loaf French bread, sliced ½-inch thick
1½ cups Swiss cheese, grated
1½ mozzarella cheese, grated
3 tablespoons onion, grated
1 teaspoon paprika
¼ cup flour
3 cups milk
1 cup white wine
3 whole eggs, beaten
1½ teaspoons salt

Cream 1/3 cup of butter with garlic and 1/2 teaspoon mustard powder until smooth. Spread on both sides of bread and line the bottom and sides of a buttered 9 x 13-inch casserole.

Combine cheeses, onion, paprika and remaining 1/2 teaspoon mustard powder. Sprinkle over the top of the bread.

Melt 1/3 cup of butter in medium saucepan. Whisk in the flour and cook 3 minutes. Gradually add milk and continue to cook until mixture comes to a boil. Stir in the wine and remove from heat. Add a little hot milk mixture to eggs and then add back to the rest of the milk. Stir well. Pour over bread and cool. Cover and let sit overnight in refrigerator. Bring to room temperature and bake at 350° for 30–40 minutes or until puffed and golden. Serve immediately.

This versatile recipe can be used as the main entree for a brunch or as a side dish for dinner. The sharp flavor of the cheese and wine give it an unexpected and surprising taste. Be sure to use a good, dry white wine as it is predominant. If desired, cheeses may be sprinkled in individual baked tart shells and filled with egg mixture. Bake 20–25 minutes or until puffed.

Spring

Spring

BRUNCHES

Spring Shad Roe
SERVES 4

4 servings shad roe, 1 set per person
1 cup flour
1 1/2 teaspoons salt
1/2 teaspoon black pepper, freshly ground
8 tablespoons butter
2 tablespoons lemon juice, freshly squeezed
1 teaspoon Dijon mustard
1/4 cup minced fresh parsley

In a small pan, combine flour, salt and pepper. Cut each shad roe set in half, taking care not to break the membrane. Coat each set with seasoned flour and set aside.

In a 10–12-inch skillet, melt the butter over medium heat. (if desired, 1/2 butter and 1/2 bacon grease may be used) When the butter begins to sizzle, place shad roe in pan. Be sure to keep the temperature at medium heat, so shad do not cook too quickly. Turn each set carefully to avoid breaking the membrane after 6–7 minutes, or when nicely browned. Remove shad roe to a heated platter and keep warm.

Remove all but 4 tablespoons of butter and add lemon juice and mustard to the skillet. Stir, scraping up any little bits of browned flour. Cook until slightly thickened and add minced parsley. Drizzle over shad rod and serve immediately.

If a lighter crust is desired, try seasoning the shad with salt and pepper. Place on a sheet of wax paper and dot with butter. Place the wrapped shad directly in the pan with melted butter and fry as above. A spritz of lemon and a garnish of parsley may be added at the last minute, along with a HOLLANDAISE SAUCE (P. 348) on the side.

Fried country bacon, cornmeal waffles and fresh slices of tomatoes make a perfect addition to this very special springtime brunch.

SUMMER

Ants are creatures of little strength, yet they store up their food in the summer.

Proverbs 30:25

Sweep off the terrace, fire up the barbeque and have a summer cookout. Entertaining this time of the year could not be more fun. The abundance of sunshine and fresh foods combine for a winner in my home. Summertime is the season for casual outdoor entertaining with as little effort as possible. Fruits and vegetables abound at the market and because of their freshness need little prep. The outdoor grill is always a must and a welcome relief from a hot kitchen. I like to take advantage of the large variety of local produce and often will not plan a menu until after I have first gone to the farmers' market to see what's available. A perfect accompaniment to a summer meal is a cold soup that can be prepared the day before and a rustic French bread; add a chopped salad of tomatoes, cucumbers, peppers and green onions to give a pretty finish to the plate. Don't forget to use your home-grown fresh herbs or a couple of flowers for garnish. Voila!

SUMMER BLESSING:

Let us rejoice in the work that we do to prepare for Your Kingdom. Bring us together on this journey with the fruits of Your early harvest, and together make us mindful of Your endless presence. Give us the strength of this meal so that we may continue to spread the Good News of Your truth in our lives and the lives of Your children.

APPETIZERS

Summer

Crabmeat Tarts
MAKES 48 TARTS

4 ounces cream cheese, softened
1 teaspoon lemon juice, freshly squeezed
1 large egg, beaten
4 tablespoons mayonnaise
2 tablespoons fresh parsley, minced
2 tablespoons Parmesan cheese, grated
1 dash cayenne pepper
1/2 teaspoon salt
1/2 pound crabmeat, picked through for shells
4 Roma tomatoes
2 recipes of CREAM CHEESE TART SHELLS
Sprigs of parsley

In medium bowl, combine cream cheese, lemon juice and egg. Beat until smooth. Stir in mayonnaise, parsley, Parmesan cheese, cayenne pepper and salt. Taste for seasoning. Gently fold in crabmeat and refrigerate until ready to use.

Just before serving, cut tomatoes in 1/4-inch slices and then cut each slice into quarters. Fill each baked tart shell with one tablespoon of crab mixture and stick one or two tomato wedges in the top of each tart. Bake at 375° for 15–20 minutes until puffed and lightly browned. Garnish each tart with a sprig of parsley and serve immediately.

Cream Cheese Tart Shells
MAKES 24 TART SHELLS

3 ounces cream cheese
8 tablespoons margarine, cold
1 cup flour

In a medium bowl, cut together the cream cheese, margarine, and flour until it resembles coarse cornmeal. Shape into walnut size balls and press evenly into miniature muffin tins. Bake in a preheated 375° oven for 15 to 18 minutes or until golden brown. Remove from pans and cool on a rack. Tart shells may be stored at room temperature for several days or frozen up to 2 months.

Summer

APPETIZERS

Tomato Pies
MAKES 48 TARTLETS

> 1 cup mayonnaise
> 1 teaspoon lemon juice, freshly squeezed
> SUMMER PESTO, (P. 152)
> CREAM CHEESE TART SHELLS (P. 75)
> 4 Roma tomatoes
> 1/2 cup Parmesan cheese, grated
> Sprigs of fresh basil

Combine mayonnaise, lemon juice and 1/4 cup of Summer Pesto. Spread one teaspoon of mixture in bottom of each baked tart shell. Coarsely chop tomatoes and layer on top of each tart. Sprinkle with Parmesan cheese and bake at 350° on a cookie sheet for 15–18 minutes. Place tarts on a platter and garnish with a sprig of basil. Pass the hors d'oeuvres immediately.

APPETIZERS

Garden Quesadillas
SERVES 12

    16 ounces cream cheese, softened
    4 green onions, minced
    4 cloves garlic, minced
    1 tablespoon fresh cilantro, minced
    2 jalapeño peppers, finely chopped
    2 cups Monterey Jack cheese, shredded
    1 teaspoon cumin seed, roasted and ground
    1 cup cooked black beans, coarsely chopped
    1 teaspoon salt
    1/2 teaspoon black pepper
    12 flour tortillas, fajita size

Combine cream cheese, onions, garlic, cilantro, jalapeños, Monterey Jack cheese, cumin, beans, salt and pepper. Mix well. Spread about 1/4 cup of mixture evenly on one tortilla, top with second tortilla. Cook on a lightly greased griddle or grill, turning to brown evenly. Let stand 2–3 minutes, cut with pizza cutter in 6–8 pieces. Serve with salsa, sour cream, extra jalapeños. Garnish with whole peppers, cilantro and green onion curls.

Summer

Summer

APPETIZERS

Goat Cheese Quesadillas
SERVES 6

4 ounces goat cheese
1 1/2 cups Monterey Jack cheese, shredded
1/4 cup red onion, minced
1/4 cup fresh basil, minced
1 teaspoon salt
1/2 teaspoon black pepper, freshly ground
1 clove garlic, crushed
12 flour tortillas

Combine goat cheese, Monterey Jack, onion, basil, salt, pepper and garlic. Spread about 1/4 cup on top of tortilla and top with second tortilla. Refrigerate up to one hour until ready to cook.

Heat skillet with one tablespoon of oil until sizzling hot. Cook tortillas 5 minutes, turning to brown. Cut in wedges and serve immediately with salsa, sour cream and lime wedges.

APPETIZERS

Greek Dolmades
SERVES 8

1 jar grape leaves
1 pound ground lamb, cooked, drained and crumbled
1 small onion, finely chopped
2 cloves garlic, crushed
1/3 cup rice, uncooked
1/4 cup water
1/4 cup lemon juice, freshly squeezed
1 1/2 teaspoon salt
1/2 teaspoon black pepper, freshly ground
1/4 cup fresh parsley, minced
1/4 cup fresh mint leaves, minced
2 cans beef broth
YOGURT DRESSING (P. 80)

Soak grape leaves in a sink of warm water to remove grit. Remove and carefully dry.

Combine lamb, onion, garlic, rice, water, lemon juice, salt, pepper, parsley, mint and meat, mixing well. Place 2–3 tablespoons of the mixture in the middle of each grape leaf, stem at bottom and shiny side down. Fold in sides of leaf first, then starting at the bottom, roll up tightly. Place each bundle in a casserole or pan that is lined with extra grape leaves. Dolmades should be packed tightly in the pan. Drizzle with a little olive oil and add beef broth to almost cover. Invert a plate or pan on top to hold down the dolmades as they are cooking. Cover with aluminum foil and bake at 300° 45 minutes or until the rice is cooked through. Let cool in broth and drain. Refrigerate until ready to serve. YOGURT DRESSING may be served on the side as a dipping sauce.

Antipasto is Italian, meaning cold hors d'oeuvres. It is not only beautiful to look at, but especially good in the summer time. An assortment of cheeses, patés, olives, marinated vegetables and the following recipe are sure to be a hit at your next party.

Summer

Summer

Seasonal Plant Materials

Hosta Leaves

Hydrangea

Oak Leaf Hydrangea

Honeysuckle

Magnolia

Fern

Rue

Lambs Ear

Artemesia

Mint

Caladium Leaves

Vitex

Beech

Ivy

APPETIZERS

Yogurt Dressing
SERVES 8

  3/4 cup yogurt
  1 green onion, minced
  1 clove garlic, crushed
  1 tablespoon lemon juice, freshly squeezed
  1 tablespoon olive oil
  1/4 teaspoon salt
  1/8 teaspoon white pepper

Combine above ingredients and chill. Serve with Greek Dolmades.

APPETIZERS

Shrimp and Cilantro Rollups
SERVES 8

- 1 pound shrimp, cooked and diced
- 1 tablespoon fresh cilantro, snipped
- 12 ounces cream cheese, softened
- 1 teaspoon cumin seed, roasted and ground
- 1 teaspoon salt
- 1 tablespoon lime juice, freshly squeezed
- 1 tablespoon green onion, minced
- 2 tablespoons green peppers, finely chopped
- 1 whole jalapeño pepper, minced
- flour tortillas

Combine all ingredients for filling and spread approximately 1/4 cup on each tortilla. Roll tortilla up tightly and place in pan seam side down. Refrigerate overnight. Slice into 1-inch pieces and serve immediately, garnishing with sprigs of cilantro and fresh whole red or green hot peppers.

You may also use the filling for Quesidillas, sprinkling with shredded jack cheese and folding tortilla in half. Brown on both sides and serve immediately.

Summer

Summer

APPETIZERS

Oriental Crab Salad
SERVES 6

1 cup mayonnaise
3 tablespoons soy sauce
1 teaspoon lemon juice, freshly squeezed
½ teaspoon cayenne pepper
1 can water chestnuts, finely chopped
4 tablespoons green onions, minced
1 pound crab meat, picked through for shells
toasted sesame seeds

Combine mayonnaise, soy sauce, lemon juice and cayenne pepper in small bowl. Taste for seasoning and stir in chestnuts and onions. Gently fold in crab meat and place in refrigerator. To serve, fill a scallop shell with ½ cup of the salad. Garnish with an onion fan, a thin slice of lemon and a sprinkling of toasted sesame seeds.

BEVERAGES

Rum Painkiller
SERVES 12

    3 cups pineapple juice
    2½ quarts orange juice
    30 ounces coconut cream
    1 quart Jamaican dark rum

In a large gallon container, combine juices and coconut cream thoroughly. Chill in the refrigerator overnight. To serve, add 1–1½ ounces of rum to a glass filled with ice. Pour in 6 ounces of juice mixture and stir well. Garnish the top of the drink with a sprinkle of cinnamon and a fresh grating of nutmeg.

Caribbean Delight
MAKES ONE DRINK

    1 cup vanilla ice cream
    1 ounce Amaretto di Amore liqueur,
        or other almond flavored liqueur
    1 ounce triple sec
    1 ounce orange juice
    1 ounce coconut rum

Scoop the ice cream into a blender and add the remaining ingredients. Blend until smooth and pour immediately into a chilled glass. Garnish with a fresh grating of nutmeg.

Summer

Summer

BEVERAGES

Café Margarita
SERVES 6

3 cups water
3 cups sugar
2 cups lemon juice, freshly squeezed
2 cups lime juice, freshly squeezed
1 cup gold tequila
½ cup triple sec
16 ice cubes
3 limes

In a medium saucepan, make a simple syrup by combining the water and sugar. Bring to a boil and stir to dissolve the sugar. Remove from the heat and cool. Add lemon and lime juice and transfer to a glass container. Refrigerate up to 1–2 days until ready to use. In a blender, combine 3½ cups of above mixture (set aside the rest of the juice for the next batch), the tequila, triple sec and ice cubes. Blend until smooth. Serve in a margarita glass rimmed first with a lime wedge and then lightly in salt.

To serve on the rocks, omit the ice cubes and serve in salt-rimmed glasses filled with crushed ice.

Bahama Mama
SERVES 12

1½ quarts orange juice
1½ quarts pineapple juice
8 ounces dark Caribbean-type rum
8 ounces coconut rum
8 ounces Nassau Royale or vanilla flavored liqueur
2 ounces Grenadine

Combine all ingredients in a large plastic container and chill overnight. Pour Bahama Mamas over ice and garnish with a sliced orange and maraschino cherry speared together.

BEVERAGES

Wine Punch
SERVES 20

    24 ounces frozen orange juice concentrate
    4 cups water
    1 cup sugar
    3/4 cup Grenadine
    1/4 teaspoon salt
    1 1/2 liters Chablis
    1/2 liter club soda

Combine first six ingredients and chill several hours in the refrigerator. To serve, pour punch into a large bowl and add club soda just before serving. Garnish with fresh mint and thin-sliced oranges if desired.

Dave's Whiskey Sour
SERVES 26

    24 ounces frozen lemonade concentrate
    12 ounces frozen orange juice concentrate
    3 quarts water
    1 1/2 liters Bourbon

Combine all ingredients and pour into jars. Refrigerate several hours to chill. To serve, pour over crushed ice in 9 ounce glasses. Garnish with skewers of orange slices and maraschino cherries.

Chilly Irishman Says Goodnight Moon
SERVES ONE

    1 1/2 ounces Irish whiskey
    1 1/2 ounces Bailey's Irish Cream
    2 ice cubes

Combine above in a 6 ounce glass. Do not use more than 2 ice cubes as it will dilute the drink too much. Makes a wonderful nightcap.

Summer

Drying Hydrangeas

Hydrangeas must be mature flowers, "papery" to the touch, when harvested to dry properly. There are 2 methods that work, I prefer the second.

- Strip off all the leaves, tie in bunches of six with twine or a rubber band. Hang in a hot, dry place, out of sunlight for approximately 2 weeks. Provide adequate circulation and do not crowd!

- Place stems in a container about ¼ full of water. Add two drops of bleach to prevent bacteria buildup. Place the container out of direct sun, and in about 2 weeks, the water will evaporate, leaving the flowers dry.

Summer

SOUPS

Creamed Zucchini Soup
SERVES 8

6 medium size zucchini, coarsely chopped
1 bay leaf
1 stick butter
1 medium onion, chopped
1/2 cup celery, chopped
4 cups chicken broth
2 tablespoons fresh parsley, minced
few sprigs fresh thyme
1 teaspoon salt
1/2 teaspoon black pepper
1 pint sour cream
2 tablespoons fresh dill, snipped

Place zucchini in a medium saucepan with one cup water and the bay leaf. Bring to a boil and cook just until zucchini is tender, 8–10 minutes. Drain well and set aside.

Melt butter in a medium skillet and sauté onions and celery until cooked through. Working in batches, depending upon the size of your processor or blender, thoroughly puree the zucchini and onion mixture, seasoning the batches with fresh herbs, salt and pepper and adding enough broth to process. Combine each batch in a large bowl and taste for seasoning. At this point soup may be frozen in one-pint or -quart bags. To serve, whisk one cup of sour cream to one quart of soup and chill thoroughly. Serve in chilled soup bowls and garnish top with one tablespoon of sour cream and a sprinkle of fresh dill.

SOUPS

Fresh Peach Soup
SERVES 4–6

> 6 cups peaches, peeled and chopped
> 2 cups orange juice, freshly squeezed
> 1 cup sour cream
> 2 teaspoons lemon juice, freshly squeezed
> 1/2 teaspoon almond extract
> 1 tablespoon sugar
> 1/4 teaspoon salt
> 1/4 cup toasted sliced almonds, chopped
> nutmeg

Place peaches in blender and add orange juice. Puree completely and pour into bowl. Whisk in sour cream, lemon juice, almond extract, sugar and salt. Taste for seasoning and if necessary, add additional sugar if peaches are not ripened. Chill thoroughly and garnish each bowl with toasted almonds and a grind of fresh nutmeg.

Summer

Summer

SOUPS

Chloknik
SERVES 10

- 5 cups buttermilk
- 2 cups sour cream
- 1/2 cup sauerkraut juice
- 1 pound shrimp, cooked, peeled and chopped
- 1 English cucumber, chopped
- 1 bunch green onions, minced
- 2 tablespoons fresh dill, snipped
- 1 teaspoon fennel seed, crushed
- 1 teaspoon white pepper
- 2 teaspoons kosher salt

In a large bowl, combine buttermilk, sour cream and sauerkraut juice. Whisk until smooth. Stir in shrimp, cucumber, green onion, dill, fennel, white pepper and salt. Taste for seasoning and chill overnight or several hours.

Serve soup in chilled bowls, garnished with fresh dill and crisp rye toasts on the side. A cold beer will round out this refreshing summer supper.

SOUPS

Gazpacho

    4 large ripe tomatoes
    2 ½ cucumbers
    1 large green pepper
    ½ Vidalia onion
    2 cloves garlic
    1 teaspoon salt
    Fresh Basil
    ¼ cup red wine vinegar
    1/3 cup olive oil
    1 teaspoon sugar
    1 tablespoon lemon juice
    3 cups tomato juice
    1 ¾ cups beef broth

Add to taste the following:

    Hot pepper sauce
    Worcestershire sauce
    Salt
    Fresh ground pepper
    Fresh parsley, chives

Peel, seed and chop the tomatoes and cucumbers in ¼ inch dice. Wash and trim the pepper and onion, and chop into ¼ inch dice. In a mortar, mash garlic, 1 teaspoon salt and fresh basil. Beat in the vinegar, oil, lemon juice and sugar. Combine this dressing with the chopped vegetables and stir in the tomato juice. Add broth. Season with a dash of hot pepper sauce, Worcestershire sauce, salt and pepper.

It is essential to hand-chop the vegetables! The soup may be easily doubled or tripled. Serve in chilled bowls and garnish with fresh herbs and cucumber slices. Serves 6.

Summer

Summer

SOUPS

Toni's Chilled Beet Borscht

> 6 cups beef stock
> 2 pounds beets, peeled and coarsely chopped
> ½ cup grated carrots
> 1 bay leaf
> 1 sprig parsley
> ½ cup fresh squeezed orange juice
> 1 cucumber
> 2-3 green onions, sliced
> 2 cups sour cream
> 1/3 -1/2 cup vodka, optional
> 2 tablespoons chopped fresh dill

Combine stock, beets, carrots, bay leaf and parsley sprig in a large pot over medium heat. Reduce heat to low, cover and simmer 30 minutes. Stir in orange juice and let cool. Discard bay leaf and parsley sprig. Cover and refrigerate for 4 hours or overnight.

Peel cucumber, remove seeds and dice. Place in a small bowl and refrigerate. Trim green onions and slice. Put in another bowl and refrigerate.

When ready to serve, remove soup from refrigerator and add 1 ½ cups sour cream, mixing well. Add vodka, stir and serve in chilled soup bowls. Cucumber and onions can be garnished on each soup bowl. Put dollop of sour cream on top and sprinkle with chopped dill.

SALADS

Summer

Black Bean and Rice Salad
SERVES 8

- 4 cups black beans, cooked and drained
- 2 cups cooked rice
- 1 cup sweet white corn
- 1/2 cup red bell pepper, diced
- 1/2 cup red onion, diced
- 1/2 cup white wine vinegar
- 2 tablespoons freshly squeezed lime juice
- 1 teaspoon cumin seed, roasted and ground
- 1 teaspoon chili powder
- 1 clove garlic, minced
- 1 teaspoon honey
- 1 teaspoon salt
- 1/3 cup vegetable oil
- 1 bunch fresh cilantro, minced

In large bowl, combine black beans, rice, corn, red pepper and onion. Measure vinegar, lime juice, cumin, chili powder, garlic, honey and salt into a small bowl. Gradually whisk in oil until smooth. Pour over black bean mixture and allow to marinate several hours. Just before serving, sprinkle with the minced cilantro.

Summer

A favorite Sunday night supper

1 slice of bread, white or wheat (You may want to allow 2 per person)

Cover bread with a thick slice of sharp cheddar or Vermont Sharp White Cheddar cheese

1 large slice of tomato, preferably from the garden

1 ½ slices of bacon, raw

1 slice of onion

Place in the above order on a slice of bread, and place on a cookie sheet. Bake at 350° 45 minutes to an hour until bacon is done.

SALADS

Roasted Corn Salad with Lime Vinaigrette Dressing
SERVES 8

6 ears of corn on the cob, unshucked
2 medium red bell peppers
1 medium green bell pepper
1 bunch green onions, finely chopped
2 chipotle peppers, minced
2 tablespoons lime juice, freshly squeezed
3 tablespoons white wine vinegar
½ teaspoon sugar
1 clove garlic, minced
1 teaspoon kosher salt
½ teaspoon cumin seed, roasted and ground
½ teaspoon black pepper, freshly ground
4 tablespoons vegetable oil
4 tablespoons olive oil
2 teaspoons fresh cilantro, minced

Peel back shucks on corn and lightly brush with olive oil. Pull shucks up around corn and place on medium heated grill. Place whole green and red peppers on grill with corn, turning often to evenly blacken vegetables, approximately 10 minutes. Place peppers in a paper bag and close tightly to steam skins. Remove corn from grill, allow to cool and cut kernels from cob. Place into a medium bowl.

After peppers have steamed 5 minutes, remove from bag and peel off blackened skins. Coarsely chop peppers and add to corn, with green onions and chipotle peppers.

In a small bowl, whisk together lime juice, vinegar, sugar, garlic, salt, cumin and pepper. Slowly drizzle in vegetable and olive oils, whisking constantly. Taste for seasoning and stir in cilantro. Pour approximately ⅓ to ½ cup of dressing over corn mixture and refrigerate 2–3 hours to allow flavors to blend. Store any leftover dressing in a glass jar in the refrigerator.

SALADS

Tomato Aspic
SERVES 35

- 4½ quarts tomato juice, divided
- 10 envelopes plain unflavored gelatin
- 2 medium onions, coarsely chopped
- 2 bay leaves
- 4 ribs celery, coarsely chopped
- 8 whole cloves
- 2 teaspoons mustard powder
- ⅓ cup sugar
- 1 cup white vinegar
- 2 teaspoons salt
- 1 teaspoon black pepper, freshly ground

Soften gelatin in a medium bowl with 2 cups of tomato juice. In a 4-quart saucepan combine remaining ingredients and heat just to the boiling point. Simmer 20 minutes to season juice. Strain through a fine sieve and stir in the softened gelatin until it is totally dissolved. Pour into 2 greased three-quart molds. Congeal overnight in the refrigerator. Serve the aspic with FRESH HERB DIP or a seasoned mayonnaise.

Summer

Summer

SALADS

Coleslaw Dressing
SERVES 12

1/3 cup cider vinegar
1/3 cup sugar
2 teaspoons salt
1/4 teaspoon cayenne pepper
2 tablespoons Dijon mustard
1 tablespoon lemon juice, freshly squeezed
1 1/2 cups mayonnaise
1 large cabbage

Heat vinegar and sugar until hot and sugar is dissolved. Whisk in the salt, cayenne, Dijon, lemon juice and mayonnaise. Add additional mayonnaise, if necessary to make a thick dressing. Chill until ready to use.

Grate or thinly slice the cabbage and store in the refrigerator up to 24 hours. When ready to serve, add the dressing to the cabbage and serve immediately. Do not overdress cabbage as it will become soggy. Add dressing just until cabbage is moist.

SALADS

Broccoli Picnic Salad
SERVES 8

- 1 head broccoli, cut into florets
- 1 cup cheddar cheese, shredded
- 1 medium red onion, thinly sliced
- 16 ounce can red kidney beans, drained
- 3/4 cup Italian salad dressing

Combine all ingredients and refrigerate overnight to allow flavors to blend. Do not cook broccoli, as it will become soggy in the dressing.

A quick and easy salad to make ahead. Perfect for that weekend tailgate and easy enough to make for a crowd at the family reunion.

Summer

Sliced Summer Tomatoes

Skin tomatoes. To do this, drop tomato in boiling water for 10 seconds! Do not overcook the tomato. Core tomato, and the skin should peel off easily. Quarter or slice the tomatoes on a platter. Sprinkle with a little kosher salt and fresh ground pepper. Top with chopped fresh basil. Sprinkle with seasoned rice vinegar.

Summer

SALADS

Cobb Salad
SERVES 8

1 head romaine lettuce, cut into thin ribbons
4 cups cooked and shredded chicken
½ pound Roquefort cheese, crumbled
2 large tomatoes, peeled, seeded and diced
4 hard boiled eggs, peeled and sliced
BUTTERMILK DRESSING (P. 27)
¼ pound bacon, cooked and crumbled

Layer romaine lettuce, chicken, tomatoes, eggs and Roquefort cheese in a large shallow sided platter. Dress lightly with Buttermilk Dressing and sprinkle with bacon bits. Serve immediately.

SALADS

Cucumbers in Sour Cream Sauce
SERVES 6

- 2 English cucumbers, unpeeled and sliced 1/4-inch thick
- 1 cup sour cream
- 2 tablespoons white wine vinegar
- 1 teaspoon sugar
- 1 teaspoon kosher salt
- 1 clove garlic, crushed
- 1/4 cup olive oil
- 1 tablespoon fresh dill, minced

In medium bowl, combine sour cream, vinegar, sugar, salt and garlic. Whisk in oil and gently stir in cucumbers and dill. Cover and refrigerate up to 6 hours. To serve, spoon cucumbers and sauce in small individual dessert size bowls, garnishing with additional dill and nasturtium blossoms if desired.

Summer

Refrigerating Fresh Herbs

Bunches of leafy herbs like parsley, mint, and cilantro can be placed in a tall glass with an inch or two of water. Do not trim the stems, but do remember to replace the water every other day. Cover the tops with plastic wrap draped loosely enough to let moisture evaporate and escape.

Woody herbs like sage, rosemary, and thyme can be wrapped or bagged in plastic and placed in the crisper. Here again, make sure the plastic is perforated to prevent moisture build up.

Summer

SALADS

Summer Rice Salad
SERVES 6–8

3 cups cooked rice
1/2 cup thinly sliced radishes
1/2 cup thinly sliced scallions
1 green pepper, slivered
1 tablespoon minced parsley
1 tablespoon minced fresh dill
1 tablespoon snipped chives
2 tablespoons finely chopped gherkins
2 tablespoons red wine vinegar
1 teaspoon salt
1/2 teaspoon white pepper
1/3 cup olive oil
1/4 cup mayonnaise
1 tablespoon Dijon mustard

Combine rice, radishes, scallions, green pepper, herbs and gherkins in a large bowl. Make a dressing by whisking together the vinegar, salt and pepper. Gradually add the olive oil and whisk in the mayonnaise and mustard. Taste for seasonings and stir into rice and vegetables. Refrigerate until ready to serve. Salad will hold for several hours, but should not be made more than 4–6 hours before serving.

SALADS

Jodi's Watermelon Tomato Salad
SERVES 8–10

4 cups seedless watermelon, cut in one inch cubes
4 cups cherry tomatoes or heirloom tomatoes, seeded and cut in chunks,
1 cup red onions, slivered
1 cup cucumber chunks, peeled and seeded
½ cup fresh basil, sliced
½ cup red wine vinegar
¼ cup olive oil
½ teaspoon salt
Pepper to taste
1 Tablespoon sugar
Optional: ¾ cup feta cheese

Combine watermelon, tomatoes, onions, cucumbers and basil. Toss lightly. Slowly whisk the olive oil into the red wine vinegar. Add the salt, pepper and sugar to the vinaigrette. Pour the vinaigrette over watermelon mixture and top with crumbled feta cheese.

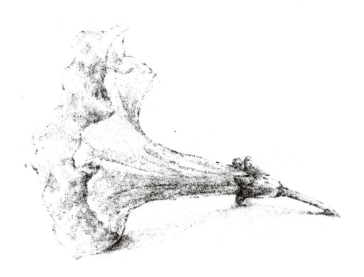

Summer

Summer

ENTREES

Shrimp and Cannellini Beans
SERVES 4

1 cup cannellini beans, picked through and washed
6 cloves garlic, divided
1 bay leaf
1 pound shrimp, peeled
6 tablespoons olive oil, divided
3 garlic cloves, minced
2 tablespoons fresh basil, minced
1 teaspoon fresh parsley, minced
1 teaspoon salt
1/2 teaspoon black pepper, freshly ground
1 pound plum tomatoes, peeled, seeded and chopped

Place cannellini beans in a 4-quart saucepan and add water to cover by 3 inches. Allow to soak overnight or at least 4 hours. Drain and add fresh water to cover by 3 inches. Add the bay leaf and 2 sliced garlic cloves. Bring to a boil and reduce until just boiling, cooking 1–2 hours until beans are soft through. You may need to add more water to keep beans covered. As beans begin to cook, allow the water to boil down. When they are cooked through, drain the beans, reserving 1/3 cup of the bean liquor. Rinse beans and set aside.

In medium skillet, heat 4 tablespoons of olive oil over medium heat. Add the shrimp and sauté 2–3 minutes until they are pink and just barely firm. Add 3 minced garlic cloves, basil, parsley, salt, pepper, beans and the reserved liquor. Heat thoroughly, 2–3 minutes.

In a separate pan, heat 2 tablespoons of olive oil until hot, but not smoking. Add remaining whole garlic cloves and cook slowly until soft and just golden in color. Remove from pan. Add tomatoes and sauté quickly for 1–2 minutes. Stir into the shrimp and beans and serve immediately. Garnish with whole leaves of basil if desired.

Great Northern beans may be substituted for the cannellini beans if they are unavailable. If you have not tried the cannellini, they are similar in size and texture to a red kidney bean.

ENTREES

Summer

Chesapeake Bay Crab Cakes
SERVES 4

- 1 pound crabmeat, jumbo lump
- 2 tablespoons capers
- 1 bunch green onions, finely minced
- 2 egg whites, slightly beaten
- 1 tablespoon fresh lemon juice
- 1 teaspoon white wine vinegar
- 1 tablespoon soy sauce
- 3 tablespoons fresh bread crumbs
- 3 tablespoons flour
- 1 teaspoon kosher salt
- 1/4 teaspoon cayenne pepper
- 1 cup flour
- 2 eggs, beaten
- 2 cups fresh bread crumbs
- 4 tablespoons butter

Carefully pick through crabmeat and place in the refrigerator until ready to use. In a medium bowl, combine the capers, onions, egg whites, lemon juice, vinegar, soy sauce, 3 tablespoons bread crumbs, 3 tablespoons flour, salt and cayenne pepper. Fold in the crabmeat until thoroughly mixed. Divide mixture into 8–10 portions and shape into cakes. Dip each one first in the flour, carefully tapping off any extra flour, then in the beaten eggs and last in the bread crumbs. The crab cakes will be very loose and at first seem they will fall apart. Press lightly after each dipping and pat back and forth between your hands to remove excess flour or crumbs. Place cakes on pan when finished, cover with plastic and refrigerate at least 30 minutes or up to 6 hours. Melt butter in 10-inch skillet until sizzling. Fry crab cakes about 5 minutes on each side until golden brown. Serve immediately with wedges of lemon.

Summer

ENTREES

Suck Mountain Barbeque Sauce
SERVES 12

1 pound vegetable shortening
1 quart apple cider vinegar
1 cup Texas Pete® hot sauce
5 tablespoons salt
3 tablespoons black pepper
3 tablespoons mustard powder

Combine all ingredients in saucepan and heat until melted.

Brush sauce on chicken quarters or pork shoulders. Soak hickory chips for 1 hour and place on a low burning charcoal fire. Add chicken or pork and cook slowly, basting frequently and adding hickory chips as needed. Cook chickens up to 3 hours or pork 4–5 hours until thermometer registers 160°. Meat should be carefully watched as you do not want it to cook too quickly and dry out.

ENTREES

Becca's Burgers
SERVES 6

- 2 pounds lean ground beef
- 2 tablespoons butter
- 1 medium onion, sliced
- 8 ounces mushrooms, sliced
- 2 tomatoes, sliced
- 6 slices cheddar cheese
- 1/2 cup bacon bits
- 3 English muffins, split and toasted
- 1 recipe of BEARNAISE SAUCE (P. 344)

Make Bearnaise Sauce according to the recipe and set aside in warm place so it will not become too cool and stiff.

Form ground beef into 6 patties and refrigerate until ready to cook. Melt butter in a small skillet and sauté sliced onion for 3–4 minutes until wilted and slightly golden in color. Remove onions and set aside. Add mushrooms and sauté until cooked through. Keep warm until ready to serve.

Begin cooking the hamburgers after you have prepared all the toppings. Season each hamburger on both sides with a good season salt and freshly ground pepper. Just before they are finished cooking, add the cheese slices to melt.

To assemble, place one tomato slice on each muffin half and then top with a cooked hamburger. Divide the cooked mushrooms and onions equally on each burger. Spoon one tablespoon of bearnaise on top and sprinkle with bacon pieces. Serve immediately as an open face sandwich. Don't forget to set your table with both a knife and fork as they will be needed.

Always use a light touch when making hamburger patties. Never press tightly or knead meat as it will result in a tough hamburger. Cook the meat on a hot fire, approximately 4–5 minutes per side for medium rare burgers, 3/4-inch thick.

Summer

Summer

ENTREES

Daddy's Barbequed Chicken
SERVES 4–6

- 1 cup red wine vinegar
- 2 cups vegetable oil
- 2 tablespoons black pepper
- 2 tablespoons salt
- 6 tablespoons Worcestershire sauce
- 4 tablespoons lemon juice
- 4 tablespoons dry thyme leaves
- 2 tablespoons garlic powder
- 4 tablespoons mayonnaise
- 2 whole chickens, cut into quarters

Combine first 9 ingredients and mix well. Place chicken in a large non-corrosive bowl and pour marinade over it, reserving one cup for basting chicken on grill. Refrigerate at least two hours or preferably overnight. Prepare a low charcoal or gas fire. Cook chicken at least 2 hours very slowly until the juices run clear or a thermometer registers 160°. Baste and turn frequently the entire time. Serve chicken immediately.

All of our neighbors' mouths would be watering when Daddy cooked his famous barbeque chicken. The secret to this moist, flavorful chicken is the slow patient grilling, basting and turning.

ENTREES

Grilled Chuck Steak
SERVES 8

> 4 pounds chuck roast, 2-inch thick
> 1/2 cup strong coffee
> 1/2 cup soy sauce
> 1 tablespoon Worcestershire sauce
> 1 tablespoon sesame seeds, toasted
> 1 large onion, finely chopped

Place chuck roast in pan. Combine rest of ingredients and pour over roast. Place in refrigerator, turning occasionally, for 3–4 hours or overnight. Remove from refrigerator and drain. Allow to sit 30 minutes before grilling.

Place steak on a hot charcoal or gas grill and cook 10–15 minutes per side until roast reaches desired temperature, 130° for medium rare. Allow roast to sit for 15 minutes before slicing meat vertically against the grain of the meat in 1/4-inch slices. Serve with a BEARNAISE (P. 344) or HORSERADISH sauce (P. 343).

This recipe will turn the cheaper cut of meat into a delicious steak dinner. The marinade tenderizes and flavors a chuck roast especially well. This is worth trying, even for company.

Summer

Summer

ENTREES

Pork Barbeque Sauce for Ribs or Roast
SERVES 8

> 1/4 cup apple cider vinegar
> 1/2 cup water
> 2 tablespoons prepared mustard
> 1 1/2 teaspoons salt
> 1/2 teaspoon black pepper, freshly ground
> 1/4 teaspoon cayenne pepper
> 2 tablespoons brown sugar
> 2 tablespoons lemon juice
> 1 large onion, minced
> 1/4 cup butter
> 1/2 cup catsup
> 2 tablespoons Worcestershire sauce
> 1 1/2 teaspoons liquid smoke

In a 3-quart saucepan, combine vinegar, water, mustard, salt, black pepper, cayenne pepper, brown sugar, lemon juice, onion and butter. Bring to a boil and simmer 20 minutes uncovered, stirring occasionally.

Stir in catsup, Worcestershire and liquid smoke. Cover sauce and continue to simmer for 1–2 hours. Sauce may be brushed on ribs or chops while cooking on the grill or used on a pork roast that has been cooked and chopped for barbeque. If using for chopped barbeque, add only enough sauce to moisten meat when heating and have available as a sauce on the table.

ENTREES

Peach Barbeque Rib Sauce
SERVES 8

1 pound can peach halves
1/2 cup brown sugar
1/4 cup catsup
3/4 cup apple cider vinegar
2 tablespoons soy sauce
1 clove garlic, minced
1 teaspoon salt
1 teaspoon ground ginger
3 tablespoons Texas Pete® hot sauce
6 pounds baby back pork ribs

Process peaches in food processor until smooth. Stir in the next 8 ingredients. Set aside.

Bring 8 quarts of water to a boil. Add one cup of vinegar and the ribs. Bring back to a boil and simmer 30 to 40 minutes until a fork sticks into the meat easily. Keep ribs in water until ready to grill. (this may be done 1–2 hours in advance) Prepare a low charcoal fire. Brush ribs with the sauce and place on the grill. Watch very carefully as the ribs will burn. Cook slowly, basting and turning often until ribs are glazed and browned. This will take 30–45 minutes, but they are well worth the wait. Cut into individual ribs to serve.

Summer

Favorite Dried Flowers

When it comes to drying, some flowers are more suitable than others. Here's a list of some tried-and-true favorites:

Allium
Belles of Ireland
Chinese lanterns
Cockscomb
Cornflower
Eucalyptus
Globe thistle
Hydrangea
Kangaroo paw
Lavender
Love-in-a-mist
Queen Anne's lace*
Statice
Yarrow

*Place head upside-down on a piece of newspaper.

Summer

ENTREES

Grilled Beef Tenderloin
SERVES 12

4 pounds beef tenderloin, fat and sinew removed
Tabasco® Sauce
Black pepper, freshly ground
Greek seasoning salt
HORSERADISH SAUCE (P. 343)

Season beef tenderloin on both sides with Tabasco®, black pepper and seasoning salt. Let stand 15–20 minutes at room temperature. Prepare a hot charcoal or gas fire and place meat on grill, timing for 8 minutes. Turn meat and continue cooking, checking every 5 minutes for doneness. A thermometer should register 130° for medium rare. If you do not have a thermometer, cut into meat and remove it from the fire when it is firm to the touch inside and dark pink in color. The tenderloin will continue to cook after it has been removed. Place the meat on a cutting board and loosely cover with aluminum foil for 10–15 minutes. To serve slice and arrange on a platter garnishing with fresh greens and with HORSERADISH SAUCE on the side.

To cook in the oven, follow above instructions, except preheat oven to 500°. Cook 8 minutes on the first side and turn. Continue to check every 5 minutes, until desired doneness is reached. An average 4 pound tenderloin will take approximately 20–25 minutes to cook to medium rare.

ENTREES

Deviled Crab Meat
SERVES 4

- 1 pound crab meat, picked through for shells
- 2 tablespoons lemon juice, freshly squeezed
- 1/2 teaspoon Worcestershire Sauce
- 1/8 Tabasco® Sauce
- 1 teaspoon Dijon mustard
- 4 tablespoons butter, melted and divided
- 2 tablespoons onions, finely chopped
- 1 tablespoon flour
- 1 cup half and half
- 1/2 teaspoon salt
- 1/4 cayenne pepper
- 1/2 cup bread crumbs
- 2 tablespoons mayonnaise

Gently combine crabmeat, lemon juice, Worcestershire, Tabasco® and mustard. Refrigerate until ready to use.

In medium saucepan, sauté onion in 2 tablespoons butter until translucent. Sprinkle flour over onion and continue cooking about 2–3 minutes, taking care not to brown. Whisk in half and half, and cook until it thickens, stirring constantly. Stir in salt and cayenne. Gently fold sauce into crabmeat. Pile mixture in 4 baking scallop shells and place on a cookie sheet. Combine breadcrumbs, 2 tablespoons butter and mayonnaise. Sprinkle on top of crabmeat mixture. Bake at 375° for 20 minutes until heated through. At last minute run under broiler to brown top.

Serve immediately with wedges of lemon and fresh watercress as a garnish.

Summer

Summer

ENTREES

Chicken Salad
SERVES 4–6

> 6 chicken breast halves, skin on and bone in
> 2 bay leaves
> 1/2 teaspoon black pepper corns
> 3 stalks celery, chopped
> 1 cup mayonnaise, maybe a bit more
> 1 teaspoon grated onion
> 1/2 teaspoon Worcestershire sauce
> 1/2 teaspoon salt
> 1/4 teaspoon black pepper
> 1 tablespoon lemon juice
> 1/2 teaspoon paprika

Place chicken breasts in a 4-quart pot and cover with cold water. Add bay leaves and pepper corns and bring to a boil. Stir once or twice to evenly distribute chicken, cover and remove from heat. When cool, place in refrigerator overnight or for several hours. Remove skin from chicken breasts, and pick meat from bones. Cut into bite size pieces and place in bowl. Stir in chopped celery. In separate bowl, combine remaining ingredients and taste for seasoning. Stir into chicken and refrigerate several hours for flavors to blend. If needed add more mayonnaise to proper consistency. Always keep chicken salad cold until ready to serve.

ENTREES

Inglewood Road Barbeque Sauce for Chicken
SERVES 8–12

    2 large bottles store-bought spicy barbeque sauce
    12 lemons, sliced and juiced, saving rinds
    1 gallon apple cider vinegar
    1 cup vegetable oil
    1/4 cup catsup
    2 tablespoons Worcestershire sauce
    1/2 teaspoon Texas Pete® hot sauce
    1 cup margarine, melted
    salt, pepper
    4 whole chickens, cut into breasts and whole legs

Combine barbeque sauce, lemon juice, lemon rinds, vinegar, oil, catsup, Worcestershire and Texas Pete® in sauce pan and boil until lemons are cooked down.

Coat chicken pieces with margarine and sprinkle well with salt and pepper. Prepare a low heat charcoal fire and place chicken on the grill. Cook slowly, approximately 1/2 hour on each side. Remove chicken and dip each piece of chicken into the barbeque sauce. Return chicken to grill and watch carefully to keep from burning. Turn chicken frequently, every 10 minutes, and brush with sauce often. Cook until meat is well coated, browned and fork tender.

George Hughes was famous in our neighborhood for his barbequed chicken. His recipe was kept a secret for many years, but was recently shared with me and now with you.

Summer

Summer

ENTREES

Crispy Baby Back Ribs
SERVES 6

6 pounds pork baby back ribs
3 tablespoons salt, divided
6 tablespoons sugar, divided
2 tablespoons cumin seed, roasted and ground
3 tablespoons black pepper, freshly ground, divided
2 tablespoons chili powder
1 3/4 cups white vinegar
2 tablespoons Tabasco® sauce

Place ribs on baking sheet. Prepare rub by mixing together 2 tablespoons salt, 4 tablespoons sugar, cumin, 2 tablespoons black pepper and chili powder. Rub both sides of ribs with mixture and roast in a 180° oven uncovered for 3 hours. In the meantime combine vinegar, Tabasco®, one tablespoon salt, 2 tablespoons sugar and one tablespoon black pepper. Brush on ribs after roasting and place them on a low fire charcoal or gas grill. Baste and turn ribs for 20–25 minutes until crispy on the outside. Remove ribs and cut into individual pieces. Serve immediately.

If you love ribs be sure to try this recipe. To roast cumin seed, heat a small skillet until hot. Add cumin seeds to dry skillet and heat, stirring constantly until they become aromatic. Cool and grind to a powder with mortar and pestle or a small processor.

ENTREES

Grilled Tandori Chicken
SERVES 6

2 whole chickens
1 cup vegetable oil
2 cups red wine vinegar
1 cup tomato juice
4 tablespoons kosher salt
1 teaspoon black pepper
1 teaspoon cayenne pepper
2 teaspoons tandori seasoning
½ teaspoon onion powder
1 clove garlic, minced
¼ small bottle hot sauce

Cut chickens into pieces, leaving the wing intact with the breast piece and then cutting the breast in half horizontally. If you use the backs for the stock pot, you will have a total of 12 pieces. Place chicken in a large zip lock freezer bag. Combine remaining ingredients, whisking until smooth. Reserve 2 cups of marinade and pour the remaining marinade on the chicken in the bag. Zip shut and place in shallow pan in the refrigerator. Allow chicken to marinate 6–8 hours (overnight is even better), turning the bag over several times. About one hour before grilling remove chicken to counter and allow to come almost to room temperature. Cook indirectly over a medium hot charcoal fire, turning frequently and brushing with reserved marinade. Grill the chicken for approximately one hour, or until juices run clear when meat is pierced.

Serve immediately with CUCUMBERS IN SOUR CREAM SAUCE (P. 97), corn on the cob and fresh sliced tomatoes.

Summer

Summer

SIDE DISHES

Grilled Yams
SERVES 8

> 2 pounds yams, about 4–5 inches each
> 3 tablespoons soy sauce, divided
> 1/4 cup rice vinegar
> 1/2 cup olive oil
> 4 green onions, minced
> 2 tablespoons fresh parsley, minced
> 1 tablespoon fresh ginger root, grated
> 1/4 cup corn oil

Place yams into a medium pot of cold water. Bring to a boil and cook for 15 minutes. They should be done when a fork can be inserted easily, but the yams are not soft. The time may vary according to the size of the yams. Rinse under cold water, peel and slice lengthwise into 1/4-inch slices. Set aside.

In a small bowl, combine 1 tablespoon of soy sauce, rice vinegar, olive oil, green onions, parsley, and ginger root. Set aside.

Combine remaining 2 tablespoons of soy sauce and corn oil. Brush onto yams and place on a medium hot, greased grill rack. Carefully turn and brown on both sides. Remove yams to a heated serving dish and spoon onion and parsley mixture over yams. Serve immediately.

SIDE DISHES

Chinese Noodles

SERVES 8

> 8 ounces Chinese noodles, broken into pieces
> 2 teaspoons chili oil
> 2 teaspoons sesame oil
> 2 tablespoons apple cider vinegar
> 1 1/2 teaspoons salt
> 1/2 teaspoon white pepper
> 1 tablespoon soy sauce
> 2 teaspoons sugar
> 1 bunch green onions, minced
> 4 tablespoons vegetable oil

Cook Chinese noodles according to directions, taking care not to overcook. Rinse and drain thoroughly. Place in a medium bowl and set aside.

Combine in small saucepan: chili oil, sesame oil, vinegar, salt, pepper, soy sauce and sugar. Heat gradually until sugar dissolves. Pour over noodles and mix well. Sprinkle green onions over noodles. Do not mix. Heat 4 tablespoons of oil until smoking hot. Carefully pour over onions and noodles. Mix well and refrigerate until ready to use. If desired, sprinkle toasted sesame seeds over top just before serving.

Summer

Summer

SIDE DISHES

Easy No-Fail Corn On The Cob
SERVES 6

        12 ears of corn, shucked and silk removed
        8 quarts water
        8 tablespoons butter, room temperature

Place the ears of corn in a large pot and add cold water to cover. Stirring occasionally, bring the water to a boil and cut off heat, leaving the corn in the hot water until ready to serve. Corn may sit in water up to 30 minutes and will not overcook. Dry each ear off with a paper towel and serve immediately with plenty of softened butter, salt and pepper.

For a southwestern flavor, brush hot cooked ears of corn with olive oil and then sprinkle with roasted ground cumin seed, salt and pepper.

SIDE DISHES

Uncle William's Corn Pudding
SERVES 6

- 2 cups corn, cooked and removed from cob
- 3 tablespoons butter, softened
- 2 eggs, beaten
- 1/4 cup sugar
- 1/2 teaspoon salt
- 1 1/2 cups milk
- pinch of nutmeg (optional)
- 1 tablespoon flour if using frozen corn

Cream together butter and sugar (add flour at this point if using frozen corn). Beat in eggs and milk. Stir in salt, nutmeg and corn last. Pour into a buttered 1 1/2-quart casserole and place in a 350° oven. Bake for 35 minutes or until a knife blade inserted in the middle comes out clean. (Note the center of the pudding may shake slightly even when fully baked) Serve the corn pudding immediately.

Uncle William didn't pick the corn until the water was boiling on the stove! He insisted on the freshest taste possible!

Summer

The Scent of Summer

Homemade pot-pourri preserves the fleeting fragrances of summer.

- 6 ml* lavender oil
- 6 ml* geranium oil
- 1 oz. ground orris root (purchase at a health food store)
- 1/2 oz. whole cloves
- 1/2 oz. dried mace
- 4 oz. dried lavender
- 8 oz. dried rose petals
- 8 oz. dried rose buds

Blend the oils together in a bottle and shake. Add a few drops at a time to the orris root, stirring until crumbly. Cover and set aside. Mix the remainder of the oil into the dried spices. Cover and let sit for 24 hours. Place the dried flowers in a bowl. Mix in the dried spices and follow with the orris root. Cover and leave in a dark spot for 6 weeks. Enjoy the fragrance through the fall and into the winter.

*Best measured with an eye-dropper

Summer

SIDE DISHES

Grilled Eggplant Pasta
SERVES 12

3 large eggplants, peeled and sliced 1/2-inch thick
1 medium red onion, sliced 1/4-inch thick
1/4 cup olive oil, plus additional oil for grilling
1 cup chopped onion
3 cloves garlic, minced
1/4 cup freshly squeezed lemon juice
1/4 teaspoon red pepper flakes
16 ounces penne pasta
1/2 cup fresh oregano, snipped
1/2 cup fresh basil, snipped
1 cup grated Romano or Parmesan cheese
3 large tomatoes, peeled, seeded and coarsely chopped
1/2 cup pine nuts, toasted
1 teaspoon kosher salt
1/2 teaspoon freshly ground black pepper

Lightly salt eggplant slices and let stand in a colander for 30 minutes. Press dry on paper towels. Brush eggplant and red onion slices with olive oil and grill until browned and cooked through. Cut slices into strips and put in a large bowl. Add 1/4 cup olive oil, chopped onion, garlic, lemon juice and red pepper flakes. Let stand for one hour.

Cook pasta as directed for al dente and rinse and drain thoroughly. Add to eggplant mixture along with the fresh herbs, Romano cheese tomatoes and pine nuts. Season to taste with salt and freshly ground pepper and serve immediately. If necessary, pasta may be refrigerated overnight. Allow to stand at room temperature for one hour before serving.

This is one of my favorite summer dishes. The vegetables are blackened on the grill until they are crisp tender and then combined with fresh tomatoes, pasta and cheeses. The result is both flavorful and full of the colors of summer vegetables.

SIDE DISHES

Three Baked Bean Pot
SERVES 8

> 6 slices bacon
> 1/2 cup green pepper, chopped
> 1 small onion, chopped
> 2 tablespoons brown sugar
> 1/2 cup catsup
> 1 tablespoon prepared mustard
> 1 envelope onion soup mix
> 1 teaspoon hot sauce
> 1 teaspoon Worcestershire sauce
> 15 ounce can baked beans
> 15 ounce can butter beans, drained
> 15 ounce red kidney beans, drained

Slice bacon in half and drop in boiling water for 2–3 minutes. Drain and set aside. Combine remaining ingredients in a large bowl, mixing well. Spoon into a 3–4-quart bean pot or casserole. Lay strips of bacon across the top and cover. Place in a 300° oven and bake slowly for 2–3 hours.

Summer

Summer

SIDE DISHES

Yellow Squash Casserole
SERVES 8

2 pounds yellow summer squash, sliced 1/2-inch thick
4 tablespoons butter, melted
1 small onion, diced
1 can cream of chicken soup
1 cup sour cream
2 tablespoons fresh basil, minced
1 teaspoon salt
1/4 teaspoon red pepper
1 small bag herb stuffing mix, crushed

In medium saucepan, sauté onion in butter. Add squash and 1/2 cup water. Bring to a boil, cover and reduce heat, cooking 8–10 minutes until tender. Do not drain. Add cream of chicken soup, sour cream, basil, salt and pepper. Layer squash mixture in a buttered 2-quart casserole, with a layer of herb stuffing, ending with stuffing. Dot with butter. Bake uncovered at 325° for 25 minutes. Serve immediately.

SIDE DISHES

Grilled Chipotle Corn on the Cob
SERVES 4

> 8 ears of corn, shucked, silks removed
> ½ cup butter, softened
> 1½ tablespoons minced chipotle peppers
> 1 teaspoon kosher salt
> 1 teaspoon sugar
> ½ teaspoon ground cumin
> 2 tablespoons fresh lime juice

In small saucepan, combine butter, chipotle peppers, salt, sugar, cumin and lime juice. Heat just until ingredients can be whisked together smoothly. Brush on ears of corn and place on charcoal grill. Cook corn either over a low fire or indirectly, approximately 15–20 minutes until lightly browned and cooked through. Serve immediately.

Summer

Summer

SIDE DISHES

Curry Stuffed Potatoes
SERVES 6

6 medium Idaho potatoes
2 teaspoons salt
1 teaspoon black pepper, freshly ground
1 1/2 teaspoons curry powder, or to taste
8 tablespoons butter, melted
1/2 cup sour cream

Wash and prick potatoes all over with tines of a fork. Grease lightly and sprinkle with kosher salt. Place on a baking sheet and bake at 425° for 45–60 minutes until they pierce easily with a fork. Remove from oven. Cut top off each potato and scoop out flesh into a mixing bowl. Beat with a hand held mixer until completely mashed. Stir in butter, sour cream, 2 teaspoons salt, pepper and curry. Refill potato shells, mounding the filling up slightly. Sprinkle tops with paprika or parsley. If using immediately, reheat at 350° for 30 minutes. If not, refrigerate until ready to use or wrap individually to freeze up to one month. Heat thawed or refrigerated potatoes at 350° for 45–60 minutes. Serve immediately with barbequed chicken or grilled steaks and a fresh garden salad.

SIDE DISHES

Indian Green Beans

SERVES 4

> 8 slices bacon, cooked and crumbled
> 1 tablespoon bacon grease, reserved
> 1 medium onion, minced
> ½ cup sugar
> ½ cup cider vinegar
> 2 (16 ounce) cans French-style green beans
> 3 tablespoons Indian pickle relish or hot pickle relish

Sauté onion in bacon grease until soft and translucent. Stir in sugar and vinegar and heat until sugar dissolves, stirring constantly. Drain green beans and place in lightly greased 1½-quart casserole. Pour sugar mixture over beans. Combine bacon bits and relish and sprinkle evenly over beans. Cover casserole tightly and bake at 275° for 1½ hours. Serve immediately.

Summer

Recipe to Whiten Yellowed Linens

Mix:

1 gallon hot water

½ cup Electrasol® dish detergent

¼ cup Clorox®

Soak linens in the above solution for ½ hour. Rinse thoroughly.

Re-soak linens in ½ cup white vinegar and 1 gallon hot water for up to one hour. Rinse thoroughly two times and launder them as usual. Let your linens dry in the sun for maximum brightness.

—Whitie Lewis

Summer

SIDE DISHES

Catherine's Tomato Casserole
NUMBER OF SERVINGS DEPENDS ON CASSEROLE SIZE

Green tomatoes, sliced
Ripe tomatoes, sliced
Vidalia onions, sliced
Salt
Brown sugar
Bread crumbs
Butter

Layer, in order, the above in a greased baking dish. Sprinkle with salt and brown sugar. Top with a layer of bread crumbs. Repeat the tomatoes, onions, salt, sugar and end with the bread crumbs. Dot with butter. Bake for 2- 3 hours at 200°.

This is a wonderful dish to prepare in the summer/early fall when tomatoes are plentiful.

DESSERTS

Kathie's Amaretti Nut Crunch Pie
SERVES 8

PIE CRUST:
- 1 ¼ cups ground Amaretti cookies or ground coconut macaroons
- 1/3 cup granulated sugar
- ½ cup chopped macadamia nuts
- 1/3 cup melted unsalted sweet butter
- ½ square (½ ounce) unsweetened chocolate, melted

Preheat oven to 400°. Mix cookie crumbs, sugar and melted butter. Stir in nuts and chocolate. Spread on bottom and sides of pie pan, that has been buttered. Bake for 8 minutes and cool.

FILLING:
- ½ cup unsalted sweet butter
- ¾ cup brown sugar
- 1 square (1 ounce) unsweetened chocolate, melted
- 2 eggs
- 2 teaspoons instant coffee

Cream butter and sugar in bowl until fluffy. Add chocolate and coffee powder. Beat until well mixed. Beat in eggs one at a time. Spoon into pie crust. Refrigerate for at least 5 hours or overnight.

WHIPPED CREAM TOPPING:
- 1 ¼ cup whipping cream
- 2 tablespoons cold liquid coffee
- 1 tablespoon powdered sugar
- ¼ teaspoon vanilla

Whip cream until there are stiff peaks. Add coffee, sugar and vanilla. Beat until fluffy. Spread this mixture on top of filling. Garnish with ground Amaretti crumbs or ground macadamia nuts.

Summer

Summer

DESSERTS

Butter Layer Cake
MAKES TWO 9-INCH LAYERS

1 cup sour cream
1/4 cup milk
1 cup butter, softened
2 cups sugar
4 eggs, room temperature
2 3/4 cups flour
2 teaspoons baking powder
1/2 teaspoon salt
1 teaspoon vanilla extract
1 teaspoon rum flavoring (optional)

Combine sour cream and milk in a small bowl. Set aside. In a medium mixing bowl, cream butter and sugar together. Add eggs, one at a time, beating well after each addition. In a separate bowl, sift dry ingredients together and add to cake batter, alternating with sour cream mixture. Begin and end with flour. Stir in the vanilla and rum. Spoon batter into 2 well-greased and floured 9-inch cake pans. Bake at 350° for 30–35 minutes. Test for doneness and cool in pan 10 minutes before turning onto racks. When completely cool, ice with frosting of your choice.

DESERTS

Raspberry Almond Cake
MAKES ONE FOUR-LAYER CAKE

    1 recipe BUTTER LAYER CAKE (PREVIOUS PAGE)
    16 ounces cream cheese, softened
    4 tablespoons butter, softened
    2½ cups powdered sugar
    ½ teaspoon almond extract
    1 teaspoon vanilla extract
    1½ cups seedless raspberry jam
    1 cup sliced almonds, toasted
    ½ pint fresh raspberries

Make one recipe of BUTTER LAYER CAKE according to directions. Combine cream cheese, butter, sugar and extracts, beating until smooth. Split each cake layer in half and place first layer on cake plate. Ice with the cream cheese frosting and spread ½ cup of the jam carefully over the frosting. Repeat with the next two layers. Ice outside of the cake with the remaining frosting. Decorate by covering side of cake with overlapping layers of sliced almonds. Place 2 or 3 rows of fresh raspberries along outer top edge of cake. Cover and refrigerate until ready to serve.

Summer

Summer

DESSERTS

Chocolate Mocha Cake
MAKES ONE FOUR-LAYER CAKE

    1 recipe Butter Layer Cake (p. 126)
    1 recipe Chocolate Mousse (p.45)
    1 cup butter, softened
    2½ cups powdered sugar
    1 tablespoon instant coffee crystals
    ¾ teaspoon cocoa
    ¾ teaspoon hot water
    2 egg yolks, beaten
    1 teaspoon almond extract
    2 tablespoons Jamaican rum

Make Butter Layer Cake according to the directions. Split each layer in half. Spread 2 cups of Chocolate Mousse between the two split halves and refrigerate until firm.

In medium bowl, beat together the butter and powdered sugar. Dissolve the coffee crystals and cocoa in the hot water and cool slightly. Stir coffee into the butter mixture, along with the egg yolks. Beat until smooth and creamy. Stir in the almond extract and rum. Spread frosting between the two refrigerated layers and on the top and sides of the cake. Refrigerate until ready to serve. If desired, decorate the top of the cake with chocolate covered espresso beans.

DESSERTS

Fresh Peach Cake
MAKES ONE FOUR-LAYER CAKE

    1 recipe Butter Layer Cake (p. 126)
    1 teaspoon almond extract
    1 1/2 cups sugar
    4 tablespoons cornstarch
    1/2 cup water
    4 cups peaches, coarsely chopped
    2 cups heavy cream
    3 tablespoons powdered sugar
    1 cup sour cream
    1 peach, peeled and sliced for garnish
    1 teaspoon lemon juice

Prepare cake as directed, replacing almond extract for the rum flavoring. In a small saucepan, combine sugar and cornstarch. Stir in water and chopped peaches and cook over medium heat, stirring until thickened. Remove from heat and cool.

Whip the cream with the powdered sugar until it is glossy and forms stiff peaks. Refrigerate until ready to use.

To assemble the cake, split each layer in half horizontally. Spread 1/3 of the peach filling and 1/3 of the sour cream on top of the peach filling between each layer. Frost top and sides of cake with the whipped cream. Lightly sprinkle one teaspoon of lemon juice over peach slices to prevent darkening and arrange slices around top edge of cake. Surround bottom of cake with sprigs of fresh mint. Refrigerate until ready to serve.

This is a beautiful cake and can be simplified by using a butter flavored cake mix. It is best if refrigerated at least 4 hours or up to 24 hours before serving.

Summer

Still, in a way, nobody sees a flower, really. It is so small. We haven't the time— and to see takes time, like to have friends takes time.

—Georgia O' Keefe

Summer

DESSERTS

Chocolate Pound Cake
MAKES ONE LARGE BUNDT CAKE

1 cup butter, softened
1/2 cup margarine, softened
3 cups sugar
5 eggs, room temperature
3 cups flour
1/2 cup cocoa
1/2 teaspoon baking powder
1/2 teaspoon baking soda
1/2 teaspoon salt
1 cup milk
2 tablespoons vanilla extract

Grease and flour an oversized (14 cup) bundt pan. Cream together the butter, margarine and sugar in a large mixing bowl. Beat in the eggs, one at a time. Sift together flour, cocoa, baking powder, baking soda and salt. Stir into the cake batter, alternating with the milk. Add the vanilla and spoon evenly into the bundt pan. Bang the pan several times on a counter top to dispel any air bubbles. Bake in a 250° oven for 2 hours. Cake will rise almost to the top and sometimes will run over the top. I usually place a cookie sheet under the cake to catch any batter that may spill over. The cake will fall back down as it becomes fully baked. When done, remove from oven and set on a rack to cool, about 30 minutes. Turn out onto a rack to completely cool. Dust with powdered sugar if desired.

This rich, dark chocolate pound cake is the best I have ever tasted. The recipe is very different from most, but it works well. An extra large bundt pan is very important to prevent too much batter from spilling over the top. If one is not available be sure to remove some of the batter and bake in a small loaf pan. I highly recommend trying this recipe.

DESSERTS

Cissa's Almond Squares
MAKES 48 SQUARES

> 3 eggs, room temperature
> 1 1/2 cups sugar, divided
> 1 cup flour, plus 1 tablespoon
> 1 1/2 cups butter, melted and cooled slightly
> 1/2 cup sliced almonds
> 1 tablespoon milk

Beat together eggs and one cup of sugar until thick and lemon colored, about 10 minutes. Gently fold in one cup of butter and one cup of flour. Spoon into a greased and floured 9 x 13-inch pan and bake in a 350° oven for 25–30 minutes or until cake tests done.

While cake is baking, combine 1/2 cup of butter, 1/2 cup of sugar, almonds, one tablespoon flour and milk in a heavy 2-quart saucepan. Bring slowly to a boil and continue to slowly boil, stirring constantly, until mixture becomes thick and golden brown.

After cake is done, immediately pour almond mixture over the top, spreading evenly. Place under the broiler and lightly brown the top, watching carefully so as not to burn. Remove from oven and place on a cooling rack. Cut in 1-inch squares when cake has completely cooled.

The almond glaze topping is also delicious poured over a round of brie and run quickly under the broiler to brown.

Summer

Summer

DESSERTS

Romanov Fruit Sauce
MAKES 6 CUPS

    1 pint heavy whipping cream
    4 cups sour cream
    3 tablespoons grated orange peel
    1 cup brown sugar
    1 dash nutmeg, freshly grated
    1 dash cinnamon
    1/4 cup Grand Marnier
    1/4 cup brandy

Whip cream until it is glossy and holds in stiff peaks. Set aside. In a large mixing bowl, combine the remaining ingredients. Gently fold in the whipped cream and store in the refrigerator 2–3 days. Additional brown sugar may be added to taste.

An elegant and easy dessert, especially for a large crowd. Serve the sauce with fresh strawberries, peaches, blueberries and raspberries beside a slice of homemade pound cake.

DESSERTS

Momma's Banana Split Pie
SERVES 6

    1 baked pie crust
    2 medium bananas, sliced
    1/2 cup margarine, softened
    1 cup powdered sugar
    1 egg, beaten
    8 ounce can pineapple tidbits
    1 pint strawberries
    1 cup heavy whipping cream, whipped

Line bottom of pie shell with sliced bananas. In a small bowl, beat together margarine, powdered sugar and egg for 15 minutes until creamy and smooth. Spread over bananas. Drain pineapple bits and layer on top of creamed mixture. Wash, cap and slice fresh strawberries, reserving a few for garnishing the top. Layer over pineapple (canned cherries or other fruit may be substituted for strawberries if not available). Ice top of pie with the whipped cream and garnish with the reserved strawberries. Refrigerate for several hours but not more than 24 hours.

Summer

Summer

Peeling Peaches

This task is easier if you blanch the fruits first to loosen their skin. Lightly score the bottom of each peach with an **X** before blanching. Working in batches of 3 or 4, add peaches to boiling water for 30–45 seconds. Use a slotted spoon to transfer them to an ice water bath to stop the cooking. Remove skin with a paring knife.

DESSERTS

Peach Ice Cream
SERVES 12

- 4 eggs, room temperature
- 2 cups sugar
- 5 cups peaches, peeled and pureed
- 4 cups heavy whipping cream
- 1/2 teaspoon salt
- 1/2 teaspoon vanilla extract
- 1/2 teaspoon almond extract

Beat eggs and sugar together until thick and lemon colored, about 10 minutes. Stir in remaining ingredients and refrigerate several hours or overnight. Pour into ice cream maker and freeze according to manufacturer's instructions. Pack in airtight plastic container and freeze 3–4 hours before serving.

DESSERTS

Strawberry Banana Nut Ice Cream
SERVES 12

    6 eggs, room temperature
    2 cups sugar
    1 cup milk
    14 ounces sweetened condensed milk
    1 1/2 teaspoons vanilla extract
    1 pint strawberries, sliced
    2 bananas, mashed
    1 cup pecans, broken in pieces
    8 ounces frozen whipped topping, thawed

Beat eggs until frothy. Gradually beat in sugar until thick and lemon colored, about 10 minutes. Stir in milk, condensed milk and vanilla. In separate bowl combine strawberries, bananas and nuts. Fold in whipped topping and then fold into egg/milk mixture. Refrigerate several hours. Pour into ice cream maker and freeze according to manufacturer's instructions. Allow ice cream to ripen in the freezer for at least 2 hours before serving.

Summer

DESSERTS

Nana's Mile High Birthday Cake
SERVES 12

1 store-bought angel food cake
1 quart orange sherbert
1 quart lime sherbert
1 quart raspberry sherbert
1 quart pineapple sherbert
1 small container frozen whipped topping, thawed
1 recipe RASPBERRY SAUCE (P.350)
1/2 pint fresh raspberries (optional)

Split angel food cake into 4 equal layers. Set aside. Working with one quart of sherbert at a time, soften slightly and "ice" (approximately 1/2-inch thick) the bottom and middle hole of the first cake layer with the orange sherbert. Place in the freezer for 30 minutes. Place the second cake layer on top and "ice" with lime sherbert as above. Freeze. Repeat with a layer of cake and raspberry sherbert and top with the fourth layer. Freeze for at least 30 minutes.

Place pineapple sherbert in medium bowl and soften slightly. Fold in the whipped topping and quickly "ice" the top and sides of the cake. Cover tightly and re-freeze immediately.

To serve, cut the cake with a very sharp knife that has been dipped into hot water. Spread 2 tablespoons of Raspberry Sauce on the dessert plate and place a cake slice on top. Garnish with additional fresh raspberries and mint sprigs if desired.

A beautiful and refreshing cake in the hot summer time. A favorite with men.

Summer

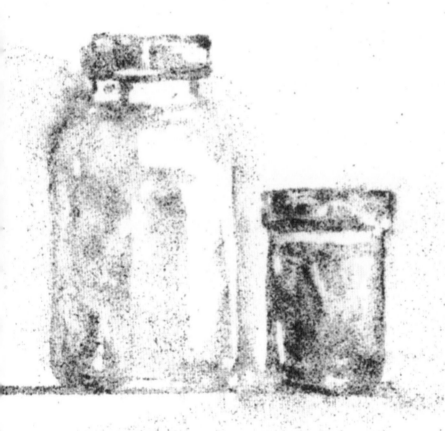

Summer

Preserving the bounty of summer through canning is not as difficult as it may seem if you follow some simple steps. Jars, lids and bands may be sterilized by running them through one cycle of the dishwasher. Remove jars to a clean towel surface and turn upside down. If needed, jars may be kept warm in an oven heated to 180°. Lids and bands should be placed in a pan of simmering water until you are ready to use them. After filling the hot jars with your product, wipe the top of the jar with a hot, damp cloth. Using tongs, place a hot lid on the top and screw down the band. Place the jars in a canning rack and lower into the boiling water for the required time. Carefully remove the jars to a draft-free area to cool. As each jar seals, it will make a popping sound and the lid will flatten out tightly on the jar. I like to use the buddy system when I am canning. It makes the chopping and peeling go by more quickly and you can split the fruits of your labor.

CANNING

Bread and Butter Pickle
MAKES 12 PINTS

    40 small cucumbers, thinly sliced
    5 medium onions, thinly sliced
    1/2 cup pickling salt
    1 quart cider vinegar
    4 cups sugar
    1 tablespoon celery seed
    2 tablespoons mustard seed
    1 tablespoon ground ginger
    1/2 teaspoon ground cloves
    1/2 teaspoon ground allspice
    1/2 teaspoon white pepper, freshly ground
    4 green peppers, cut in slivers

In a ceramic bowl or 3-gallon crock, combine cucumbers and onions. Sprinkle salt on top and mix well. Cover with ice and allow to sit 2–3 hours until crisp, adding ice as needed to cover top. Drain well.

In a large stockpot, combine cider vinegar, sugar and spices. Bring to a boil and boil 10 minutes. Gently stir in drained cucumbers, onions and green peppers. Return to a boil and remove from heat. Pack in hot, sterile pint jars and process in boiling water bath for 30 minutes to seal.

Summer

Note about canning

During the summer months, take advantage of doing some canning since the summer produce is so flavorful and relatively inexpensive. You may want to can for your own pantry or make something special as gifts for the Christmas season. A homemade loaf of bread with a jar of Tomato Marmalade makes a wonderful gift that is always appreciated.

Summer

CANNING

Green Tomato Pickle
MAKES 15 HALF PINTS

- 2 quarts green tomatoes, 2 inches in diameter and sliced 1/8-inch thick
- 3 tablespoons kosher salt
- 2 cups apple cider vinegar
- 2/3 cup dark brown sugar
- 1 cup sugar
- 3 tablespoons mustard seeds
- 1/2 teaspoon celery seed
- 1 teaspoon turmeric
- 3 cups onions, thinly sliced
- 2 large red bell peppers, chopped
- 1 hot chili pepper, finely minced (wear protective gloves)

Mix tomatoes and salt together in a large ceramic bowl or crock. Cover and allow to stand at room temperature for 12 hours. Drain well.

In large 8-quart saucepan, combine vinegar, sugars and spices. Bring to a boil and add onions. Boil gently 5 minutes, stirring occasionally. Add tomatoes and peppers and return slowly to a boil. Boil 5 more minutes, stirring gently with a wooden spoon. Pack and seal pickles and juice in hot, sterile half-pint jars. Process in a boiling water bath for 5 minutes. Remove and allow to cool in draft-free place.

CANNING

Cucumber Relish
MAKES 12 PINTS

    24 medium cucumbers
    4 cups onions, coarsely ground
    5 tablespoons pickling salt, divided
    6 cups sugar
    6 cups cider vinegar
    1 teaspoon turmeric
    1 1/2 teaspoons mustard seeds
    1 1/2 teaspoons celery seeds
    1 teaspoon ground cloves

Coarsely grind unpeeled cucumbers and place in a ceramic bowl. Sprinkle 4 tablespoons of salt over cucumbers and stir well. Place ground onions in a separate bowl and sprinkle one tablespoon of salt over the top. Stir well. Let both mixtures stand for 2 hours and then drain well. In a heavy 8-quart Dutch oven, combine sugar, vinegar, turmeric, mustard seeds, celery seeds and cloves. Bring to a boil, stirring to dissolve the sugar. Stir in the cucumbers and onions and return to a rolling boil. Pour into hot, sterile pint jars and wipe jar rim with a hot damp cloth. Place lids on jars and tighten down with bands. Process in boiling water bath for 15 minutes. Remove jars and allow to cool in a draft-free place.

Summer

Summer

CANNING

Pickled Dilly Beans
MAKES 4 PINT JARS

2 pounds green beans
1 teaspoon red pepper flakes
8 cloves garlic, peeled
1/4 cup fresh dill, snipped
2 1/2 cups water
2 1/2 cups white vinegar
1/4 cup kosher salt

Choose very thin, tender green beans. Wash and cut off just the stem end. Pack the beans, lengthwise in 4 hot, sterile pint jars, leaving 1/4-inch headroom. In each jar, place 1/4 teaspoon of pepper flakes, 2 garlic cloves, one tablespoon dill weed and one tablespoon kosher salt. Heat the water and vinegar just to a boil and pour over beans to cover. Wipe the rims of jars well with a wet cloth and place lids on jars and tighten down with bands. Process in a boiling water bath for 15 minutes. Remove jars and allow to cool in draft-free place until sealed.

Try using these homemade Dilly Beans in a Bloody Mary instead of a stalk of celery or use them on an antipasto tray as an hors d'oeuvre.

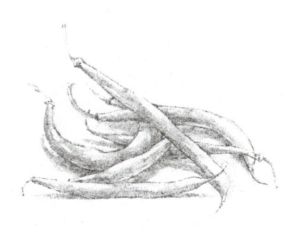

CANNING

Pickled Eggplant
MAKES 2 QUARTS

    6 Japanese eggplants
    1 tablespoon kosher salt
    4 tablespoons red wine vinegar
    8 fresh basil leaves, whole
    3 cloves garlic, peeled and slivered
    3 dried red chili peppers, whole
    2 cups extra virgin olive oil

Trim the stems on the eggplant and cut into 2-inch sections. Slice each section lengthwise 1/2-inch thick and then cut each slice into 1/2-inch strips. Place in a bowl and sprinkle with the salt, tossing to coat. Cover and let sit at room temperature for 24 hours. Remove excess moisture by pressing eggplant strips with toweling. Return to the bowl and stir in vinegar. Allow to rest for one hour. Layer the eggplant, basil and garlic in a 2-quart Mason jar or crock type container. Slip red chili peppers along the sides of the jar. Press down gently and pour in enough olive oil to cover. Screw on lid or cover with plastic wrap. Place in refrigerator and check in a few hours, adding more oil if it is absorbed. Pickled Eggplant is ready to eat within a few days or may be kept in the refrigerator for several months. Allow the eggplant to sit at room temperature for an hour so that the olive oil will liquefy.

This recipe is delicious as an accompaniment for an outdoor barbeque or on the antipasto tray. Make it in the summer when the garden vegetables and herbs are at their peak and it will last into the Fall.

Summer

Summer

CANNING

Dill Pickles
MAKES 15 PINTS

- 14 large seedless cucumbers
- 1 large bunch fresh dill weed
- 15 garlic cloves, peeled and cut in half
- 15 dried red chili peppers
- 3 quarts water
- 1 quart cider vinegar
- 1 cup pickling salt

Wash and slice unpeeled cucumbers in $1/4$-inch thickness. Pack in pint jars, along with several sprigs of fresh dill weed, 2 garlic halves and a red chili pepper. Combine water, vinegar and salt in saucepan and bring to a boil. Carefully pour hot liquid over cucumbers and screw lids on jars. At this point, I do not process the pickles, but rather refrigerate the jars and allow them to age for a month before using. Because the jars have not been sealed, you will need to keep them refrigerated. They will however last for several months, if they are not eaten first.

CANNING

Pickled Jalapeño Peppers
MAKES 8 PINTS

- 4 cups white vinegar
- 4 cups water
- 4 teaspoons kosher salt
- 4 pounds jalapeño peppers, washed and stems trimmed
- 16 garlic cloves, peeled and cut in half
- 8 whole bay leaves
- 16 whole allspice
- 48 whole black pepper corns
- ½ cup olive oil

Combine white vinegar, water and salt in stainless saucepan and heat just to the boiling point. Keep warm until ready to use.

Pack jalapeño peppers in hot, sterilized pint jars, placing 4 garlic halves and one bay leaf in as you pack them. Drop 2 allspice and 6 peppercorns in each jar. Carefully pour the hot vinegar to within ½ inch of the top of the jar, covering the peppers completely. Drizzle one tablespoon of olive oil over the top of the peppers, taking care that the rims do not have any oil on them. Wipe rims clean with a hot, wet towel and tighten lids and bands. Process in a boiling water bath for 20–25 minutes, depending upon the size of the peppers. Allow to cool at room temperature until sealed. Peppers are best if stored for one month before using.

Summer

Summer

CANNING

Tomato Marmalade
MAKES 6 HALF PINTS

4 pounds tomatoes, peeled and coarsely chopped
2 pounds lemons, sliced paper thin
3 oranges, sliced paper thin
1/2 ounce whole cinnamon sticks
1/2 ounce whole cloves
4 pounds sugar, approximately

Drain the tomatoes in a colander, reserving the juice. Measure and discard 1/2 the juice and transfer the tomatoes to a bowl. Re-weigh and stir in an equal amount of sugar. Place in a heavy saucepan and add lemon and orange slices. Tie spices in a cheesecloth bag and add to tomatoes. Cook over low heat until sugar dissolves. Increase the heat and stir marmalade frequently until it begins to thicken. Skim off any scum as it rises. Continue to cook until the temperature reaches 124°–125°, or a soft ball stage. Immediately pour into hot, sterilized half-pint jars. Seal and process in a boiling water bath for 15 minutes. Allow to cool in a draft-free spot until jars seal.

An unusual jam, that is good not only on breakfast toast, but is also a delicious condiment for pork or chicken.

CANNING

Ginger Preserves
MAKES 6 HALF PINTS

    1 1/2 pounds young ginger
    3 cups sugar, divided
    1 cup white corn syrup
    1 lemon, thinly sliced and seeded
    8 cups water

Peel and slice ginger 1/4-inch thick. Combine ginger and water in a large, non-corrosive saucepan. Bring to boil, cover and simmer 20 minutes until tender. Add one cup of sugar. Bring back to a boil, cover and remove from heat. Let stand 3 hours or overnight. Return to a boil, cover and continue to boil 15 minutes, stirring occasionally. Stir in the corn syrup and lemon slices. Again bring to a boil, cover pan and continue to boil 15 minutes, uncover and boil an additional 15 minutes, stirring at times. Remove from heat and let stand 3 hours or overnight. Bring back to a boil, add one cup of sugar and boil covered 30 minutes. Add one more cup of sugar and bring back to a boil covered. Uncover and cook mixture until it reaches 230°. Do not stir mixture during this last cooking. When preserves have reached this soft ball stage, ladle into hot, sterilized half-pint jars. Wipe rims with a hot, wet towel and tighten down lids and bands. Process in water bath 5 minutes to seal, or refrigerate if unprocessed. Ginger Preserves will keep several weeks in the refrigerator unsealed.

Ginger Preserves must be made with very young ginger. It will have a very thin outer peel and is juicy light pink or yellow on the inside. This is usually available in markets in January and February or July and August. It is delicious served over ice cream or as a complement to a pork roast. The ginger may be chopped and used as a seasoning in sauces and stir frys.

Summer

Summer

CANNING

Strawberry Preserves
MAKES 5 HALF PINTS

1 pound strawberries, washed and capped
2 cups sugar

Place strawberries in a heavy 4-quart Dutch oven and sprinkle the sugar on top. Heat slowly until the strawberries give up their juice and the sugar begins to dissolve. Bring the mixture to a boil, stirring constantly, and remove any scum that rises to the surface. Continue to boil for 10 minutes, until preserves darken slightly and reach the soft ball stage, 225°–230°. You may test a bit of preserves by dropping a small amount in a glass of cold water. The mixture should hold together in a soft ball at the bottom of the glass. The cooking time may vary according to the amount of water in the strawberries. When the preserves have reached the proper stage, remove from heat and carefully ladle into hot, sterilized half-pint jars. Wipe rims with a hot, wet towel and screw the lids and bands on the jars. Process in a water bath for 15 minutes. Remove and cool in a draft-free area until sealed.

This recipe may be substituted with other fruits, such as raspberries, blackberries or blueberries. Be sure to weigh fruit carefully and allow for an equal amount of sugar.

CANNING

Tomato Juice
MAKES 15 QUARTS

    30 pounds tomatoes
    5 tablespoons salt

Wash tomatoes and dip in boiling water for 30 seconds to loosen skins. Peel, core and cut into fourths. Place in a heavy 20-quart stock pot. Bring the tomatoes to a boil, stirring frequently. Pour in batches into a cone shaped strainer and mash through with the wooden pusher. Remove seeds and tough flesh after straining each batch. Fill the jars to within a half inch with the hot juice. Add one teaspoon of salt to each quart of juice. Wipe the rims with a hot, wet towel and screw on hot lids and bands. Process in a water bath for 30 minutes. Remove and cool in a draft-free place.

You can enjoy the taste of summer tomatoes all year long by canning the juice. It is a wonderful addition to sauces and soups, but its best use is as the base for a Bloody Mary. You will never be satisfied with the store-bought version again.

Summer

Ripening Tomatoes

Tomatoes should ALWAYS be kept at room temperature. never refrigerate! Place under-ripe tomatoes in a sunny spot or in a brown paper bag for 2–4 days. Check daily for desired ripeness.

Summer

CANNING

Peach and Habanero Salsa
MAKES 6 PINTS

6 pounds peaches, peeled and chopped
4 bunches green onions, minced
6 red bell peppers, finely chopped
20 cloves garlic, crushed
12 Habanero peppers, finely diced (use rubber gloves)
2 tablespoons salt
1 cup white wine vinegar
2 tablespoons cumin seeds, roasted and ground
1/3 cup sugar
1 cup lime juice, freshly squeezed
1 bunch fresh cilantro, minced

In a heavy saucepan, combine peaches, green onions, bell peppers, garlic, Habaneros, salt, vinegar, cumin and sugar. Bring to a boil and cook, stirring frequently until the mixture cooks down slightly. Remove from heat and stir in lime juice and cilantro. Ladle into 6 hot, sterilized pint jars and wipe rim clean with a hot, wet towel. Process in water bath for 20 minutes and remove to a draft-free area to seal.

CANNING

Summer Marinara Sauce
MAKES 12 QUARTS

28 pounds tomatoes
1 1/2 pounds mushrooms, sliced
24 cloves garlic, minced
2 large onions, chopped
2 red bell peppers, chopped
2 green peppers, chopped
1 tablespoon sugar
1 tablespoon black pepper, freshly ground
3 tablespoons kosher salt
1 tablespoon ancho chili powder
1/4 cup fresh basil, minced
1/3 cup fresh oregano, minced
1/4 cup fresh parsley, minced
1/2 cup olive oil, divided

Bring a large pot of water to a boil and dip each tomato in the water to split the skin. Allow to cool and peel off skin. Cut tomatoes in wedges and place in a large stock pot. Bring the tomatoes to a boil and allow to boil slowly for 1–2 hours until they have begun to thicken and break apart.

Heat 1/4 cup of olive oil until sizzling and sauté the garlic, onions and peppers until tender. Remove and add to pot of tomatoes. Heat remaining oil and sauté mushrooms until done. Stir mushrooms into tomatoes, along with the sugar, black pepper, salt and chili powder. Continue to simmer until sauce thickens. Add fresh herbs and cook an additional 25–30 minutes. Ladle into 12 hot, sterilized quart jars and carefully wipe rims with a hot, wet towel. Process jars in boiling water bath for 25–30 minutes. Remove to a draft-free area and allow to cool and seal.

Summer

Summer

CANNING

Summer Pesto
MAKES 2 CUPS

- 3 cups fresh basil, stems removed
- 2 cups spinach, stems removed
- 4 cloves garlic, peeled
- 1/2 cup pine nuts
- 1 cup fresh parsley, stems removed
- 1 cup grated Parmesan cheese
- 3/4 cup olive oil
- 2 teaspoons salt
- 1 teaspoon black pepper, freshly ground

Combine in food processor basil, spinach, garlic, pine nuts, parsley and Parmesan cheese. Turn on machine and slowly pour olive oil into bowl. If all the greens will not fit in the bowl at first, add them gradually as they are processed. Season to taste with salt and pepper. Continue to process until it forms a smooth paste. Serve pesto over hot, drained pasta or use as a seasoning in sauces or casseroles.

Although better when served fresh, pesto freezes relatively well and is worth the loss in quality to preserve the flavor of fresh garden basil all winter long. I freeze it in small half-pint containers or snack size ziplock bags.

CANNING

Tomato Chutney
MAKES 4 CUPS

    2 tablespoons vegetable oil
    ½ teaspoon panch phoran
        (available in Indian speciality shops)
    2 whole red chilies, dried
    1-inch piece fresh ginger, slivered
    6 cloves garlic, crushed
    4 medium tomatoes, peeled, seeded and chopped
    1 teaspoon salt
    ½ cup sugar
    5 dried apricots, chopped
    2 fresh jalapeño peppers, finely chopped
        (use rubber gloves)

Heat oil in heavy 4-quart saucepan. Add the panch phoran and heat until the spices pop. Stir in the red chilies, ginger and garlic. Cook until very fragrant and stir in tomatoes, salt and sugar. Bring to a boil and slowly cook, stirring frequently, until mixture begins to thicken slightly, usually about 2 hours. Add apricots and jalapeño peppers and cook an additional 15 minutes. Ladle into 4 hot, sterilized half-pint jars and process in water bath for 20 minutes. Remove to a draft-free area to cool and seal. Chutney may also be refrigerated unsealed for 2–3 weeks.

This flavorful chutney gets its distinctive taste from the Indian spice mixture, panch phoran. This spice mix is made by combining equal amounts of fennel seeds, mustard seeds, fenugreek seeds, cumin seeds and kalonji. It should be available in Indian specialty markets.

Summer

Summer

CANNING

Peach Chutney
MAKES 15 PINTS

15 pounds peaches, peeled and coarsely chopped
5 pounds dark brown sugar
1 pound raisins
10 ounces currants
2 cups cider vinegar
2 cups frozen lemon juice
4 tablespoons crushed red pepper
1 tablespoon ground ginger
4 tablespoons mustard seeds
4 tablespoons salt
8 cloves garlic, crushed
2 pounds onions, finely chopped
1 pound crystalized ginger, finely chopped

Peel peaches by dipping first in boiling water for 30 seconds. Remove peels and coarsely chop. Place peaches in heavy 20-quart stock pot. Add remaining ingredients, except crystalized ginger and place over medium heat. Bring to a slow boil, stirring frequently to prevent sticking. Remove any scum that rises to the top. Continue to boil until mixture begins to thicken and darken in color. Be sure to keep mixture at a low boil so it will not scorch on the bottom. Chutney is done when it coats a wooden spoon, usually 3–4 hours. At this point stir in the crystalized ginger and pour into hot, sterilized pint jars. Wipe rims clean with a hot, wet towel and tighten bands and lids down. Process in a boiling water bath for 20–25 minutes. Remove to a draft-free area and allow to cool and seal.

This recipe is time consuming, but the rewards are worth it. It is a must for many Indian recipes and is excellent served as an accompaniment to chicken or pork. Be sure to use peaches that are fully ripe, as they provide the correct sugar content to thicken the chutney. You will find several recipes in this cookbook that call for Peach Chutney, although you may substitute a store-bought brand.

CANNING

Picking Cherries Jubilee
MAKES 4 PINTS

> 5 pounds cherries, washed and pitted
> 3 cups sugar
>   (you may need extra sugar if tart cherries are used)
> 1 cup orange-flavored liqueur
> 1/4 cup peach-flavored liqueur

Place the cherries and sugar in a heavy saucepan and bring to a slow boil, stirring until the cherries begin to juice and the sugar dissolves. Continue to cook for 15 minutes. Remove from the heat and stir in the orange and peach liqueurs. Ladle cherries and juice into hot, sterilized pint jars and process in a boiling water bath for 15 minutes. Remove and allow to cool in a draft-free area, until jars seal.

To serve the cherries jubilee, slowly heat the cherries and liquid until hot, but not boiling. In a small bowl, dissolve one teaspoon of arrowroot in one tablespoon of water for every one cup of cherry liquid. Add to cherries and continue to heat until mixture thickens. Carefully pour 1/4 cup of brandy over the top and light with a long stick match. Spoon immediately over ice cream or cake as an impressive flaming dessert.

Summer

Summer

CANNING

Figs in Wine Sauce
MAKES 6 PINTS

4 quarts fresh figs, washed and stems left on
4 cups water
2 cups sugar
1/2 cup dry sherry
1 tablespoon lemon juice, freshly squeezed
1/4 teaspoon nutmeg, freshly grated

In a 4-quart saucepan, bring the water to a boil. Stir in the sugar until completely dissolved. Return to a boil and stir in the sherry, lemon juice and nutmeg. Reduce to a simmer and add the figs. Cover and cook on low for 10 minutes. Turn off heat and allow to sit for 10 more minutes. Pack figs in hot, sterilized pint jars, adding enough liquid to come within 1/2 inch of the top of the jars. Wipe the rims clean with a hot, wet towel and tighten on seals and bands. Process in a boiling water bath for 20 minutes and remove to a draft-free place to cool.

APPETIZERS

Roasted Garlic Spread
MAKES 1 1/2 CUPS

    2 heads of garlic
    2 tablespoons olive oil
    8 ounces cream cheese, softened
    1/4 cup sour cream
    3/4 teaspoon kosher salt
    1/4 teaspoon black pepper, freshly ground
    1/4 teaspoon lemon pepper

Separate the unpeeled garlic into individual cloves. Place in a oven-proof dish and coat well with the olive oil. Place in a 375° oven and roast for 25–30 minutes or until the cloves are soft to the touch. Remove from the oven and allow to cool slightly. Peel the cloves and place in the bowl of a food processor. Add the remaining ingredients and process until smooth. Taste for seasoning and pack in a pint jar. Refrigerate until ready to use. It will keep up to 3–4 days. Bring to room temperature before serving.

This versatile spread is delicious served with assorted crackers or roasted potato wedges. I have also used it as a filling for boned chicken breasts. Spread on a flattened chicken breast, roll in a cylinder and secure with a toothpick. Dip in beaten egg, then bread crumbs and bake at 350° for 45–60 minutes.

Fall

APPETIZERS

Spicy Crab and Artichoke Dip
SERVES 15

1 green bell pepper, minced
1 tablespoon olive oil
2 (16 oz) cans artichoke hearts, drained and chopped
2 cups mayonnaise
½ cup green onion, minced
½ cup chopped pimientos
1 cup Parmesan cheese, grated
2 tablespoons lemon juice
4 teaspoons Worcestershire sauce
3 whole jalapeño peppers, minced
1 teaspoon Greek seasoning salt
1 pound crab meat, picked over
1 package pita bread, split and cut in 6 triangles
olive oil

Lightly brush pita triangles with olive oil. Season if desired with salt and cayenne pepper. Place on a cookie sheet in a 300° oven for 45–60 minutes, or until crisp and dry. Remove to a rack to cool. Sauté the bell pepper in one tablespoon olive oil until soft. Remove from heat and stir in artichoke hearts, mayonnaise, green onion, pimiento, Parmesan cheese, lemon juice, Worcestershire, jalapeño peppers and season salt. Gently fold in crabmeat and place in a greased 2-quart casserole. Bake at 350° for 25–30 minutes or until heated through, being careful not to overheat or it will separate. Serve in a chafing dish with the pita chips or tortilla chips if preferred.

APPETIZERS

Sausage Swirl Canapés
MAKES 50 PIECES

- 4 cups flour
- 1/4 cup fine ground white corn meal
- 1/4 cup sugar
- 2 tablespoons baking powder
- 1 teaspoon salt
- 2/3 cup vegetable oil
- 1 cup milk
- 2 pounds pork sausage, uncooked

In a large bowl, combine flour, cornmeal, sugar, baking powder and salt. Make a well in the center and quickly stir in oil and milk until thoroughly mixed. Turn out onto a lightly floured board and knead several times until smooth. Divide dough in half and roll each half into an 8 x 12-inch rectangle. Turn dough with the long side toward you and spread uncooked sausage on dough to within a 1/2 inch of the bottom. Roll up jelly roll–style to make a 12-inch cylinder. Wrap in plastic wrap and refrigerate 4 hours or overnight. When ready to bake, cut in 1/2-inch slices and place on a lightly greased cookie sheet. Bake at 350° for 20 minutes or until lightly browned. Pass or serve immediately.

Fall

APPETIZERS

Mushroom Pâté
SERVES 16

- 1 pound mushrooms, sliced
- 1 clove garlic, minced
- 2 tablespoons butter
- 1 tablespoon fresh tarragon
- 1 tablespoon fresh marjoram
- 1 tablespoon fresh thyme
- 1/2 teaspoon fresh rosemary (dried herbs may be substituted by substituting 1 teaspoon for 1 tablespoon)
- 8 ounces cream cheese, softened
- 3 tablespoons dry sherry
- 1 teaspoon black pepper, freshly ground
- 1 teaspoon lemon pepper
- 1/2 teaspoon salt

Melt butter in medium skillet and sauté mushrooms and garlic until soft and all liquid has been absorbed. Remove from heat and process until smooth. Mince fresh herbs and add to processor, pulsing once or twice. Add remaining ingredients and process until smooth. Taste for seasoning and press mixture into an oiled 3-cup mold or loaf pan. Refrigerate overnight. When ready to serve, unmold on a platter lined with fresh hosta or lemon leaf. Garnish with additional herbs and Aztec mushroom caps.*

*To make Aztec mushroom caps use a small paring knife. Start in the center of the mushroom top and gently press just the point of the knife into the flesh, making a triangular impression. Continue to press into the cap, moving in concentric circles around the mushroom, until the entire cap is covered with the indentations. Store loosely wrapped in the refrigerator until ready to use.

APPETIZERS

Fresh Tomato Bruschetta
SERVES 6–8

    1 French baguette, sliced in 1-inch thickness
    8 Roma tomatoes, cut in small cubes
    2 tablespoons minced fresh basil
    2 tablespoons minced fresh parsley
    3 cloves of garlic, minced
    1/2 cup crumbled feta cheese
    1 cup fresh mozarella, diced
    2 tablespoons good quality olive oil, divided
    1/2 teaspoon salt
    1/4 teaspoon freshly ground pepper

Combine tomatoes, herbs, garlic, cheeses, one tablespoon olive oil, salt and pepper in a bowl and allow to stand at room temperature for 30 minutes. Lightly brush each baguette slice with remaining oil and toast lightly on both sides. Top each piece with a couple of tablespoons of tomato mixture while still warm and serve immediately.

Fall

Fall

APPETIZERS

Party Crab Mold
SERVES 25

1 envelope plain gelatin
1/4 cup lemon juice, freshly squeezed
1 can cream of mushroom soup, undiluted
1 cup mayonnaise
3/4 cup minced green onions
3/4 cup finely chopped celery
16 ounces cream cheese, softened
1 pound crab meat, picked over

Soften gelatin in lemon juice and heat until dissolves. Combine next 5 ingredients, stirring well. Taste for seasoning and fold in crab meat. Pack mixture in an oiled 1 1/2-quart mold. Refrigerate several hours until congealed. Unmold on lettuce bed, garnishing with lemon slices and fresh parsley. Serve immediately with a light wafer type cracker.

APPETIZERS

Beer Cheese
MAKES 2 CUPS

- 1 pound extra sharp cheddar cheese
- 3 cloves garlic, mashed
- 1/2 teaspoon Tabasco® sauce
- 1 tablespoon Worcestershire sauce
- 1 teaspoon mustard powder
- 1 teaspoon salt
- 1/2 can beer

Grate the cheese and place in the bowl of a food processor. Add the garlic, Tabasco®, Worcestershire, mustard, salt and half the amount of the beer. With the processor running, add additional beer until it makes a soft spread. The cheese will firm after it has been refrigerated several hours. Taste for seasoning and pack mixture in a crock or small jars. Refrigerate until ready to use. Allow to stand at room temperature before serving with assorted crackers and of course beer.

Fall

APPETIZERS

Smoked Trout Spread
SERVES 12

- ½ pound smoked trout, cut in small pieces
- 2 tablespoons shallots, minced
- 1 teaspoon capers, minced
- 1 teaspoon parsley, snipped
- ½ cup sour cream
- ½ cup mayonnaise
- ½ teaspoon lemon juice, freshly squeezed
- ¼ teaspoon salt
- ¼ teaspoon black pepper

Combine all ingredients and taste for seasoning. Place in a small bowl or crock and refrigerate overnight to allow flavors to blend. If desired, garnish top with additional parsley and fresh ground black pepper. Serve with small rounds of rye bread or an assortment of crackers.

Smoked salmon may be substituted for the trout. Add additional onion and substitute fresh dill for the parsley.

APPETIZERS

Lucy-and-Her Shrimp
SERVES 8

½ cup cider vinegar, plus 2 tablespoons, divided
2 tablespoons shrimp seasoning
1½ pounds shrimp, 36 count
20 bay leaves
2 medium onions, thinly sliced
1 teaspoon paprika
¼ teaspoon cayenne pepper
½ teaspoon salt
¼ cup Worcestershire sauce
1½ cups vegetable oil

Bring two quarts of water to a boil. Add 2 tablespoons of vinegar, 2 tablespoons shrimp seasoning and the shrimp. Cook 3–5 minutes or until the shrimp turn pink and the water boils. Drain immediately and turn shrimp out on paper towels to cool and air dry. Peel and reserve shells for stock if desired.

Place ½ cup vinegar in a small stainless pan. Add 20 bay leaves and bring almost to a boil. Gently simmer 15 minutes. Remove bay leaves and allow vinegar to cool completely.

Layer the peeled shrimp, the bay leaves and the onions in a large glass jar or plastic container. In a small bowl, whisk together the cooled vinegar, paprika, cayenne, salt and the Worcestershire. Slowly whisk in the vegetable oil until it is well blended. Pour over the shrimp and refrigerate at least 24 hours.

To serve, drain the shrimp, onions and bay leaves. Separate each and make a ring of onions around the edge of a glass compote or bowl. Fill in the middle with the shrimp and decorate around the onions with the bay leaves. Serve with toothpicks and saltine crackers if desired.

Fall

Fall

APPETIZERS

Oven Fried Oysters
SERVES 6

    1 clove garlic, finely minced
    1/2 cup olive oil
    3/4 cup Parmesan cheese
    1/2 cup cracker crumbs, finely ground
    1/2 teaspoon salt
    1/4 teaspoon black pepper
    1 pint select oysters

Combine garlic and olive oil in a small bowl and set aside. Stir together the Parmesan cheese, cracker crumbs, salt and pepper. Drain the oysters well and dip in garlic olive oil. Roll in the cracker crumb mixture to coat well. Place on a well-greased cookie sheet and bake at 450° for 12 minutes or until golden. Serve immediately.

APPETIZERS

Smoked Salmon Lox
SERVES 12–15

- 3–5 pounds fresh salmon filet, skin removed
- 6 tablespoons kosher salt
- 3 tablespoons sugar
- 7 tablespoons hickory smoked salt

Combine salts and sugar and completely cover the salmon, both sides. Wrap tightly in several layers of plastic wrap. Refrigerate 6 days, turning once or twice daily. Remove from wrap and wash off any clinging salts. Slice thinly on the diagonal. If desired the salmon may be cold smoked or cooked over a low charcoal fire, with a water pan, for 1–2 hours. Care should be taken not to overcook the fish, which has already been cured.

Fall

Collecting Fall Leaves

Place leaves between waxed paper and put under a rug. Leaves will dry in several weeks and can be used to decorate cheese/fruit platters and your Thanksgiving table.

SOUPS

Corn Chowder
SERVES 6–8

12 ears white or yellow corn
2 quarts chicken broth
4 ounces salt pork, diced and cooked until crisp
4 tablespoons butter
1 green pepper, diced
1 red pepper, diced
2 medium onions, diced
2 teaspoons kosher salt
1 teaspoon cumin, roasted and ground
1 tablespoon dried cilantro
2 bay leaves
1/2 teaspoon red pepper flakes
1 teaspoon southwest seasoning
2 cups half and half
1/2 cup flour
fresh minced cilantro
1/2 cup sour cream

Remove shucks from corn and place in a large pot. Add cold water to cover and place over high heat. When water boils, remove from heat and allow to stand 5 minutes. Cut kernels from ears and set aside. Return the corn ears to the pot and boil until corn water is reduced to one quart. Strain and place in 8-quart stock pot. Add chicken broth and salt pork to stock pot and heat to simmer. In a medium sauté pan, melt butter and stir in peppers and onions. Cook until soft and stir into stock pot. Add corn kernels, salt, cumin, cilantro, bay leaves, pepper flakes and southwest seasoning. Bring to a boil and reduce to simmer. Continue to cook over low heat for 45 minutes. Just before serving, place flour in a small bowl. Slowly whisk in the half and half until smooth. Stir into the soup and cook until slightly thickened. Taste for seasoning and serve immediately in warmed soup mugs. Garnish with sprinkle of fresh cilantro and a dollop of sour cream if desired.

SOUPS

White Chili
SERVES 8

    4 cups cannellini beans, soaked overnight and drained
    2 pounds chicken breasts, boneless and skinless
    8 cups chicken stock
    2 medium onions, diced
    6 cloves garlic, minced
    1 tablespoon peanut oil
    2 teaspoons cumin seeds, roasted and ground
    1 tablespoon dried cilantro
    1 tablespoon kosher salt
    ½ teaspoon red pepper flakes
    1 ½ cups canned green chili peppers, diced
    2 cups Monterey Jack cheese, grated
    2 medium avocados, diced
    2 medium tomatoes, diced
    ½ cup diced onion
    1 cup sour cream
    ½ cup jalapeño peppers, sliced

Place cannellini beans in a 6-quart saucepan. Add water to cover by 3 inches and bring to a boil. Cook 45 minutes to an hour or until beans begin to soften. (You may need to add more water to keep beans just covered). Drain beans after they are completely cooked through, reserving 2 cups of bean liquid.

Place chicken breasts in a 2-quart saucepan with cold water to cover by 2–3 inches. Bring to a slow boil and when water boils, remove from stove and cover. Allow chicken to cool in water. Shred chicken breasts and strain chicken broth, reserving 6 cups.

In a large 8-quart stock pot, sauté onions and garlic in peanut oil until tender. Add 6 cups of chicken stock, bean liquid, beans and chicken. Bring to a boil and reduce to simmer. Cook chili, stirring occasionally for about one hour. Add more chicken stock or reserved broth if necessary. When beans are thoroughly cooked, add cumin seed, cilantro, salt and pepper flakes. Continue to simmer chili for one hour, stirring often. Add green chilies the last 30 minutes and taste for seasoning.

Serve the chili in large heated soup bowls and garnish with grated cheese, avocado, tomato, onion, sour cream and jalapeño peppers.

Fall

SOUPS

Virginia's Brunswick Stew
SERVES 20

    6 pounds pork loin, cooked and chopped
    2 small chickens, cooked, boned and chopped
    3 (28 ounce) cans diced tomatoes
    4 small boxes frozen corn
    1½ cups catsup
    2 medium onions, finely chopped
    1 tablespoon salt
    1 teaspoon black pepper
    1 teaspoon cayenne pepper
    2 tablespoons Worcestershire sauce
    4 small boxes frozen lima beans
    3 quarts chicken stock
    ½ pound butter
    1 cup flour

Combine first 12 ingredients in a large stock pot. Bring to a boil and simmer 1–2 hours, stirring occasionally. In a small saucepan, melt the butter and whisk in the flour. Cook over medium heat, stirring constantly, until flour begins to brown. Carefully stir spoonfuls of roux into the soup pot. Continue to simmer until soup thickens slightly. Serve immediately or continue to barely simmer until ready to serve.

Tabasco® sauce and oyster crackers make great accompaniments.

Brunswick stew is the perfect ending to a clear October afternoon. The stew can be fixed in advance and is hearty enough to stand on its own. Leftovers are easily frozen for a later date.

SOUPS

Brunswick Stew For A Crowd (and I'm not kidding)
SERVES 50–60

- 4 whole chickens, cooked, picked from bone and chopped, discarding skins
- 15 pounds Boston butts, cooked and chopped
- 4 pounds fat back, diced and cooked until fat is rendered (reserve fat)
- 3 gallons chicken stock
- 5 pounds onions, chopped
- 6 pounds white potatoes, cubed
- 4 pounds sweet potatoes, cubed
- 4 pounds frozen butter beans
- 6 pounds frozen sweet corn
- 4 #10 cans diced tomatoes
- Tabasco® to taste
- 6 ounces Worcestershire sauce
- ½ cup salt, may use less according to saltiness of stock
- ¼ cup black pepper

I like to cook my stew in a large, black, cast iron kettle on an open fire, built with oak and hickory logs. You may use a propane cooker stand and a large pot to get almost the same results.

Begin cooking with approximately one cup of fat from fat back (you may need vegetable oil to make a full cup) in the bottom of a 40-quart pot. When fat begins to sizzle add onions and cook until softened. Pour in chicken stock and bring to a boil. Add potatoes and bring back to a boil, cooking until they are soft. Stir in chopped chicken and pork and return to a boil. Reduce to a simmer and stir often. After cooking for one hour, add butter beans and corn and simmer an additional 45 minutes, stirring often. (At this point you may want to solicit the help of a friend with a strong arm) Stir in the seasonings and the tomatoes and continue to stir to prevent the stew from sticking. This is a very crucial place in the cooking, as the stew can easily scorch if left unattended. I like to cook my Brunswick stew until it thickens, the meat falls apart, but the vegetables are still recognizable. Taste for seasoning and add as desired. Serve the soup with extra hot sauce and small oyster crackers.

Fall

Fall

Fragrant Osage Oranges

Osage oranges or "hedge apples" emit a pleasant, orange-peel scent and are inedible. The chartreuse wrinkled fruits drop to the ground in September and October when ripe. They may be used in wreaths, arrangements, or grouped in a bowl for an easy seasonal centerpiece.

SOUPS

Potato Leek Soup with Truffle Oil

SERVES 6

4 tablespoons butter
4 leeks, white parts only
4 cloves garlic, minced
6 medium potatoes, peeled and cubed
2 tablespoons fresh parsley, minced
2 tablespoons fresh thyme
1 bay leaf, crumbled
2 tablespoons celery leaves, minced
1 tablespoon kosher salt
1 teaspoon black pepper, freshly ground
1/2 cup vermouth
1 cup cream
1 1/2 teaspoons truffle oil

Cut leeks into 1/4-inch slices, reserving one leek for garnish. Melt the butter in a 4-quart pot and add the leeks and garlic. Sauté until they are soft and add 2 quarts of water. Bring to a boil and add the potatoes. Make a bouquet garni by combining the parsley, thyme, bay leaf and celery leaves. Tie with a string in a square of cheese cloth and add to the pot. Simmer for 30 minutes until the potatoes are cooked through. Strain the solids, reserving the liquid, and place in the bowl of a food processor. Process the leeks and potatoes until smooth, adding reserved liquid if needed. Return the pureed mixture to the pot and stir in the remaining stock to make a thick soup. Season with salt, pepper and vermouth and simmer an additional 15 minutes. Add cream and taste for seasoning. Keep warm until ready to serve, but do not allow soup to boil.

While soup is simmering, slice the reserved leek as thinly as possible. Heat 2 inches of oil to 375° and fry leek rings until lightly browned and crisp. Drain on a paper towel and salt lightly. Set aside.

To serve soup, ladle into heated cream soup bowls. Garnish top of soup with the fried leeks and drizzle with a 1/2 teaspoon of truffle oil.

SOUPS

Sweet Potato and Jalapeño Soup
SERVES 6

3 tablespoons butter
1 cup onion, minced
2 cloves garlic, minced
6 cups chicken stock
1 1/2 pounds sweet potatoes, peeled and cubed
1 fresh jalapeño pepper, thinly sliced
1 cup sweet white corn
2 teaspoons salt
1/4 teaspoon cayenne pepper
1/2 teaspoon ground roasted cumin seeds
1/2 teaspoon ancho chili powder
1/2 cup cream
1/2 cup sour cream
1 1/2 teaspoons lime juice, freshly squeezed
1/2 teaspoon lemon zest
2 tablespoons fresh cilantro, minced

In a 6-quart stockpot, melt butter and sauté onion and garlic until tender. Add chicken stock, sweet potatoes and jalapeño pepper. Bring to a boil and reduce to simmer. Cover and cook 25 minutes, until potatoes are thoroughly cooked. Strain solids, reserving liquid and place in the bowl of a food processor. Add enough liquid to process to a smooth consistency. Return to stockpot and add the remaining liquid back into the soup. Stir in corn, salt, cayenne pepper, cumin and chili powder. Simmer 15 minutes and whisk in cream. Heat thoroughly, but do not boil.

In a small bowl, combine sour cream, lime juice and lemon zest. Ladle soup into heated bowls and garnish with small dollops of sour cream around the edge of the bowl. With the point of a knife, pull through the edges of the sour cream dollops to make a star design. Sprinkle with fresh cilantro and serve immediately.

Fall

Fall

SOUPS

Beans and Greens Soup
SERVES 6

- 1 cup dried navy beans
- 1/4 pound bacon, chopped
- 1 medium onion, chopped
- 1 pound smoked kielbasa type sausage, cut into 1/2-inch slices
- 1 quart chicken stock
- 1 tablespoon kosher salt
- 1 teaspoon black pepper, freshly ground
- 1 pound kale, chopped
- 1 pound mustard greens, chopped
- 1 medium potato, peeled and chopped
- 1 small red bell pepper, chopped
- 1 tablespoon cider vinegar

Soak navy beans overnight in cold water and drain. Place in a 4-quart pot and add fresh water to cover by 3 inches. Bring to a boil and cook until beans are soft, adding more water if necessary, but eventually cooking most of the water out. Remove from heat.

In an 8-quart stockpot, cook bacon until it begins to render some of the fat. Add the onion and sausage and continue to cook until the onion is translucent. Drain off the bacon grease and add the beans and liquid to the stockpot. Stir in the chicken stock, greens, salt and pepper. Bring to a boil and simmer 30–45 minutes. Add the potato and red pepper and continue to simmer 30 minutes until the potato is soft. Add more stock or water if necessary to keep a nice soup consistency. Stir in the vinegar and taste for seasoning. Serve the soup in large heated soup bowls with JUDY'S CORN STICKS (P 329) and sweet butter.

Heating your bowls first will keep your soup from cooling off too quickly. You can do this in advance by heating them 15–20 minutes in a 250° oven. Carefully remove the hot bowls and place in a cooler lined with towels and just big enough to hold them. If you leave them shut tightly, they will stay warm at least an hour or more. This works well with dinner plates and is a great way to heat for a crowd when oven space is at a premium the last few minutes.

SOUPS

Westport Fish Chowder
SERVES 4

- 1 pound haddock, hake or cod fillets
- 1/4 pound salt pork, diced
- 1 medium onion, chopped
- 4 green onions, minced
- 2 medium potatoes, peeled and diced
- 2 cups fish stock or 1 cup clam juice and 1 cup water
- 3/4 teaspoon marjoram
- 1/4 teaspoon oregano leaves
- 1 pinch nutmeg, grated
- 1 1/2 cups half and half, divided
- 1 teaspoon salt
- 1/2 teaspoon black pepper, freshly ground
- 2 tablespoons butter
- 2 tablespoons minced chives

In heavy, four-quart saucepan, sauté the salt pork 10 minutes, until it is crisp and the fat has been rendered. Remove and discard all but 3 tablespoons of the fat. Add the onions and sauté 2–3 minutes until softened. Add the potatoes, stock, plus one cup of water (or 2 cups of water with clam juice), marjoram, oregano and nutmeg. Bring to a boil, lower heat, cover and simmer until potatoes are done, about 8–10 minutes.

While chowder is simmering, cut the fish into 1-inch pieces. Add to the chowder and stir in one cup of half and half. Cook over low heat until the fish is cooked through, about 3 minutes. Add the remaining half and half and heat thoroughly. Season to taste with salt and pepper. Stir in butter and serve chowder in warmed soup bowls. Garnish with minced chives if desired. I find that the chowder is even better if it is made the day before and held in the refrigerator overnight.

This is one of my favorite soups. My first introduction to this chowder was in Westport, Maine during the summer of 1998. The fish were freshly caught out of the cold Atlantic waters. We would usually combine several of the firm white fish and add lots of onion and potatoes. The salt pork adds a hint of meat flavor to the broth. Although it was the summer time, the cool Maine evenings made this soup a perfect evening meal.

Fall

Skeletonizing Leaves

Lacy, delicate, skeletonized leaves appear naturally in autumn, but the process is long and the results are imperfect. To speed things up:

Pour 1 cup of detergent in to a pot of water.

Add leaves and bring the pot to a boil.

Reduce heat and simmer for a half hour.

Remove leaves and rinse in cold water.

Using a soft toothbrush, gently sweep away remaining tissue to reveal the vein structure. Dull looking skeletons can be perked up by a bath of weak bleach solution, followed by a thorough clear rinse.

Use the leaves in floral arrangements or add to a gift package for decoration.

SOUPS

Shrimp Bisque
SERVES 6

2 tablespoons butter
2 carrots, peeled and diced
1 medium onion, chopped finely
1 stalk celery, chopped finely
1 medium potato, peeled and diced
2 pounds shrimp, peeled, shells reserved for stock
2 cups shrimp or chicken stock
2 cups half and half
1 teaspoon thyme leaves
1 bay leaf
1 teaspoon kosher salt
1/2 teaspoon white pepper, freshly ground
1 tablespoon fresh parsley, minced

Melt butter in 4-quart saucepan. Stir in carrots, onion, celery, potatoes and shrimp shells. Sauté 3–4 minutes, until onion is translucent and shells turn pink. Add stock, half and half, thyme and bay leaf. Bring to a boil and reduce to simmer 20–25 minutes. Remove bay leaf and discard.

Remove vegetables and shells with a slotted spoon to food processor bowl. Puree mixture, adding enough liquid to blend. Force the puree through a strainer, pressing with a spoon to remove all the liquid. Set aside the solids in the strainer to add at the end. Return the stock to the saucepan and stir in the shrimp. Bring to a boil and cook just until the shrimp turns pink and is cooked through. Remove shrimp and process until finely chopped. Add back to the stock, along with the pureed vegetables. Season to taste with salt and pepper and heat gently for 10–15 minutes. Serve the bisque in heated soup bowls, garnishing with the fresh parsley.

You will never know the shrimp shells are in the bisque if you puree them thoroughly. They add a wonderful flavor to the soup.

SOUPS

Mulligatawny Soup
SERVES 12

- 4 tablespoons olive oil
- 3 medium onions, finely chopped
- 4 cloves garlic, minced
- 4 green chili peppers, seeded and minced
- 2 teaspoons ginger root, grated
- 12 cups chicken stock
- 1 28 ounce can diced tomatoes
- 2 carrots, peeled and diced
- 3 medium Granny Smith apples, peeled and diced
- 2 tablespoons curry powder
- 1 1/2 tablespoons kosher salt
- 1 teaspoon black pepper, freshly ground
- 4 cups cut up leftover turkey
- 2/3 cup uncooked rice
- 1/2 cup plain, low fat yogurt
- 1 tablespoon fresh mint leaves, minced
- 1 tablespoon freshly squeezed lemon juice

In a large 8-quart stock pot, heat the olive oil and sauté the onion, garlic, peppers and ginger until translucent. Add the chicken stock, tomatoes, carrots, apples, curry, salt and pepper. Bring to a boil and simmer 30–45 minutes. Stir in the turkey and rice, and continue to simmer for an additional 30–45 minutes or until the rice is completely cooked, stirring often.

In a small bowl, combine the yogurt, mint and lemon juice. Serve the Mulligatawny in warm, shallow soup bowls with a dollop of yogurt sauce on top. Split, buttered and toasted pita bread makes a nice alternative to crackers.

Mulligatawny is an Indian soup that is fragrantly spiced with curry, ginger, onions and garlic. It is an unusual way to use up that leftover turkey, but you may also substitute chicken if desired.

Fall

SALADS

Fresh Pear Salad
SERVES 6

> 6 pears, Anjou or Bartlett
> 1 small red onion, thinly sliced
> 1 head Bibb lettuce, washed and chilled
> 1/2 pound blue cheese, crumbled
> 3/4 cup FRENCH VINAIGRETTE DRESSING (see next page)
> 1/3 cup sliced and toasted almonds
> lemon juice

Select pears that are free of blemishes and give slightly when pressed. If the pears are hard, buy them several days in advance and place them on the counter in a paper bag. Check daily for ripeness.

To prepare salad, peel pears, cut in half and scoop out the center seed core. Spritz lightly with lemon juice. Place a large "leaf cup" of Bibb lettuce on each plate. Arrange two pear halves on lettuce and several onion rings on top. Drizzle with 2 tablespoons of dressing and sprinkle with blue cheese and almonds. Serve immediately.

SALADS

French Vinaigrette Dressing
MAKES 3/4 CUP

    4 tablespoons red wine vinegar
    1 tablespoon fresh lemon juice
    1/2 teaspoon sugar
    1 teaspoon salt
    1/2 teaspoon black pepper, freshly ground
    1–2 teaspoons Dijon mustard
    1 clove garlic, crushed (optional)
    8–10 tablespoons olive oil

In a small, deep mixing bowl, combine vinegar, lemon juice, sugar, salt, pepper, mustard and garlic. Whisk well to dissolve salt and sugar. Gradually whisk in olive oil in a thin, steady stream. Taste for seasoning and store in the refrigerator for up to 24 hours.

Because there are so few ingredients in this dressing, it is important to use top quality products to obtain the best results. Use a high acidity wine vinegar and only extra virgin olive oil. A teaspoon of water may also be added if the vinaigrette is too strong for your individual taste.

Fall

Seasonal Plant Materials

Bittersweet
Persimmon Tree
Arbelia
Sweet Annise
Witch Hazel
Rose Hip
Crabapple
Ivy Blossom
Vitex
Chinese Lantern
Colored Leaves
Magnolia Pods

SALADS

Nutty Oriental Slaw
SERVES 12

16 ounces broccoli cole slaw (in the produce section)
1 bunch green onions, minced
1/2 cup slivered almonds, toasted
1/2 cup sunflower seeds, toasted
2 packages Top Ramen noodles, oriental flavor
1/3 cup rice wine vinegar
1/4 cup sugar
1/2 cup vegetable oil

In large bowl, combine broccoli slaw and green onions. Set aside. In a separate bowl, break up the noodles into pieces, reserving the seasoning packs and toss in the almonds and sunflower seeds. Set aside. To make the dressing, heat the vinegar and sugar in a small saucepan. Whisk in the oriental seasoning packs and the oil. Stir together the broccoli and the noodles and pour the dressing over both. Mix well and refrigerate one hour to chill. Serve immediately.

This salad will keep for several hours, but will become soggy if held overnight.

SALADS

Jellied Seafood Salad
SERVES 8

- 1½ tablespoons plain gelatin
- 2 tablespoons cold water
- 2 cups boiling water
- 3 tablespoons fresh lemon juice
- ½ cup white wine vinegar
- 2 teaspoons dry mustard
- 1 tablespoon Worcestershire sauce
- 1 teaspoon salt
- 1 tablespoon sugar
- 2 teaspoons grated onion
- 24 medium shrimp, cooked and peeled
- ½ pound crab meat, picked through for shells

Soften gelatin in cold water and stir in boiling water to dissolve. Cool slightly and add lemon juice, vinegar, mustard powder, Worcestershire, salt, sugar and onion. Set aside, but do not refrigerate.

Pour a small amount of gelatin mixture into the bottom of 8 individual salad molds. Place 3 shrimp in the bottom and add just enough liquid to hold in place. Set molds in refrigerator for 20 minutes or until congealed. Divide crab meat between the molds and add liquid to hold in place and form next layer. Refrigerate to congeal. Add additional liquid to fill the molds to the top and refrigerate several hours.

To serve, unmold salads and serve with a dollop of Seafood Cocktail Sauce (p. 346) or Caper Sauce (p. 346).

A beautiful first course that is worth the effort. Be sure to put in enough liquid to hold each layer and allow plenty of time to congeal.

Fall

Collecting Bittersweet

Bittersweet berries add a flourish of vibrant color to fall arrangements. Collect them while the casings are yellow. Remove leaves and hang overnight in a dry place. The casings will pop open to reveal bright orange berries.

Try to avoid handling the bittersweet once casings have opened as they will drop off.

Act before the first frost! Cool nights will soften the berries.

SALADS

Indian Salad
SERVES 6

> 3 tablespoons plain gelatin
> 1 cup water
> 1/2 cup sugar
> 1/2 teaspoon salt
> 1/2 cup fresh lemon juice
> 1 cup peach or mango chutney, cut into small pieces if necessary
> 1/2 cup mayonnaise
> 1/2 cup sour cream
> 1/2 teaspoon curry powder
> 1/2 teaspoon kosher salt
> 1 tablespoon lemon juice

Soften gelatin in 1/4 cup of cold water. Heat the remaining water to a boil and stir into the softened gelatin. When completely dissolved, add the sugar, 1/2 teaspoon salt, 1/2 cup lemon juice and chutney. Pour into small individual molds or a one-quart salad mold. Refrigerate several hours or overnight to congeal.

In small bowl, combine mayonnaise, sour cream, curry powder, kosher salt and one tablespoon lemon juice. Serve in a small bowl as a sauce for the Indian Salad.

An unusual salad that complements a roasted chicken or pork roast.

SALADS

Apple and Fennel Salad
SERVES 4

- 1 fennel bulb, julienned
- 1 tart red apple, julienned
- 1 Granny Smith apple, julienned
- 1/4 cup shredded carrot
- 1/4 cup green onion, chopped
- 1 tablespoon water
- 1 tablespoon white wine vinegar
- 1/2 teaspoon sugar
- 1/4 teaspoon salt
- 2 teaspoons light vegetable oil

Combine fruits and vegetables in a bowl. Whisk together the water, vinegar, sugar and salt. Gradually whisk in the oil to make a dressing. Pour over the salad and refrigerate up to one hour before serving.

A pretty and refreshing salad.

SALADS

Congealed Cranberry Salad
SERVES 18

2 pounds cranberries
4 oranges, juice and rind
4 tablespoons lemon juice, freshly squeezed
3 cups sugar
3 ounce box cherry flavored gelatin
2–3 ounce boxes lemon flavored gelatin
2 tablespoons plain gelatin
4 cups boiling water
2 8 ounce cans crushed pineapple

Coarsely grind the cranberries and combine with the juice and rind of the oranges, lemon juice and sugar. Cover and let sit overnight in the refrigerator.

The next day, mix together the cherry and lemon gelatin. In a small bowl, mix ¼ cup of the fruit juices with the unflavored gelatin and allow to soften. Pour boiling water over the gelatin, add the unflavored gelatin and stir until completely dissolved. Add to the cranberry mixture and stir in the pineapple. Pour into an 11-cup mold and refrigerate overnight to congeal. Unmold on a large platter lined with lettuce and serve with a small dish of mayonnaise on the side.

A nice change from the usual cranberry relish dish at Thanksgiving.

ENTREES

Muffulettas
SERVES 6

- 1 2/3 cups pimiento stuffed olives
- 1 1/2 cups Kalamata olives
- 4 ounces pimientos
- 2/3 cup olive oil
- 1/3 cup fresh parsley, minced
- 3 anchovies, mashed
- 2 tablespoons capers
- 1 tablespoon garlic, minced
- 1 tablespoon fresh oregano, snipped
- 1/2 teaspoon black pepper, freshly ground
- 1 tablespoon red wine vinegar
- 1 loaf French bread
- 1/4 pound Provolone cheese, thinly sliced
- 1/4 pound coppacola sausage, thinly sliced
- 1/8 pound Mortadella sausage, thinly sliced

Coarsely chop the olives and pimientos. In medium bowl mix together the olives, pimientos, olive oil, parsley, anchovies, capers, garlic, oregano, black pepper and red wine vinegar. Refrigerate for one day, but will keep for several weeks.

The day before serving, split the French bread lengthwise. Press 1/2 of the olive mixture into the bottom section of the bread and cover with the slices of meat and cheese. Spread the other 1/2 of the olives on the meat and place the top of the bread on the olives. Wrap tightly in aluminum foil and place on a cookie sheet. Place another cookie sheet on top and balance a three pound weight on top, pressing the sandwich down firmly. Refrigerate overnight.

To serve, slice the Muffulettas into 3-inch pieces and secure each with a frilly toothpick or a toothpick with an olive stuck through the top.

If the Italian salami or sausage is not available, any delicatessen meats such as ham, Genoa salami or bologna may be substituted. If desired the loaf may be wrapped in foil and heated 20 minutes at 300°. Slice immediately and serve as above.

Fall

ENTREES

Aged Standing Rib Roast
SERVES 8

> 6 pound standing rib roast
> 2 teaspoons Tabasco® sauce
> 1 teaspoon minced garlic
> 2 teaspoons kosher salt
> 1 teaspoon black pepper, freshly ground

Remove the roast from the plastic wrappings and Styrofoam tray. Place on a cooling rack on a baking sheet and cover loosely with a clean linen towel. Place in the coolest part of the refrigerator, maintaining a temperature between 34° and 38°. Allow roast to age 3–5 days, changing the toweling daily. When ready to cook, remove roast and rub all over with the Tabasco® and garlic. Sprinkle liberally with the salt and pepper and let stand at room temperature for one hour. Preheat oven to 300°. Place roast on a rack which fits into a roasting pan. Place in the oven and cook approximately 1½ hours or until internal temperature reaches 118°. Remove from oven and cover loosely with foil. Allow to stand for 30 minutes, or until temperature levels off at approximately 130°. Increase oven to 400° and (return roast to oven for 15 minutes to brown outside crust). Remove from oven, let stand again for 10–15 minutes and carve in ½-inch slices. The rib bones may be cut away from the roast itself to make carving easier. Serve with Horseradish Potatoes and Yorkshire Pudding if desired.

This roast is wonderful cooked on a charcoal grill. Be sure to have an accurate thermometer monitoring the grill temperature. The coals should be at a medium heat, where you can hold your hand over them for 10 seconds. A few pieces of soaked hickory add just a hint of smoke to this delicious cut of meat.

ENTREES

Pork Chops with Creamy Chipotle Sauce
SERVES 4

 1 cup sour cream
 1/4 cup mayonnaise
 1–2 canned chipotle peppers
 1 clove garlic, crushed
 1/4 cup cider vinegar
 1/2 teaspoon sugar
 1 teaspoon salt
 4 half-inch pork chops
 2 tablespoons peanut oil
 2 tablespoons fresh cilantro, chopped
 1 lime, thinly sliced

Combine sour cream, mayonnaise, peppers, garlic, vinegar, sugar and salt and process until smooth. Place in a double boiler and heat until just warm. Lightly season the pork chops with salt and pepper. Heat the oil until hot and cook the pork chops, 4 minutes per side. To serve, spoon 2–3 tablespoons of the sauce on the dinner plate. Place the cooked chop on the sauce and sprinkle with the cilantro and garnish with a lime slice.

Fall

ENTREES

Pork Roast with Apple Cider Sauce
SERVES 6

2 pounds boneless pork roast, tied
1 tablespoon vegetable oil
1 teaspoon salt
1/2 teaspoon black pepper, freshly ground
2 tablespoons dark brown sugar
1/4 cup cider vinegar
1 1/2 cups apple cider
2 carrots, diced
1 rib celery, finely chopped
1/2 teaspoon dried thyme leaves
1 tablespoon fresh parsley, minced
1 bay leaf
2 tablespoons softened butter
2 tablespoons minced green onions

Heat vegetable oil in a heavy roasting pan, just large enough to hold the pork. Sprinkle the roast with salt and pepper and brown all sides in hot oil. Remove roast from pan and discard oil.

Stir in vinegar and brown sugar into roasting pan and cook over medium heat until reduced by half. Stir in the cider, scraping up any bits on the bottom of the pan. Add the vegetables, thyme, parsley and bay leaf. Season to taste with salt and pepper and add pork roast back to pan. Bring the liquid to a boil, cover and place in a preheated 350° oven. Roast the pork for approximately 45 minutes or until a meat thermometer registers 140°. Remove the pork to a carving board with a lip to catch any juices. Cover loosely with foil and allow to stand 15 minutes before carving.

Carefully strain the vegetables and juices, pressing the vegetables to remove all liquid. Pour the broth into a saucepan and heat over low fire. Whisk in the softened butter and taste for seasoning. Serve the sauce over the sliced pork with a sprinkling of green onions for garnish.

ENTREES

Spicy Baby Back Ribs with Salsa Verde
SERVES 6–8

6 pounds baby back ribs
1/2 cup paprika
1/2 cup brown sugar
1/4 cup ground cumin
1/4 cup ground coriander
1/4 cup kosher salt
1/4 cup black pepper
1/4 cup chopped fresh garlic
1/4 cup chopped fresh cilantro
7 ounce can salsa verde
1 tablespoon fresh lime juice
1/4 cup minced roasted red peppers
2 tablespoons chopped fresh cilantro

Combine paprika, brown sugar, cumin, coriander, salt, pepper, garlic and 1/4 cup cilantro. Rub on both sides of rib racks and place on cookie sheets. Bake in a 200° oven for 2–3 hours.

At this point the ribs may be refrigerated overnight and reheated, covered lightly with foil for 30 minutes at 350° before serving.

In small bowl combine the salsa, lime juice, peppers and 2 tablespoons cilantro. Allow flavors to blend for at least one hour. Serve the salsa on the side with the ribs.

I like to use cumin and coriander seeds that have been roasted for a few minutes in a dry skillet. I then allow them to cool and grind the seeds to a fine powder. The flavor is very intense and superior to the store-bought spices that are already ground.

Fall

Fall

ENTREES

Southwest Seared Tuna
SERVES 4

2 pounds sushi quality tuna, cut in 4 1-inch steaks
2 tablespoons ancho chili or mild chili powder
1 tablespoon black pepper, freshly ground
1 tablespoon lemon pepper
1 tablespoon kosher salt
1 tablespoon sugar
1/2 teaspoon garlic powder
1 tablespoon peanut oil

Mix together chili powder, black pepper, lemon pepper, salt, sugar and garlic. Coat each tuna steak on both sides with rub and place in refrigerator one hour before cooking.

Pour oil in heavy skillet and heat over medium fire. Sear tuna steaks for 4 minutes on each side for pink interior, or 2–3 minutes for red. Serve the fish immediately with lime wedges and Chipotle Mayonnaise (p. 345) on the side.

It is important to buy very fresh tuna for this recipe and not to overcook the tuna. By searing the fish in this manner, it will stay moist and tender, with a crispy coating on the outside.

ENTREES

Elegant Shrimp Crêpes
SERVES 4–6

CRÊPES
1/2 cup milk
1 cup flour
3 tablespoons melted butter
3 eggs, beaten
1/2 cup beer

SAUCE
6 tablespoons melted butter
6 tablespoons flour
2 1/2 cups milk, divided
1/2 cup heavy cream
2 teaspoons lemon juice, freshly squeezed, divided
salt
pepper

SHRIMP FILLING
1 pound shrimp, peeled and cut into 1/4-inch pieces
2 tablespoons green onions, chopped
1 tablespoon fresh dill, snipped
1/2 teaspoon cayenne pepper
1 tablespoon bread crumbs
1 tablespoon Swiss cheese, shredded

To make crêpes, place 1/2 cup of milk in blender. Add one cup flour, 3 tablespoons melted butter, eggs and beer. Mix until completely smooth and allow to sit for 30 minutes. Heat an 8-inch skillet over medium high heat and brush lightly with vegetable oil. Pour a scant 1/4 cup of batter into pan and tilt to evenly distribute. Cook until bubbles appear and pop and turn, continuing to cook until lightly browned. Remove and place on wax paper. Cook crêpes and place between sheets of wax paper until ready to use. Do not refrigerate, but crêpes may be frozen for later use.

To make sauce for crêpes, combine 6 tablespoons melted butter and 6 tablespoons of flour in medium saucepan. Cook flour, whisking constantly, for 3–4 minutes. Slowly stir in 2 cups of milk and cook until thickened. Remove 3/4 cup of sauce for shrimp filling and set aside. Return pan to heat and stir in 1/2 cup milk and cream. Bring just to a boil and season to taste with 1/2 teaspoon salt, 1/4 teaspoon black pepper and one teaspoon lemon juice. Remove from heat and set aside.

Continued on next page

Fall

ENTREES

Elegant Shrimp Crêpes, continued

To make shrimp filling, sauté green onions in 2 tablespoons of butter for one minute. Add shrimp and sauté until just pink. Remove from heat and add reserved ¾ cup of cream sauce, fresh dill, one teaspoon lemon juice, ¾ teaspoon salt and ½ teaspoon cayenne pepper, stirring well. Grease a 9 x 13-inch Oven-proof casserole and spread ½ cup of sauce in the bottom. Use approximately ¼ cup of the filling for each crêpe. Place in the lower center of the crepe and roll up tightly. Place in the prepared casserole, seam side down, leaving a ½-inch space between each crepe. If necessary use 2 casseroles, rather than crowding. Spoon remaining cream sauce over the top of the crêpes. Combine the bread crumbs, cheese and one tablespoon melted butter and sprinkle over the top. Bake the crêpes for 10–15 minutes at 375° until bubbly. Place under a hot broiler to brown the top if necessary. Crêpes may be made a day ahead. Cooking time may need to be increased by 15–20 minutes.

ENTREES

Rosemary Chicken Thighs
SERVES 4

    2 pounds chicken thighs
    2 tablespoons olive oil
    3 cloves garlic, minced
    2 teaspoons fresh rosemary, snipped
    1 1/2 cups chicken broth
    2 tablespoons red wine vinegar
    salt and pepper to taste

Season chicken thighs with salt and pepper. Heat olive oil in large skillet and brown thighs on both sides. Cover and simmer 20 minutes or until thermometer registers 160°. Remove thighs and discard all but 2 tablespoons of drippings. Add garlic and rosemary to drippings and cook until fragrant. Add broth and vinegar, continue cooking until reduced by half. Add chicken back to skillet and heat thoroughly, spooning sauce over thighs. Serve immediately.

I find myself often turning to this entree, both for my family and for a casual dinner with friends. The chicken is fragrant from the rosemary, and the red wine vinegar adds just the right lift to the sauce. This dish is highly recommended.

ENTREES

Easy Chicken Divan
SERVES 6

1 head broccoli, cut into 4-inch spears
2 pounds bone-in chicken breasts
2 cans cream of chicken soup, condensed
1 cup mayonnaise
2 teaspoons lemon juice, freshly squeezed
1/2 teaspoon curry powder
1/2 cup cheddar cheese, shredded
1 tablespoon butter
1 cup fresh bread crumbs

Place chicken breasts in a four-quart saucepan and cover with cold water. Bring to a boil, stir once or twice to distribute chicken, cover and remove from heat. Allow to cool in water for one hour.

Steam or microwave broccoli until just barely tender when pierced with a fork. Place into the bottom of a greased 9 x 13-inch casserole.

In a small saucepan, combine chicken soup, mayonnaise, lemon juice, curry powder and cheddar cheese. Heat slowly, stirring constantly until cheese melts.

Melt butter in small skillet and toss in bread crumbs. Cook until crumbs are crispy and browned. Set aside.

When chicken has cooled, slice into 1/4-inch slices and place over broccoli spears. Pour sauce over chicken and top with bread crumbs. Bake at 350° for 25–30 minutes until heated through. Serve immediately.

This casserole may be made in advance and refrigerated 1–2 days, or it may be frozen. Thaw completely before baking.

ENTREES

Chicken Enchiladas
SERVES 4–6

- 2 bone-in chicken breasts
- 1 1/2 cups sharp cheddar cheese
- 8 ounce can Mexican tomato sauce
- 8 ounce can enchilada sauce
- 1 small onion, diced
- 1 green pepper, diced
- 2 garlic cloves, minced
- 1/2 teaspoon ground cumin
- 1 teaspoon chili powder
- 1/2 teaspoon salt
- 12 corn tortillas

Place chicken in a small saucepan and add water to cover. Bring to a boil and remove from heat. Cover and let stand in water until cool. In small saucepan, combine the tomato and enchilada sauces. Set aside 1/2 cup for filling and heat the remaining sauce until hot. Shred chicken into a medium bowl. Add one cup of cheese, 1/2 cup sauce, onion, green pepper and seasonings. Mix well. Take one tortilla at a time and dip it into the hot sauce until soft, about one minute. Remove to a plate and place 1/3 cup of filling in the middle. Fold over the top and bottom to form a roll. Continue filling and rolling the tortillas as above. Spoon a thin layer of sauce on the bottom of a 9 x 13–inch pan. Carefully place the enchiladas, seam side down, in the casserole. Spoon on any sauce that is left over and sprinkle with the reserved 1/2 cup of cheese. Place in a 350° oven for 30 minutes until hot and bubbly. Serve with shredded lettuce, sliced avocados, minced green onions, fresh salsa and wedges of lime.

Fall

Preserving Peak Fall Foliage

Collect and preserve branches of leaves as soon as they peak, using drug-store glycerin. Don't wait! Older leaves will not absorb the solution.

Mix 1 part glycerin (from your local pharmacy) to 2 parts hot water and shake well.

Pour about 3 inches into a narrow-necked vase or jar.

Remove damaged leaves from branches (or vines).

Snip stems at an angle, then cut vertical slits into the base.

Wait 2-3 weeks, adding glycerin solution as needed.

Dried leaves should have a soft, supple, "leathery" feel.

Collect Copper Beech in August. Magnolia leaves may also be done using this method and used in floral arrangements over the winter.

Fall

Brining Turkey
Juicy, Tender, Tasty

Brining is a sure-fire way to prevent lean meats like poultry and pork from drying out during cooking. All it takes is cold water, kosher salt, and a glass or plastic container.

The amount of salt needed varies by brand. For every 2 quarts of water dissolve 1 cup of Diamond Crystal Kosher Salt or 5/8 cup Morton Kosher Salt. (Another option is substituting apple juice for water and adding your own flavor-boosting spices.)

Submerge meat, cover, and refrigerate.

Brining Times:

Thick Pork Chops 3–4 hours

Whole Chicken 3–4 hours

Pork Roast 5–6 hours

Whole Turkey* 12–18 hours

Rinse thoroughly and pat dry before cooking.

Brining longer than recommended will make the meat too salty. Brined meats may cook a little faster than usual and retain a pinkish color.

* Do not use a pre-basted turkey.

ENTREES

Roasted Turkey and Gravy
SERVES 12

- 1 15 pound turkey
- 2 tablespoons butter, melted
- 2 quarts water
- 3/4 cup butter
- 3/4 cup flour
- 1 teaspoon salt
- 1/2 teaspoon black pepper, freshly ground

Remove giblets and neck from inside turkey and set aside. Wash turkey inside and out and pat dry. Brush outside of turkey with melted butter and sprinkle with salt and pepper. Set in a large roasting pan and place in a preheated 350° oven, uncovered.

While turkey is roasting, place giblets and neck into a 4-quart saucepan and add water. Bring to a boil and reduce to a simmer for 2–3 hours. You can also add a few extra turkey wings or legs for added richness.

Check turkey for doneness with a meat thermometer around 2 1/2 hours. Internal temperature should be at least 160° in the breast and upper thigh region. When done, remove turkey to a cutting board and cover with foil. Allow to rest 15–20 minutes before carving.

Strain giblets through a fine sieve and dice fine if desired for giblet gravy. Set stock aside. Remove any drippings from roasting pan and skim off grease.

Melt 3/4 cup of butter in 4-quart saucepan. Whisk in 3/4 cup of flour and cook, stirring constantly, for 3–4 minutes. Whisk in 6–8 cups total of hot stock and skimmed drippings from turkey. Continue to cook, stirring frequently until gravy thickens. Season with salt and pepper to taste and keep warm until ready to serve. Heat the gravy bowl before filling, so the sauce will not cool down too quickly.

This would seem a bit simple a recipe for a cookbook, but I am often asked how to roast a turkey and make a well-seasoned gravy. Be sure to cook your turkey thoroughly, but not overcook it. Allowing the turkey to rest after roasting will keep the juices sealed inside. The secret to good gravy is a rich, homemade broth, the pan drippings and seasoning with just enough salt and pepper.

ENTREES

Venison
SERVES 6–8

This recipe is simple but very good. The secret to this recipe is in the proper preparation of the venison.

    Venison haunch or tenderloin
    1 quart whole milk
    1 cup dry red wine
    2 cups flour
    Lawry's seasoned salt
    Cooking oil

Preparation of venison: Dissect and separate the muscle bundles of the haunch. Using the larger muscles, cut crosswise into small cutlets about ½ inch thick. With a sharp knife, trim the edges of the cutlets to remove all the fascia (silver skin) and fat. This is important since it is the fat which carries much of the "gamey" flavor.

Place about 18 cutlets in a large bowl and cover with milk. Allow to marinate in the milk about 4 hours. About ½ hour before cooking, add the red wine to the milk marinade.

In a large skillet, heat about ½ inch deep cooking oil to hot but not smoking. Remove the cutlets from the marinade, dredge them in flour, season with Lawry's seasoned salt and cook them a few at a time in the oil. When the red meat juices appear on the surface of the meat, about 3–4 minutes, turn and cook the other side. They are best when pink in the center.

This recipe was a favorite of Eddie Baker, Commander on the Lynchburg Police Force, who was an ardent hunter and excellent cook.

Fall

Fall

Rose Hip Wreath

In the early fall, plump glossy rose hips ripen in the sun, bringing a welcome burst of color to fast-fading rose gardens.

The long, unwieldy branches of climbing and rambling roses, heavy with hips, are easy to cut and bend into elegant, primitive wreaths.

Grab a pair of thorn-proof gloves, pruning shears, and a reel of florist's wire. Cut 2 or 3 long branches and use the wire to bind both ends. Create a circle and fasten. Fill in as needed, twisting and binding extra stems into the frame.

ENTREES

Doves
SERVES 6

12 doves at room temperature
1 cup melted butter
1 cup dry vermouth, warmed
12 strips lean bacon

Gently warm the butter and vermouth in a small saucepan. Place the doves in a large bowl. Pour the vermouth mixture over and allow to marinate 1–2 hours, stirring occasionally. The marinade will congeal when it is poured over the cooler doves.

Pre-heat grill.

When ready to cook, remove the doves and wrap each in a slice of bacon secured with a toothpick. Cook over a medium-hot charcoal grill about 7 minutes, turning frequently and occasionally dipping into the reserved marinade. Cook until done, but the breast meat is still pink for best flavor.

ENTREES

Quail
SERVES 6

12 quail
1 cup flour
salt, pepper
cooking oil
butter
1 small onion, minced
¼ carrot, peeled and minced
½ celery stalk, sliced
½ cup dry vermouth or dry white wine
2 cans mushroom soup
2 cups chicken broth

Pre heat the oven to 350°

Lightly dust the quail in the flour, salt and pepper to taste, then brown them in oil and butter in a large skillet over medium high heat. Remove the birds and set aside. Lower the heat, add the onion, carrot and celery and cook until translucent, 2–3 minutes. Remove the vegetables and deglaze the pan with the vermouth, scraping up all the bits stuck to the pan. Return the birds and vegetables to the pan, add the mushroom soup and chicken stock to cover the quail. Bring to a simmer, cover and place in 350° oven and continue cooking for about 1½ hours until the birds are very tender and almost falling from the bone.

Serve two birds on a dinner plate and cover with pan sauces.

ENTREES

Pheasant Breast

SERVES 6

>3 pheasants
>oil
>salt and pepper
>4 medium shallots, minced
>1/4 cup sherry vinegar
>1/2 cup red wine
>1 cup chicken stock
>10 tablespoons butter, divided

Preheat oven to 450°.

Remove the wings and legs from the birds and set aside. Heat a heavy skillet over medium heat, add a little oil, season the breasts with salt and pepper, then one at a time brown the birds on all sides. Remove from pan.

Place the reserved wings, legs, and necks in the bottom of a roasting pan large enough to hold the pheasants. Arrange the pheasants on top and roast about 20 minutes until the meat is medium rare. Remove the birds from the pan and keep them warm. Discard the wings, necks and excess fat from the pan.

Sauté the shallots in the roasting pan 1–2 minutes adding a little butter if necessary.

Deglaze both the skillet and roasting pan with the vinegar and combine the liquids into one pan. Add the wine and reduce it over high heat until the liquid becomes a little like syrup. Pour in the stock and reduce it by half. Whisk in the 8 tablespoons of butter, a little at a time. Season to taste with salt and pepper and strain the sauce into a clean saucepan, keeping it warm.

To serve, carve each pheasant breast half into 4 nice slices, arrange on a dinner plate and spoon a little sauce over each serving.

Pheasant legs may be used for something else since they are pretty tough when cooked. They may be used for stock or in a paté.

ENTREES

Flossie's Turkey Pot Pie
SERVES 10

- 4 cups all purpose flour
- 2 teaspoons salt
- 1 cup cold margarine
- 1/3 cup cold butter
- 2/3 cup ice water
- 4 cups turkey meat, chopped
- 2 medium onions, diced
- 2 large potatoes, uncooked, peeled and diced
- 4 carrots, peeled and diced
- 2 stalks celery, diced
- 8 ounces frozen green peas
- 4 cups herb stuffing mix
- 6 cups turkey gravy

In a food processor bowl combine flour and salt. Pulse once or twice and add margarine and butter, cut into pieces. Pulse several times, until mixture resembles coarse cornmeal. Turn out into a large bowl and sprinkle water over the top. Lightly toss the crumbs until they begin to hold together, adding additional water by the tablespoons if necessary. Press together in ball and divide in half. Flatten each half into a cylinder and wrap in plastic film. Refrigerate one hour.

Lightly grease a large lasagna-size casserole, 2–3 inches deep. Roll one pastry disc to fit the bottom and sides of the dish. Layer the turkey, onions, potatoes, carrots, celery, peas and stuffing mix. Carefully pour the gravy over the top, allowing it to seep into the casserole. Roll out the second pastry to fit across the top and pinch along the sides to seal. Cut slits over the top of the pastry for steam vents and bake in a 350° oven for one hour and 45 minutes. Serve immediately with a salad of crisp greens and citrus sections.

You have never tasted pot pie until you have a homemade one. Be sure to have a little extra gravy on the side to serve at the table. You can also substitute any other vegetables that appeal to you. If you are feeling creative, cut out shapes such as leaves or vegetables and place them across the top. Brush lightly with an egg wash to give them an extra shine.

ENTREES

Picnic Chicken Strips
SERVES 8

4 pounds boneless, skinless chicken breasts
1 cup whole buttermilk
1 1/2 tablespoons lemon juice
3/4 teaspoon soy sauce
1 tablespoon Greek seasoning salt
1 teaspoon black pepper
2 cloves garlic, minced
1 1/3 teaspoons Worcestershire sauce
3/4 teaspoon paprika
1/2 teaspoon salt
1 tablespoon cayenne pepper, optional
2 cups flour
1/2 teaspoon baking powder
peanut oil

Cut chicken breasts in strips, 3/4 x 3 inches long and place in a plastic zip lock bag. Stir together the buttermilk and the next 9 ingredients. Pour over chicken strips and marinate in the refrigerator overnight. Heat 3 inches of peanut oil in deep, heavy-bottom pan to 375°. Combine flour and baking powder in large bowl. Drain chicken strips well and roll in flour, shaking off any excess. Fry in small batches until golden brown, turning often. Drain on paper towels and keep warm until all the chicken has been fried. Serve in a basket lined with a colorful napkin and a bowl of PLUM SAUCE (P. 343) or spicy mustard on the side.

These chicken strips are a great tailgate item because you can quickly fry them at the last minute. Do not wrap them too tightly or they will sweat. I usually place a clean towel over the chicken, before placing them in a cooler for the game. Whether you make them spicy or not, everyone will agree that they are a favorite.

SIDE DISHES

Potatoes Au Gratin
SERVES 4

- 3 medium baking potatoes
- 1/2 cup low fat cottage cheese
- 1/2 cup buttermilk
- 2 tablespoon snipped chives
- 2 teaspoons cornstarch
- 1/2 teaspoon salt
- 1/4 teaspoon cayenne pepper
- 1/4 cup shredded mozzarella cheese
- 1/4 teaspoon paprika

Place potatoes in medium saucepan and add water to cover. Bring to a boil and cook about 20 minutes until potatoes can be easily pierced with a fork. Remove from water and allow to cool 15 minutes.

Combine cottage cheese and buttermilk in a food processor until smooth. Stir in chives, cornstarch, salt and pepper. Set aside. Peel and thinly slice potatoes and place in a buttered 2-quart casserole. Pour cottage cheese mixture over potatoes and bake at 350° until bubbly. Sprinkle cheese and paprika on top and bake an additional 5 minutes. Serve immediately.

A tasty low fat side dish, that is both light and easy.

SIDE DISHES

Rosalie's Deviled Eggs
SERVES 12

24 eggs
2/3 cup mayonnaise
2 teaspoons apple cider vinegar
1 teaspoon Dijon mustard
1 tablespoon sour cream
1/2 teaspoon Worcestershire sauce
1 teaspoon grated onion
1/2 teaspoon sugar
1/2 teaspoon salt
1/4 teaspoon curry powder
1/4 teaspoon cayenne pepper
1 teaspoon celery seed

Place eggs in a large stainless pot and add water to cover eggs by 1 inch. Add one tablespoon of salt to the water to help release the shells when peeling. Slowly bring the water to a boil, reduce to simmer and cook 12 minutes. Remove from heat, drain and cool eggs with running cold water. Peel eggs. Split in half lengthwise and place yolks in bowl of food processor. Add remaining ingredients to processor and process until smooth. Fill egg white halves with mixture. Garnish with fresh parsley. Cover lightly with slightly damp paper towels. Cover with plastic wrap and refrigerate up to 24 hours.

If you are going to be traveling with deviled eggs wait to fill them at your destination. Spoon the egg yolk mixture into a large freezer zip lock bag and cut one corner in a zig zag pattern, approximately ½-inch across. Wrap a rubber band around the end to close until ready to use. Carefully pipe the egg yolk into the white halves already arranged on the platter.

SIDE DISHES

Green Bean and Potato Salad
SERVES 10

2 pounds green beans, washed and stemmed
10 small red potatoes, washed and quartered
1 cup celery, chopped
1 cup green onions, chopped
8 ounces blue cheese, crumbled
FRENCH VINAIGRETTE DRESSING (P. 181)

Bring 2 quarts of water to a boil and add green beans. Blanche 8–10 minutes until tender and remove from water. Add quartered potatoes and boil 15–20 minutes or until cooked through. Drain well and place in a large bowl. Add green beans, celery, onion, blue cheese and one cup of dressing. Refrigerate until ready to serve. Spoon into a large wooden bowl and garnish with green onion fans and fresh nasturtiums.

To make green onion fans, cut off the bottom root end of the onions and the top 4 inches of the green end. With a small, sharp knife, make 6 or 8 one-inch slits on either end of the onion. Place in a bowl of ice water for several hours. Remove from water when curled and store in a plastic bag until ready to use.

Fall

SIDE DISHES

Stuffed Banana Peppers
SERVES 4

>8 large banana peppers
>8 ounces feta cheese, crumbled
>1 tablespoon olive oil
>1/4 teaspoon salt
>1/4 teaspoon black pepper

Cut top off banana peppers, leaving stem intact. Using a small paring knife, remove the membrane and seeds. Stuff inside of pepper with crumbled feta cheese. Place cap on top of pepper and skewer top and bottom together with two or three toothpicks.

Heat a 10-inch skillet over medium heat. Add olive oil and heat until sizzling. Reduce heat slightly and add peppers, turning every 4–5 minutes, until evenly browned and cheese has begun to melt, approximately 15–20 minutes. Sprinkle with salt and pepper and serve immediately.

SIDE DISHES

Spicy Chiles and Grits
SERVES 8

    8 ounces cream cheese, softened
    10 ounces Rotel® diced tomatoes and chiles, undrained
    1 cup extra sharp cheddar cheese
    6 cups water
    1 teaspoon salt
    1 cup quick cook grits
    Tabasco® to taste

Combine cream cheese, Rotel® tomatoes and cheese. Microwave 1–2 minutes until soft and stir until smooth. Bring water to a boil in a medium saucepan. Stir in salt and gradually stir in grits. Reduce to a simmer and cover. Cook for 5–10 minutes until mixture thickens, stirring occasionally. Remove from heat and stir in cream cheese mixture. Turn into a greased 3-quart casserole, sprinkle with paprika and bake at 350° for 30 minutes.

Fall

Fall

SIDE DISHES

Creamy Herb Risotto
SERVES 4

> 1 1/2 cups risotto
> 4 tablespoons butter, melted
> 2 tablespoons fresh basil, minced
> 1 tablespoon fresh parsley, minced
> 1 1/4 cups mozzarella cheese, shredded
> 2/3 cup Parmesan cheese, grated
> 2 teaspoons salt
> 1/2 teaspoon black pepper

Cook risotto according to directions, using water or chicken broth. When done, quickly stir in remaining ingredients until cheeses are beginning to melt. Turn into a heated bowl and serve immediately.

SIDE DISHES

Curry Butter Bean Casserole
SERVES 8

2 boxes frozen butter beans
½ pound bacon
½ cup onions, chopped
1 can cream of mushroom soup, undiluted
1 cup sour cream
1 ½ teaspoons curry powder
½ teaspoon salt

Cook butter beans as directed and drain well. Slice bacon in half and then crosswise into ½-inch pieces. Cook in a small skillet, stirring frequently, until bacon begins to foam and is crisp. Drain on paper towels, reserving one tablespoon of bacon grease. Fry chopped onions in reserved bacon grease until transparent. In medium bowl, combine butter beans, bacon, onions, mushroom soup, sour cream, curry powder and salt. Turn into a 2-quart casserole and bake for 30 minutes in a 350° oven. Serve immediately with roasted chicken or beef roast.

SIDE DISHES

Apricot Kugel
SERVES 8

> 2 2/3 cups milk
> 1/4 teaspoon salt
> 1/4 pound wide egg noodles
> 5 tablespoons butter
> 3 tablespoons white sugar
> 3 tablespoons brown sugar
> 3 large eggs, separated
> 1 teaspoon almond extract
> 1 box golden seedless raisins
> 8 ounces apricot jam, heated slightly
> 1/2 cup sliced almonds

Bring the milk to a boil and add the salt and noodles. Cook until tender, about 8–10 minutes. Cool slightly without draining milk.

Beat together butter and sugars until creamy. Add egg yolks and beat well. Stir in almond extract, raisins and warm noodles. Beat egg whites until stiff and gently fold into noodle mixture. Pour 1/2 of the mixture into a buttered 2-quart casserole. Drizzle apricot jam over noodles and layer remaining noodles on top. Sprinkle sliced almonds over top and bake at 350° for 30–35 minutes. Cool 10 minutes and sprinkle with powdered sugar. Cut into squares and serve immediately or refrigerate overnight.

A delicious and light variation of the traditional noodle pudding. It may be served warm or cold.

SIDE DISHES

Thanksgiving Dressing for Turkey
SERVES 12

- ½ cup butter
- 1 cup onion, diced
- 1 cup celery, diced
- 2½ cups chicken stock
- 12 ounces unseasoned croutons
- ¼ cup fresh parsley, minced
- ¼ cup fresh rosemary, snipped
- ¼ cup fresh thyme, minced
- ¼ cup fresh sage, minced
- 2 teaspoons kosher salt
- ½ teaspoon cayenne pepper

Melt butter in large skillet and sauté onion and celery until tender. Stir in chicken stock and set aside. In large bowl combine remaining ingredients, mixing well. Pour onion and celery mixture over croutons and stir until thoroughly moistened. If dressing is too dry, add more stock. Spoon dressing in buttered 2-quart casserole, but do not pack tightly. Bake in a 350° oven, 45–60 minutes until browned and slightly dried out. Serve immediately with turkey and gravy.

Fall

Fall

SIDE DISHES

Southwestern Sweet Potato Casserole
SERVES 6

4 medium sweet potatoes, baked
6 tablespoons butter
½ cup sour cream
1 tablespoon salt
freshly ground black pepper
1 teaspoon ground cumin
pinch nutmeg
2 fresh jalapeños, seeded and chopped fine

Scoop out sweet potatoes into medium bowl while still hot. Beat with electric mixer until smooth and free of lumps. Stir in butter, sour cream, and remaining seasonings. Spoon into 2-quart casserole and bake at 350° for 30 minutes until hot. Serve immediately with extra jalapeños and freshly snipped cilantro, if desired.

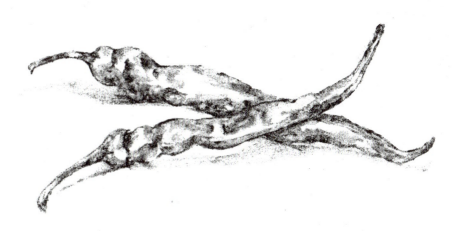

DESSERTS

Estelle's Oatmeal Lace Cookies
MAKES 100 COOKIES

    1 cup shortening
    1 cup brown sugar
    1 cup white sugar
    2 eggs, beaten
    1 teaspoon vanilla extract
    1 1/2 cups flour, sifted
    1 teaspoon salt
    1 teaspoon baking soda
    3 cups quick cook oats
    1/2 cup pecans, toasted and coarsely broken

In a large mixing bowl, cream together shortening, brown sugar and white sugar. Add eggs and vanilla. Sift together flour, salt and baking soda. Stir into dough, with oats and pecans. Mix well. Divide dough into 3 or 4 parts and form each into a long roll, approximately 2 inches in diameter. Wrap in plastic film, pressing dough into a smooth, even roll. Refrigerate rolls overnight.

Slice each roll very thinly and place on a cookie sheet lined with parchment paper. Bake at 350° for 6–8 minutes or until lightly browned. Remove paper and cookies to a cooling rack. Store in a tightly lidded container for 1–2 weeks.

Keep rolls of uncooked cookie dough in the freezer for a last minute dessert. If you do not have parchment paper to bake on, buy some. It will make it worth your while, especially with this recipe. The cookies will not stick or break apart when removing from the baking sheets. Simply slide the entire piece of paper with cookies onto a wire rack and peel off when cool.

Fall

Fall

DESSERTS

Mrs. Jones' Fried Pies
SERVES 12

3 cups flour
1 teaspoon salt
1 cup shortening, chilled
1/2 cup ice cold water
4 cups dried, sliced apples or peaches
3 quarts water
2 cups sugar
1 teaspoon cinnamon
1/2 teaspoon nutmeg, freshly grated
1/2 teaspoon ground allspice

Combine flour and salt. Cut in shortening until it resembles coarse cornmeal. Sprinkle iced water on flour and mix just until incorporated and it holds together. Divide in half and press each half into a flat cylinder. Wrap in plastic film and refrigerate until ready to use.

In a 6-quart saucepan, combine 3 quarts of water, sugar and the dried fruit. Bring to a boil and reduce to simmer. Cook 1–2 hours until the water has been absorbed and the mixture is thick. Stir occasionally. Season with cinnamon, nutmeg and allspice. Remove from heat and cool slightly.

Roll out dough to 1/8-inch thickness and cut into 4-inch circles. Place a heaping spoonful of fruit mixture in the center and fold dough in half. Seal edges with a bit of water and press together with the tines of a fork.

In a 10-inch skillet, heat one tablespoon of butter flavored shortening until it just begins to sizzle. Carefully place 3 or 4 pies in the pan and fry until golden brown and crisp. Turn carefully and fry on the other side. Remove from pan and place on toweling to cool. Sprinkle with additional cinnamon sugar if desired. Serve with ice cream while still warm.

Mrs. Jones' fried pies are a long-standing tradition with the neighborhood picnics. We all stand around in anticipation of her arrival and they disappear as quickly as they are placed on the table.

DESSERTS

Pecan Pie
MAKES 2 PIES

    2 pie crusts, unbaked
    2 cups sugar
    1/2 cup butter, room temperature
    2 tablespoons flour
    5 eggs, room temperature
    1 cup dark corn syrup
    1 cup half and half, room temperature
    1 tablespoon vanilla extract
    4 cups chopped pecans, reserve pecan halves for top of pie

Before starting, all ingredients should be at room temperature. In large mixing bowl, combine sugar, butter, flour and eggs. Beat together well. Add in order, mixing after each addition, the corn syrup, half and half and vanilla. Cover the bottom of each pie shell with the chopped nuts. Carefully pour the filling over the nuts. Garnish the top of the pie with the reserved pecan halves and place the pies on a cookie sheet to catch any drippings. Bake in a 350° oven for 50–60 minutes. Pies will jiggle slightly in the middle when done, but they will set up as they cool. Place on a cooling rack until completely cool. Serve alone or with a dollop of whipped cream or (my favorite) espresso swirl coffee ice cream.

A friend brought this pie to me when I came home from the hospital with our newborn daughter. I thought it was the best pecan pie I had ever tasted. It has a light custard filling, lots of pecans and it is not too sweet. It freezes well, which means you can also provide a new mother with a last minute gift.

Fall

DESSERTS

Easy Apple Crisp
SERVES 8

    8 crisp, tart apples
    1 cup brown sugar
    1/2 cup water
    1 pinch salt
    1/2 box yellow cake mix
    1/2 cup butter, melted
    1/4 cup sugar
    1 teaspoon cinnamon

Peel and cut apples into thin wedges. Place in the bottom of a buttered 3-quart shallow casserole. Sprinkle brown sugar over the top of the apples and pour water over this. Combine salt and cake mix. Sprinkle over the apples and then drizzle the melted butter evenly over the cake mix. Combine sugar and cinnamon and dust evenly over the top. Bake at 350° for 35–40 minutes until the top is golden brown and bubbly. Serve crisp with vanilla or coffee ice cream.

DESSERTS

Cranberry Dessert Cheese
SERVES 50

2 envelopes plain gelatin
½ cup lemon juice, freshly squeezed
24 ounces cream cheese, softened
1 cup butter, softened
2 teaspoons lemon peel, grated
1 cup sour cream
1 ½ cups sugar
6 ounces dried cranberries, coarsely chopped

In a small bowl, stir the gelatin into the lemon juice and set aside to soften. Combine the cream cheese, butter, lemon peel, sour cream and sugar in the bowl of a food processor. Process for 1–2 minutes until thoroughly mixed. Add gelatin and pulse just until incorporated. Pulse in the cranberries, scraping down the sides as needed.

Turn the cranberry cheese into a lightly greased 6 cup mold and refrigerate overnight to congeal. To serve, unmold the cheese on a platter and serve with thin ginger cookies. Decorate with fresh flowers and greens if desired.

A slightly sweet cheese spread that can be used as a light dessert or as an hors d'oeuvre at a cocktail party.

DESSERTS

Black Forest Cake
SERVES 12

CAKE
6 large eggs, room temperature
18 tablespoons sugar
1 cup flour
1/2 cup cocoa
10 tablespoons butter, melted and cooled

SYRUP
14 tablespoons sugar
1 1/2 cups water
Kirsch

FROSTING
3 1/2 cups heavy whipping cream
2/3 cup whole milk, very cold
2/3 cup powdered sugar
1/2 teaspoon vanilla extract
16 ounces canned sour cherries, pitted

CURLS
Bittersweet chocolate

CAKE: Preheat oven to 350°. Grease 3 9-inch cake pans, line the bottom of pans with wax paper and grease and flour wax paper and pans. Beat together eggs and 18 tablespoons sugar until thick and lemon colored. Sift together flour and cocoa and fold into egg mixture. Carefully fold in cooled butter and divide among 3 cake pans. Bake for 25 minutes until cake tests done. Turn out onto rack to cool.

SYRUP: While cake is baking, combine 14 tablespoons of sugar and 1 1/2 cups water. Bring to a boil and boil gently for 5 minutes. Allow to cool a few minutes and add Kirsch to taste. Brush syrup on hot cake, allowing to soak in.

FROSTING: Combine cream, milk, powdered sugar and vanilla. Whip until it makes stiff peaks or holds its shape. Spread frosting on first layer and arrange cherries on top. Repeat with next layer. Ice top and sides of cake and cover with chocolate curls. Garnish top with additional cherries if desired. Refrigerate until ready to serve.

CURLS: Warm a bittersweet chocolate bar with a hair dryer for a few minutes. Push a carrot peeler across the top to make long curls of chocolate. Refrigerate until ready to use.

DESSERTS

Caramel Cake
MAKES 1 LAYERED CAKE

> 1 recipe Butter Layer Cake (p. 126), 2 layers baked as directed
> 3 cups sugar, divided
> 1 tablespoon flour
> 1 cup milk
> ¾ cup butter, room temperature
> 1 teaspoon vanilla extract

To make frosting, combine 2½ cups of sugar and flour in small saucepan. Stir in milk and bring to a boil. Reduce heat to just keep warm.

Sprinkle remaining ½ cup of sugar in a heavy 4-quart saucepan. Cook and stir over medium heat until it melts completely and turns light amber in color. Remove from heat. Gradually add ¼ cup of milk mixture, stirring constantly. Continue to slowly add the milk until it is incorporated, stirring the entire time. Return pan to the heat and bring to a boil. Brush side of pan down with a wet brush to remove sugar crystals. Cover and boil slowly for 2 minutes. Uncover and cook without stirring until a thermometer registers 238° or to the soft ball stage. Remove from heat and pour into a mixing bowl. Allow to cool for 45 minutes. Beat frosting on high, adding tablespoons of butter gradually. Continue to beat until creamy, pale tan in color and frosting holds its shape. This may take awhile. Beat in vanilla and ice cake immediately. If icing becomes too hard, add drops of hot water to loosen. You may also dip the frosting knife in a glass of hot water to prevent the icing from pulling off the cake.

This frosting is more trouble than most, but it is well worth the effort. It has a rich caramel taste that cannot be matched by any other method.

Fall

DESSERTS

Toffee Ice Cream Torte
SERVES 8

1 1/2 packages lady fingers, split
2 tablespoons boiling water
4 teaspoons instant coffee
1/2 gallon vanilla ice cream, softened
10 English toffee bars, frozen and crushed
1 cup whipping cream
4 tablespoons crème de cacao

Line an 8-inch spring form pan with the lady fingers, covering the bottom and sides. Combine the boiling water and the instant coffee, stirring to dissolve, and allow to cool.

In a medium bowl, fold together the ice cream, cooled coffee and the crushed toffee bars, reserving 1/4 cup of the candy for a top garnish. Spread carefully over the lady fingers and freeze for several hours.

Before serving, whip the cream until it forms stiff peaks. Fold in the crème de cacao and spread over the torte. Sprinkle with reserved candy and re-freeze. Release the sides of the torte and, if desired, garnish with chocolate leaves before serving.

To make chocolate leaves, pick 2-to 3-inch glossy, wax type leaves, such as camellia. Paint back side of leaves with melted semi-sweet chocolate, taking care that chocolate does not get on the front side. Freeze or refrigerate a few minutes until firm. Immediately peel leaf from chocolate leaf and store in refrigerator.

DESSERTS

Fresh Apple Cake
SERVES 15

- 1½ cups vegetable oil
- 2 cups sugar
- 3 eggs, beaten
- 3 cups flour
- 1 teaspoon baking powder
- ¼ teaspoon salt
- 2 teaspoons vanilla extract
- 3 cups tart baking apples, coarsely chopped
- 1 cup shredded coconut
- 1 cup raisins
- 1 cup pecans, toasted and broken into pieces
- 6 tablespoons butter
- ¼ cup milk
- 1 cup brown sugar

Grease and flour a 10-inch tube pan or two 5 x 9-inch loaf pans. In a large mixing bowl, combine oil, sugar and eggs. Sift together flour, baking powder and salt. Stir into the batter along with the vanilla. Mixture will be stiff. Combine apples, coconut, raisins and pecans. Stir into the batter until it is well mixed. Spoon into the tube or loaf pans. Place in a 325° oven and bake for 1½ hours or until it tests done. While cake is baking, make the glaze by combining the butter, milk and brown sugar in small saucepan. Bring the mixture to a boil and cook for 1½ minutes. After baking allow the cake to cool in the pan for 15 minutes and then turn out onto a rack. Place a pan under the rack and carefully brush the hot glaze over the top of the cake. Cool cake completely before slicing or wrap tightly in plastic wrap for storage. This cake keeps for one week at room temperature or may be frozen for up to one month.

Fall

Freshly Grated Coconut

Nothing beats the delicious flavor of grated coconut, fresh from the shell! Here's an easy way to do it:

- Pierce the soft spots at the top of the coconut with an ice pick or a clean screwdriver, and drain the milk.

- Place the coconut in a 400° oven for 15 minutes.

- Remove the coconut and wrap it in a kitchen towel, bringing all four corners of the towel together. Holding the corners, strike the wrapped coconut with a hammer.

- Remove the coconut meat from the shell with a knife. A thin brown skin will still cover the meat; remove this with a vegetable peeler or paring knife.

- Grate the coconut, using a microplane grater or the fine side of a box grater.

Yield: 2 ½ to 3 cups grated coconut

Fall

DESSERTS

Cider Sorbet
SERVES 8–10

1 cup port wine
3/4 cup sugar
3 strips of orange peel, (3 inches)
2 cinnamon sticks
5 whole cloves
4 cups apple cider

Combine port wine, sugar, orange peel, cinnamon and cloves in a heavy saucepan. Bring to a boil and simmer for 3–4 minutes, stirring occasionally. Cool to room temperature and refrigerate overnight. Strain mixture through a fine sieve and stir in cider. Freeze in ice cream maker as directed. Sorbet may be made up to 3 days in advance.

Serve this refreshing sorbet as a palate cleansing course for pork or chicken or as a dessert accompaniment with FRESH APPLE CAKE *or* CARAMEL CAKE.

DESSERTS

Greg's Best Chocolate Chip Cookies
MAKES 100 3-INCH COOKIES

    3 eggs
    2 1/4 cups brown sugar
    1 1/2 cups white sugar
    1 cup butter, softened
    1 cup margarine, softened
    2 tablespoons vanilla extract
    6 cups flour
    1 1/2 teaspoons salt
    1 1/2 teaspoons baking soda
    24 ounces semi-sweet chocolate chips
    2 cups pecans, toasted and coarsely broken

In a large mixing bowl, beat eggs for 5 minutes, until thick and lemon colored. Beat in sugars, butter, margarine and vanilla. Sift together flour, salt and baking soda. Gradually stir into egg mixture, beating just until incorporated. Stir in chocolate chips and pecans. Drop by the tablespoons on parchment paper–lined cookie sheets. Bake in a 350° oven for 15 minutes. Remove parchment with cookies to a rack to cool. Cookies may be frozen up to one month, but should not be held more that a few days at room temperature.

Fall

Fall

DESSERTS

Mississippi Mud Squares
MAKES 30 SQUARES

> 1/2 cup butter, softened
> 1 cup white sugar
> 2 eggs, separated
> 1 teaspoon baking powder
> 1 1/2 cups flour
> 1/8 teaspoon salt
> 2 teaspoons vanilla extract, divided
> 3/4 cup pecans, toasted and broken into pieces
> 1 cup brown sugar

Cream butter and white sugar together until light and fluffy. Beat in egg yolks. Sift together baking powder, flour and salt. Stir into dough, along with one teaspoon of vanilla and the nuts. Press into a greased 9 x 13-inch pan. Set aside. Beat egg whites until stiff and glossy, gradually adding brown sugar. Spread evenly across top of dough and bake at 325° for 30 minutes. Remove from oven and cut into squares with a serrated knife, but do not remove from pan. Bars will be soft and sticky at this point. Allow to completely cool and remove from pan. Store in an airtight container, up to 5 days.

DESSERTS

Date Nut Filled Cookies
MAKES 100 COOKIES

- 1 cup butter, softened
- 2 cups brown sugar
- 2 eggs, beaten
- 2 tablespoons milk
- 1 teaspoon of vanilla extract
- 1 teaspoon baking soda
- 1/2 teaspoon salt
- 3 1/2 cups flour
- 1/2 cup pecans, toasted and coarsely broken
- 3/4 cup white sugar
- 2 cups dates, chopped
- 3/4 cup water
- 1 cup powdered sugar
- 1 tablespoon milk

In a large mixing bowl, combine butter and brown sugar until smooth and creamy. Beat in eggs, milk and vanilla. Combine baking soda, salt and flour and stir into dough just until incorporated. Divide into 4 parts and shape into 2 1/2-inch rolls. Wrap in plastic film and refrigerate overnight.

In a small saucepan, combine pecans, white sugar, dates and water. Cook over low heat, stirring constantly, until mixture begins to thicken. Cool and set aside.

Slice each roll into 1/4-inch slices. Spread a small amount of filling on one cookie slice. Top with a second slice and place on a parchment–lined cookie sheet. Bake in a 350° oven for 10–12 minutes until lightly browned. Remove paper and cookies to a cooling rack.

Combine powdered sugar and milk and drizzle across cooled cookies. Allow to air dry for 30 minutes and store in tins for up to one week.

Fall

BREAD

Cheese Biscuits
SERVES 8

2 cups flour
1/2 teaspoon salt
3 teaspoons baking powder
1/4 teaspoon cayenne pepper, optional
4 tablespoons margarine, chilled
1 1/2 cups grated extra sharp cheddar cheese
3/4 cup milk

In the bowl of a food processor, combine flour, salt, baking powder and cayenne pepper. Cut up butter into pieces and add to processor, along with the cheese. Pulse the mixture until it resembles coarse crumbs. Transfer to a large bowl. Make a well in the center of the mixture and add the milk all at once. Stir quickly, mixing from the sides to the middle. Do not over beat. Mix until all ingredients are moistened. Let stand 3–5 minutes. With floured hands, make 2-inch balls, pressing lightly to form. Place on an ungreased cookie sheet or parchment paper and bake at 425° for 10–12 minutes or until lightly browned. Place on a cooling rack. I like to butter these biscuits before reheating. If you ever have leftovers, they are delicious split and toasted.

Better make plenty of these family favorites. I don't think you ever have enough. You can also vary the recipe by substituting Monterey Jack cheese and adding 1 tablespoon snipped fresh herbs and 1 clove of garlic. Bake as directed.

BREAD

Jalapeño Hush Puppies
MAKES 36 PUPPIES

1 3/4 cups self-rising white cornmeal
1 1/2 cups self-rising flour
1 1/2 cups yellow cornmeal, finely milled
2 teaspoons baking powder
1 teaspoons salt
1/2 teaspoon garlic powder
3/4 teaspoon red pepper
1 1/2 cups milk
3/4 cup buttermilk
1 egg, beaten
1/2 cup onion, finely minced
1/2 cup jalapeño pepper, finely minced

Combine dry ingredients in large bowl. Mix together milk, buttermilk and egg. Make a well in the center of the dry ingredients and add the liquid all at once. Stir quickly to combine. Stir in the onions and peppers.

Heat 3–4 inches of vegetable oil in a deep heavy fryer or pot until it reaches 375° (or a cube of bread sizzles when dropped in the oil). It is important to maintain this temperature as you cook the hush puppies. Drop the batter by the tablespoon and fry until golden brown, turning often. Hush puppies are done when they float freely to the top and are golden in color. Keep warm in an oven or serve immediately.

Fall

Fall

Freezing Fresh Blueberries

To prolong your enjoyment of summer's berry bounty, freeze unwashed, dry blueberries in a zip-lock freezer bag. Remove berries as needed, and rinse quickly under cold running water. Add them to your recipe while frozen, or pop them in your mouth for a delicious snack!

BREAD

Refrigerated Blueberry Muffins
MAKES 2 DOZEN

>2/3 cup butter, room temperature
>1 cup sugar
>3 eggs, beaten
>3 cups flour
>2 1/2 teaspoons baking powder
>1 teaspoon salt
>1 cup milk
>1 cup fresh or frozen blueberries

In a mixing bowl, cream together the butter and sugar, beating until light and fluffy. Add eggs, one at a time, beating well after each addition. Combine dry ingredients in a small bowl, and add to creamed mixture alternating with the milk. Begin and end with the dry ingredients. Stir in blueberries. Spoon the batter into greased muffin cups, filling 2/3 full. Bake in a 375° oven for 20–25 minutes. Serve immediately or cool and reheat briefly before serving. Batter may be stored in an airtight container for up to 2 weeks in the refrigerator.

Who can resist fresh blueberry muffins and these are made easy by having them ready to bake in the refrigerator. Whether for breakfast or dinner I know you and your family will enjoy these homemade treats.

BREAD

Risen Muffins
MAKES 16 MUFFINS

    2 teaspoons dry yeast
    1 teaspoon sugar
    4 tablespoons butter
    8 tablespoons margarine
    1 tablespoon sugar
    2 eggs, lightly beaten
    1 teaspoon salt
    2 1/2 cups flour
    1/2 cup milk

Dissolve yeast in 1/2 cup of warm water (110°). Stir in one teaspoon sugar and set aside to proof.

In a medium bowl, cream together the butter, margarine and one tablespoon of sugar. Stir in the eggs and yeast mixture. Sift together the salt and flour and add to the muffin dough, alternating with the milk. Begin and end with the flour. Spoon into greased muffin tins and set in a warm, draft-free place. Let rise 2 hours or until doubled in size. Bake in a 400° oven for 12–15 minutes until lightly browned. Serve immediately.

These old fashioned muffins combine the ease of making quick breads with the yeasty flavor of a more time-consuming roll. If you do not feel successful with homemade dinner rolls, try these as a possible substitute. As with any muffin recipe, a light touch is always best.

Fall

BREAD

Honey Sweet Wheat Bread
MAKES 2 LOAVES

2 tablespoons dry yeast
1/2 cup warm water (110°)
pinch of sugar
1 3/4 cups milk
2 tablespoons butter, softened
1/3 cup honey
10 tablespoons brown sugar
1 tablespoon salt
4 cups whole-grain wheat flour
1 1/2 cups unbleached all purpose flour

Combine water, yeast and a pinch of sugar in a small bowl. Stir until the yeast dissolves and set aside to proof.

Heat milk just until warm. Pour into a large bowl and stir in butter until it melts. Add honey, brown sugar and salt. Stir in wheat flour, one cup at a time and then add yeast mixture. Beat in unbleached flour, adding maybe 1/2 cup additional flour to make a soft dough. Turn out onto a floured board and knead 10 minutes until smooth and satiny. Place in a large greased bowl and cover with plastic wrap. Set in a warm draft-free place to rise. When dough has doubled in size, punch down and turn out onto a dough board. Divide in half and knead each half a couple of times. Roll out to make two 2 x 6-inch rectangles and roll up tightly, pinching edges and tucking in the ends to make a loaf. Place each in a well-greased 8 x 4 x 2-inch loaf pan. Set in a warm, draft-free place to rise, approximately 45 minutes. Bake in a 375° oven for 25–30 minutes. Brush top of bread with melted margarine and turn out onto a cooling rack.

BREAD

Black Russian Yeast Bread
MAKES 2 LOAVES

- 2 cups rye flour
- 3 cups unbleached flour
- 1/2 cup wheat bran
- 2 cups toasted fresh bread crumbs
- 1 tablespoon salt
- 1/4 cup cocoa
- 2 tablespoons carraway seeds
- 1/2 teaspoon crushed fennel seeds
- 1/4 teaspoon ground ginger
- 4 tablespoons butter, melted
- 1/4 cup molasses
- 8 tablespoons dry yeast
- 1 teaspoon sugar
- 1 tablespoon instant coffee, dissolved in 1/4 cup hot water

Combine flours, bran, bread crumbs, salt, cocoa, seeds and ginger. Set aside. In small bowl, stir together melted butter and molasses. Cool to lukewarm and whisk in yeast and one teaspoon sugar. Set aside. Add 2 cups lukewarm water to the dissolved coffee. In a large bowl, stir together half of the dry mixture with the coffee mixture. Add the yeast/butter and gradually beat in the remaining dry ingredients. When thoroughly incorporated, turn out onto a floured board and knead 5–8 minutes. Shape into a ball and place in an oiled bowl. Cover and let rise until doubled in volume. Punch down and divide dough in half. Knead each half until smooth and firm. Shape into a round loaf and place on a cookie sheet that has been dusted with cornmeal. Cut a cross slash on the top of each loaf. Cover and let rise until double. Bake in a 375° oven for 20–25 minutes. Take out and brush the tops of the loaves with a mixture of one egg, beaten, one teaspoon hot water and one teaspoon instant coffee. Return to the oven and bake an additional 10 minutes. Test for doneness and cool before serving.

BREAD

Onion Dill Bread
MAKES 1 LOAF

1 tablespoon dry yeast
1/4 cup warm water (110°)
1 pinch sugar
1 cup cottage cheese
1 tablespoon butter
2 tablespoons sugar
1/4 cup finely minced onion
2 tablespoons dried dill weed
1 teaspoon salt
1 egg, beaten
1/4 teaspoon baking soda
2 1/2 cups flour

In a small bowl, combine yeast, water and a pinch of sugar. Set aside to proof. Heat cottage cheese and butter in the microwave until warm. Pour into a medium mixing bowl and add sugar, onion, dill, salt, egg, baking soda and yeast mixture. Add flour one cup at a time, beating well after each addition. Cover with plastic wrap and let rise in a warm, draft-free place until doubled in size, 50–60 minutes. Punch down and turn into a well-greased loaf pan. Let rise again for 30 minutes and bake in a 350° oven for 25–30 minutes until browned. Allow to cool before slicing.

This bread makes an excellent sandwich bread for cucumbers or chicken salad or sliced turkey. To ensure even slices, cut the loaf from left to right. (if you are right handed) Turn the bread away from your cutting hand and rest your other hand against the cut side; using it to gauge the thickness of each slice.

BRUNCHES

Jammin' Muffins
MAKES 12 MEDIUM MUFFINS

1 2/3 cups flour
1 tablespoon baking powder
1/4 teaspoon freshly ground nutmeg
1/2 cup sugar
1/2 teaspoon salt
6 tablespoons margarine, chilled
3/4 cup milk
1 egg, beaten
1/2 cup jam
1/2 cup finely chopped nuts

Combine dry ingredients in a medium bowl. Cut in shortening until it resembles cornmeal. Make a well in the center and quickly stir in the milk and egg. Spoon into greased muffin pan, about 3/4 full. Spoon one teaspoon of jam on top of each muffin, pressing lightly into batter. Sprinkle with a few nuts and bake at 400° for 20–25 minutes. Remove from pan and serve immediately.

Fall

Fall

BRUNCHES

Swiss Apple Quiche
SERVES 12

2 9-inch pie crusts, uncooked
1 pound country sausage with sage
2 cups apples, peeled and sliced
2 cups Swiss cheese, shredded
¼ pound mushrooms, sliced
4 eggs, beaten
1 tablespoon flour
1 teaspoon salt
1 cup milk
1 cup half and half
1 ½ tablespoons butter, melted

Crumble and cook sausage until no longer pink. Drain well and set aside. In the bottom of each pie shell, layer apples, sausage, mushrooms and cheese. Combine remaining ingredients and pour over the two pies. Bake in a 375° oven for 45 minutes. Allow pies to set for 5 minutes before cutting in slices. Serve immediately.

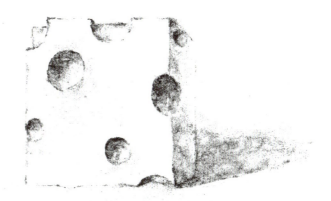

BRUNCHES

Sante Fe Granola
SERVES 40

- 2 pounds old fashioned oats, uncooked
- ½ cup wheat bran
- ½ cup wheat germ
- ½ cup oat bran
- 1 cup walnuts, broken into pieces
- 1 cup slivered almonds
- 1 cup sunflower seeds
- 2 cups canola oil   [1½ c]
- 1 cup honey
- 1 cup maple syrup
- 1 tablespoon salt
- 4 tablespoons vanilla extract
- 2 cups raisins
- 2 cups shredded coconut
- 1 cup dried apricots, diced
- 1 cup dates, chopped

In a large 8-quart bowl, combine oats, wheat bran, wheat germ, oat bran, walnuts, almonds, sunflower seeds, canola oil, honey, maple syrup, salt and vanilla. Mix thoroughly and spread in shallow pans. Bake for approximately 45 minutes in a 350° oven, stirring every 5 minutes. Do not overbake. Cool completely and return to large bowl. Mix in raisins, coconut, apricots and dates. Store in zip lock bags in the freezer until ready to use. Serve with bowls of fresh fruit and vanilla yogurt

Try serving side dishes of granola, fresh fruit and yogurt for your next buffet brunch. The lighter fare is appealing to many people and this homemade version is especially good. The recipe makes a large quantity, but it keeps well in the freezer. Use it as a hostess gift or at Christmas in a breakfast gift basket.

Fall

Drying and Storing Seeds

The seeds of many plants can be dried and saved for future planting. Here's how to prepare and store your seeds for future growing and enjoyment:

- **Detach seedpods as they are turning tan, but before they split open.**

- **Let seeds dry for several days, then place them in small paper envelopes.**

- **Store in a dark, well-ventilated location; or, for long-term storage, put envelopes in a refrigerator or freezer.**

- **To test for adequate germination, sprinkle seeds onto a moist paper towel and roll it up. Keep moist, and check often for sprouts. Most seeds will take 1 to 2 weeks to germinate.**

BRUNCHES

David Hugh's Blueberry Pancakes
SERVES 4

1 1/2 cups flour
1 teaspoon salt
1 teaspoon baking soda
1 teaspoon sugar
1 egg, beaten
2 tablespoons butter, melted
2 cups buttermilk
2 cups blueberries, washed and picked over

In a large bowl, combine dry ingredients. Stir in egg, butter and buttermilk. Mix until smooth. Stir in blueberries. Heat a large skillet until medium hot. Brush with a little vegetable oil and cook pancakes on both sides until golden brown. Serve immediately with lots of sweet butter and maple syrup.

There is nothing better than a plate full of fresh blueberry pancakes on a crisp August morning in Maine. The wild Maine blueberries are smaller and sweeter than their grocery store counterparts. If they are available to you in July and August, buy plenty and store in plastic containers in the freezer for use year round.

BRUNCHES

Cornmeal Waffles
SERVES 4

      1 1/2 cups white cornmeal, finely milled
      3/4 cup flour
      2 tablespoons sugar
      1 tablespoon baking powder
      1/2 teaspoon salt
      1/2 teaspoon baking soda
      1 3/4 cups buttermilk
      2 eggs, separated
      3 tablespoons vegetable oil

In a medium mixing bowl, combine cornmeal, flour, sugar, baking powder, salt and baking soda. Combine buttermilk, egg yolks and oil in a small bowl. Quickly stir in dry ingredients. Beat egg whites until they are stiff and fold into batter. Spread one cup of batter on a greased waffle iron and cook until golden brown. Serve immediately with softened butter and maple syrup.

The cornmeal makes the waffles extra crispy and flavorful.

Fall

BRUNCHES

Cornbatter Cakes
SERVES 6

    1 cup cornmeal
    1 tablespoon flour
    1 teaspoon baking soda
    1 teaspoon salt
    2 cups buttermilk
    2 eggs, separated
    2 tablespoons vegetable oil

Combine dry ingredients in a medium bowl. Stir in the buttermilk, beaten egg yolks and vegetable oil until smooth. Beat egg whites until stiff and fold into batter. (The mixture will be thin and very light). Heat a griddle until it is just smoking and brush liberally with vegetable oil. Use 1/4 cup of batter per cake and cook until golden brown on both sides. Serve immediately with melted butter, maple syrup or sorghum molasses.

When cooked, these cakes should be thin and crispy outside. It is not unusual to eat 8 or 10 of these at a time. Be sure to use a well-seasoned and oiled griddle to prevent the cakes from sticking.

BRUNCHES

Hot Fruit Compote
SERVES 12

    8 ounces dried apricots, cut in half
    6 ounces dried and pitted prunes
    6 ounces dried cherries
    16 ounce can pear halves
    16 ounce can peach halves
    16 ounces can pineapple chunks
    1/3 cup melted butter
    1 tablespoon curry powder
    3/4 cup brown sugar
    1/2 cup slivered almonds

In separate bowls, soak apricots, prunes and cherries in warm water for 20–30 minutes. Drain dried fruits, pears, peaches and pineapple chunks, keeping fruit separated. Lightly grease a 9 x 13-inch oven-proof baking dish and layer the fruits, ending with the cherries. Combine the butter, curry powder and brown sugar. Pour over the fruit and top with almonds. Cover tightly with aluminum foil and bake for one hour in a 325° oven. Remove foil and allow to cool. Re-cover casserole with plastic wrap and refrigerate overnight. To serve, reheat uncovered for 25–30 minutes, basting occasionally with the juices at the bottom of the casserole.

A delicious alternative to the brunch fruit one is used to seeing. Easy because it can be made ahead.

Fall

BRUNCHES

Smoked Salmon Hash with Poached Egg
SERVES 12

> 16 ounces smoked salmon or lox
> ½ cup red onion, finely chopped
> 6 tablespoons capers
> ½ cup sour cream
> 3 tablespoons horseradish
> 1 tablespoon whole grain Dijon mustard
> 4 tablespoons butter
> 1 pound diced hash brown potatoes, frozen
> 2 dozen eggs, chilled
> 1 recipe HOLLANDAISE (P. 348)

Cut salmon in small strips and place in a microwave bowl. Combine onion, capers, sour cream, horseradish and Dijon mustard until thoroughly mixed. Gently fold into salmon. Set aside.

In a large skillet, melt butter and sprinkle hash brown potatoes evenly over the bottom of the pan. Cook uncovered 6–10 minutes, turning often, until potatoes begin to brown. Remove from heat and cover to keep warm.

Fill a large braising pan with 4 inches of water. Add 2 tablespoons of cider vinegar and bring to a boil. Reduce to just below boiling. Break eggs one at a time into a small cup. Gently slide the egg into the simmering water. Continue to add eggs until they are just barely touching (usually 12 eggs per batch). Cook the eggs a total of 3–4 minutes or until the eggs float to the top and the whites are firm. You may need to gently loosen the egg from the bottom of the pan with a spatula. Remove the eggs to a pot of hot water to keep them warm, but to stop them from cooking. Continue

BRUNCHES

to cook and remove the eggs until you have the desired number (usually 2 eggs per person).

While the last batch is cooking, microwave the salmon mixture 1–2 minutes, stirring often until the salmon is just warm. Reheat the potatoes and fold into the salmon. Heat over low until the hash is warm throughout. Place the salmon hash on a heated platter, mounding slightly. Make small indentations and place a poached egg in each. Drizzle warmed HOLLANDAISE over each egg, garnish with parsley sprigs and serve immediately.

Any number of poached eggs may be cooked by using this method. The trick to serving them together is to keep them warm in a container of hot water. If you are serving a large buffet, place the cooked eggs in an oblong chafing dish that is lined with a bed of mustard or spinach greens. Each guest may choose from a variety of additions to the more traditional Eggs Benedict, such as a spicy cheese sauce, sautéed mushrooms, peppers or onions, chili, shrimp grits or a creamed spinach. Bowls of fresh fruit and homemade breakfast pastries will make your meal complete.

BRUNCHES

Open Faced Crab Sandwich
SERVES 6

    4 ounces cream cheese, softened
    1 teaspoon lemon juice, freshly squeezed
    1 large egg, beaten
    4 tablespoons mayonnaise
    2 tablespoons fresh parsley, minced
    2 tablespoons grated Parmesan cheese
    salt and cayenne pepper to taste
    1/2 pound crab meat, picked through
    2 tablespoons olive oil
    1 small loaf sourdough bread, cut into 1/2-inch slices
    6 slices tomato

In a medium bowl, combine cream cheese, lemon juice, egg, mayonnaise, parsley, Parmesan, salt and pepper. Gently fold in crab meat and set aside. Heat a 10-inch skillet with 2 tablespoons of olive oil. Lightly brown both sides of the sourdough bread and remove to a baking sheet. Place one slice of tomato on each slice of bread and mound crab mixture on each. Place in a 350° oven and bake 20–25 minutes until puffed and golden. Serve immediately with a grapefruit and orange salad or a cup of BLACK BEAN SOUP.

BRUNCHES

Bran Raisin Muffins
MAKES 40 2½-INCH MUFFINS

1 cup boiling water
3 cups bran cereal buds, divided
1½ cups sugar
⅔ cup shortening
2 eggs
2 cups buttermilk
2½ cups flour
2½ teaspoons baking soda
½ teaspoon salt
2 cups raisins

In a small bowl, pour one cup of boiling water over one cup of bran cereal buds. Set aside to cool. In a medium mixing bowl, cream sugar, shortening and eggs. Stir in buttermilk and cooled cereal mixture. In a large bowl, sift together flour, baking soda and salt. Mix in 2 cups of bran cereal. Make a well in the center of the dry ingredients and quickly stir in the buttermilk mixture, mixing just until moistened. Stir in raisins. At this point the batter may be kept in the refrigerator for several days until ready to bake. Fill greased or paper lined muffin pans to ⅔ full and bake in a 400° oven for 15–20 minutes. Remove to a rack to cool or serve immediately.

Fall

BRUNCHES

Orange Swirl Sweet Rolls
MAKES 36 ROLLS

1 tablespoon dry yeast
1 cup warm water, 110°
3 tablespoons sugar
2 tablespoons shortening
1 egg, lightly beaten
¾ teaspoon salt
3½ cups flour, divided
½ cup butter, softened and divided
½ cup sugar
2 tablespoons grated orange rind
¼ cup sour cream
1 tablespoon orange juice

Combine yeast, warm water and a pinch of sugar in a small bowl. Set aside in a draft-free area to proof. In a large mixing bowl, combine sugar, shortening, egg and salt. Stir in the yeast mixture and half of the flour. Beat until smooth and continue to add flour until you have a soft dough. Place in a greased bowl or refrigerate up to 5 days. Allow to rise until doubled and punch down. Knead 1–2 minutes and roll out onto a floured board in a 14 x 9-inch rectangle. Combine ¼ cup of butter, 2 tablespoons sugar and orange rind in a small bowl. Spread on dough to within ½ inch of long edge. Roll up dough tightly beginning with the long side. Cut a piece of thread or fishing line about 18 inches long. Holding each end, place the string under the dough approximately ½ inch from the end of the roll. Cross the two ends and pull tightly, cutting down through the dough as you pull (I hope that you now have a cleanly cut slice through the dough). Continue to move the string along the length of the roll, cutting ½-inch slices. Grease a 9 x 13-inch pan and place the rolls in the pan ½ inch apart. Let rise 45 minutes. Bake in a 400° oven for 20–25 minutes. While rolls are baking, combine ¼ cup of butter, 6 tablespoons of sugar, ¼ cup of sour cream and orange juice in a small saucepan. Heat until just warm. After rolls have baked, turn out onto a rack and drizzle with orange sauce. Allow to cool and enjoy.

BRUNCHES

Rhonda's Banana Bread
MAKES ONE LOAF

    1 teaspoon baking soda
    4 tablespoons sour cream
    1 cup banana, mashed
    ¼ cup buttermilk
    1½ cups flour
    ½ teaspoon salt
    1 cup sugar
    ½ cup butter, softened
    1 egg, slightly beaten
    1 teaspoon vanilla extract
    ½ cup pecans, toasted and coarsely chopped

In a small bowl, dissolve baking soda and sour cream. Set aside. In another bowl, combine the bananas and buttermilk. Set aside. In another bowl, combine the flour and salt.

In a large mixing bowl, cream together the sugar and butter. Beat in the egg and then the sour cream mixture, stirring well. Stir in the flour, alternating with the banana mixture, beginning and ending with the dry ingredients. Be careful to mix only until incorporated. Stir in the vanilla and pecans. Pour into a well-greased and floured loaf pan or small fluted bundt pan. Rap sharply on counter top to remove any air bubbles. Bake in a 350° oven for 50 minutes. Remove from oven and set on a cooling rack for 15 minutes. Turn out and allow to cool completely before slicing.

This moist and rich banana bread is the best I have ever had. It can be made a few days ahead or may be frozen for 2–3 months if wrapped well.

Fall

Fall

BRUNCHES

Fresh Peach Coffee Cake
SERVES 18

½ cup sliced almonds
3 cups flour
3 cups sugar
1 teaspoon salt
1 teaspoon baking powder
¼ teaspoon baking soda
¾ cup buttermilk
1 cup butter, softened
1 teaspoon almond extract
4 extra large eggs, beaten
1 cup finely chopped peaches
½ cup water
½ cup sugar
1 tablespoon butter

Grease and flour a bundt pan. Sprinkle the sliced almonds evenly around the bottom. Sift dry ingredients into a large mixing bowl. Stir in the buttermilk, butter, almond extract and eggs. Beat for 2–3 minutes until smooth. Stir in peaches and pour into prepared pan. Bake in a 350° for 60 minutes or until a straw inserted into the middle comes out clean. Place on a cooling rack for 15 minutes before turning out. While cake is cooling, combine water and a ½ cup of sugar in a small saucepan. Bring to a boil and cook 5 minutes. Remove from heat and stir in one tablespoon of butter. Brush over top of cake after it has been removed from pan, allowing the syrup to soak in. Cake may be frozen up to one month in advance.

APPETIZERS

Mississippi Cheese
SERVES 12

- 1/3 cup JOHN TUCKER PERCY'S DRESSING (P. 284)
- 2 cloves garlic, peeled
- 2 tablespoons mayonnaise
- 3 cups cheddar cheese, shredded
- 3 ounces cream cheese, softened
- 1 teaspoon paprika

Add in the following order to a blender or food processor bowl: dressing, garlic, mayonnaise, cheddar cheese, cream cheese and paprika. Blend or process until smooth. Pack in a small crock or glass container and refrigerate until ready to serve. Remove from refrigerator 1/2 hour before serving. Serve with an assortment of crackers.

Winter

Forcing Bulbs

Water forcing and soil forcing can be accomplished in under a month.

Store bulbs in brown paper bags at room temperature in dark room

Paperwhites do not require a cold period to flower

BEST BULBS FOR FORCING

Hyacinths

Crocuses

Paperwhites*

Tulips

Amaryllis

* Cannot be used again after forcing!

Winter

Rules for Forcing Branches

- Requires 6 weeks of cold weather (below 40°F)
- The closer the branches are cut to their natural blooming time, the quicker they will blossom
- Gather Branches on a warm day
- Cut 2" slash in stem, place in hot water (125° - 150°F)
- Keep branches in "holding pattern" – unheated space (60°F)
- Regulate blooms by bringing in house, where warmer
- Recut about an inch off the bottom of stems, every couple of days. Refill container with clean warm water
- Remove bud's side shoots under the water line.
- Think outside the box!

APPETIZERS

Cheese Straws
MAKES 100 MEDIUM STRAWS

2 cups flour
1 teaspoon salt
1/4 teaspoon cayenne pepper
1/4 pound margarine, chilled
1/4 pound butter, chilled
1/2 pound extra sharp cheddar cheese, grated

In a large bowl, mix flour, salt and cayenne pepper. Cut in margarine and cheese until it resembles coarse cornmeal. Press together in a ball and flatten on a sheet of wax paper. Refrigerate for one hour to chill. When ready to bake, roll as you would a pie pastry until it is about 1/4-inch thick. Cut in 3-inch long strips, 1/2-inch wide. If desired the pastry may also be cut in decorative shapes, such as hearts, stars or rounds. Place on a cookie sheet, 1/2-inch apart and bake at 375° until lightly browned. Remove immediately to a cooling rack. Store in an airtight container when completely cooled.

One of my favorite before dinner hors d'oeuvre. The crisp cheese taste goes well with any drink. Handle these delicate pastries carefully as they break easily. Store between layers of wax paper to protect the straws, which will last for up to 2 weeks. Use only top grade sharp cheese for the best results.

APPETIZERS

Holiday Stuffed Mushrooms
SERVES 8

- 1 pound large mushroom caps, stems discarded
- 8 ounces cream cheese, softened
- 1/2 cup Parmesan cheese, grated
- 1 tablespoon Worcestershire sauce
- 1 tablespoon dried dill weed

Lightly oil outside of mushroom caps and place on cookie sheet. In a small bowl, combine remaining ingredients and mound into each cap. Bake in 350° oven until puffed and golden, approximately 15 minutes. Serve immediately.

Winter

Branches for Forcing

*Bradford Pear

Crabapple

Dogwood

Flowering peach

Forsythia

Fruit trees: pear, apple, cherry, peach

Pussy willow

*Quince

Red-Bud

Spirea

Star Magnolia

Witch Hazel

*quickest to come in bloom

APPETIZERS

Country Layered Pâté
SERVES 35

½ cup beef consommé
1½ teaspoons unflavored gelatin
14 tablespoons butter, softened, divided
3 tablespoons minced onions
1 pound chicken livers
1 teaspoon mustard powder
½ teaspoon salt
¼ teaspoon nutmeg, freshly grated
½ can anchovy, mashed
⅛ teaspoon cayenne pepper
2 cups country cured ham, ground
4 tablespoons mayonnaise
1 tablespoon Dijon mustard
16 ounces cream cheese, softened
1 tablespoon sour cream
1 teaspoon grated onion

Spray a 6-cup loaf pan or decorative mold with cooking spray. Combine consomme and gelatin in a small bowl. Microwave until hot, stirring to dissolve gelatin. Pour in prepared mold and refrigerate until firm. Melt 2 tablespoons of butter in a sauté pan. Add onions and livers and cook until livers are barely pink on the inside, about 8–10 minutes. Cool. In a food processor bowl, place livers, dry mustard, salt, nutmeg, anchovy and cayenne. Process until smooth. Gradually add butter while running, processing until smooth and thoroughly combined. Set aside. Combine country ham, mayonnaise and Dijon mustard in small bowl. Set aside. Combine cream cheese, sour cream and grated onion. Spread mixture gently over congealed consommé. Spread the country ham for the next layer and then add the layer of liver pâté, spreading evenly. Chill overnight. When ready to serve, unmold on a platter and garnish with thinly sliced cucumbers, sliced hard cooked eggs and saltine crackers. Pâté may be decorated with sprigs of fresh herbs and flowers.

APPETIZERS

Christmas Pâté
SERVES 24

- 3 tablespoons olive oil
- 3 tablespoons butter
- 1 cup onion, finely chopped
- 1 tablespoon garlic, minced
- 1 teaspoon dried thyme leaves
- 2 teaspoons green peppercorns, lightly crushed, divided
- 1 pound chicken livers, drained
- 2 tablespoons cognac
- 1 tablespoon cherry brandy
- 1/2 teaspoon ground allspice
- 1/4 teaspoon nutmeg, freshly grated
- 1 teaspoon salt
- 4 tablespoons heavy cream
- 3/4 cup dried cherries, chopped
- 1/2 cup toasted pecans, coarsely chopped

Melt butter with olive oil in small saucepan. Sauté onions, garlic, thyme and one teaspoon of green peppercorns until translucent. Add chicken livers and cook until barely pink on the inside, about 5–8 minutes. Put liver mixture, cognac, cherry brandy, allspice, nutmeg and salt in the bowl of processor. Process until smooth, adding cream gradually. Fold in cherries and one teaspoon green peppercorns, and spoon into crock. Store in the refrigerator until ready to use. Remove from refrigerator one hour before serving. Put crock on board with crusty french bread or crackers. Garnish top of pâté with additional dried cherries and fresh sprigs of thyme.

Winter

"A gift of nature is fleeting, to be enjoyed in the moment. Others will always come, yet none will ever quite be the same. Though sometimes small and at first glance insignificant, each is a souvenir that lives on in remembrances."

—Ethel Brennan from *Souvenirs: Gifts from the Garden*

Winter

How to Make your Amaryllis Bloom Again

- After flowers fade, cut off the stalks and watch foliage emerge
- Keep plant watered and fertilized through remainder of cold weather season
- Slowly introduce bulb outside once outside temperatures are consistently above 55°F at night
- Keep pots in warm, semi-shaded position
- In September, begin withholding water to encourage dormancy
- Do not give anymore water, if you do, you probably won't get flowers next winter
- Once foliage dies back, and before frost comes, store bulbs (totally dry) in a cool dark place

APPETIZERS

Smoked Oyster Spread
SERVES 12

1 clove garlic, minced
1 tablespoon onion, finely chopped
16 ounces cream cheese, softened
1 tablespoon mayonnaise
1 tablespoon milk
2 teaspoons Worcestershire sauce
1/4 teaspoon salt
1/8 teaspoon white pepper, ground
1 dash Tabasco® sauce
7 1/3 ounces smoked oysters, finely chopped
chopped nuts
fresh parsley

In medium bowl, combine garlic, onion, cream cheese, mayonnaise, milk, Worcestershire, salt, pepper and Tabasco®. Mix well and spread in 8 x 10-inch rectangle on a cookie sheet lined with plastic food film. Sprinkle oysters evenly over the top. With the long side nearest you, firmly grasp the top corners of the food film. To begin rolling, slightly lift and gently push the spread until it begins to roll on itself. Continue to lift and push until it is a long cylinder. Wrap the food film around the outside and refrigerate overnight until firm. Before serving, sprinkle chopped nuts or fresh parsley on the outside. Serve with crackers or toast points. Garnish platter with additional bunches of fresh parsley and small seashells if desired.

APPETIZERS

Shrimp Mousse
SERVES 25

¹/₂ cup white wine, divided
1 ¹/₂ envelopes unflavored gelatin
1 pound shrimp, cooked and peeled
2 eggs, hard boiled
3 tablespoons lemon juice, freshly squeezed
1 small onion, grated
¹/₂ cup Miracle Whip®
1 cup mayonnaise
1 teaspoon salt
¹/₄ teaspoon cayenne pepper

Measure ¹/₄ cup of wine into a small bowl and sprinkle gelatin over the top. Stir and allow to soften about 5 minutes. Heat the remaining wine almost to a boil and stir into softened gelatin until it is completely dissolved.

Place shrimp in the bowl of a food processor, reserving 3 or 4 shrimp for garnish, and pulse chop until the shrimp are finely minced. Transfer to a bowl. Place eggs in the food processor and pulse until finely minced, but not mashed. Stir in the remaining ingredients, including gelatin mixture. Spoon into a well-greased 4-cup mold, cover tightly and refrigerate overnight.

To serve, place on a platter lined with greens. Slice the reserved shrimp lengthwise and decorate the sides of the mousse with the shrimp halves. Add thinly cut and twisted lemon slices and fresh flowers if desired. Serve with Bremner® Wafers or toast rounds.

Winter

Winter

Water Forcing Bulbs

Do not force expensive bulbs in water

Bulbs must be thrown away after blooming

Hyacinths, paperwhites, and Crocuses are good for water forcing

Store bulbs (purchased in fall) in brown paper bag @45°F. Do not place with fruit in refrigerator

Use either pebble or traditional method:

PEBBLE METHOD:

- Fill bowl with several inches of pebbles
- Place bulbs on top and fill in around bulbs with more pebbles
- Fill the vase/bowl with water until it almost touches the bottom of the bulb
- Make sure water levels remain steady
- Roots will sprout in about 1–2 weeks

(continued on next page)

APPETIZERS

Creamed Mushrooms and Peppers
SERVES 25

- 1 cup butter
- 8 small red, green and yellow sweet peppers, diced
- 2 pounds mushrooms, sliced thickly
- 1 cup flour
- 1 quart cream
- 1 teaspoon white pepper
- 2 teaspoons salt
- 1/2 teaspoon cayenne pepper
- 1 teaspoon Worcestershire Sauce
- 1/2 cup Parmesan cheese, grated

Melt butter in a large skillet. Sauté peppers until soft and cooked through. Remove peppers, reserving liquid. Cook mushrooms in reserved liquid until cooked through, about 10 minutes. Drain mushrooms, reserving liquid. Gradually whisk flour into liquid and cook stirring constantly until thickened. Add cream, white pepper, salt, cayenne pepper, Worcestershire and Parmesan. Continue cooking until just comes to a boil. Stir in mushrooms and peppers and heat through. Serve in a chafing dish with split, buttered and toasted biscuits or toast points.

APPETIZERS

Meatballs in Chutney Sauce
MAKES 150 BALLS

- 5 pounds country style sausage
- 2 tablespoons butter
- 2 tablespoons flour
- 1 cup half and half
- 1 pint sour cream
- ½ teaspoon salt
- 1 cup Peach Chutney (p. 154) or store-bought mango chutney

Form balls from sausage, approximately 1½ inches in diameter and place on an ungreased cookie sheet. You should be able to make 30 balls to a pound. Place in a 400° oven for 15 minutes, until browned and cooked through. Drain off grease and place on paper toweling to cool.

In a small saucepan, melt the butter and whisk in the flour. Cook over medium heat for 2–3 minutes, stirring constantly. Do not let sauce brown. Whisk in the half and half and continue to stir until it thickens. Remove from the heat and stir in the sour cream, salt and chutney. Taste for seasoning and refrigerate until ready to serve.

Place the sausage balls in a large covered casserole. Pour the sauce over the balls and carefully mix to coat. Bake the sausage balls covered in a 350° oven for 30–40 minutes until hot. Be careful not to overheat the sausage as it will become separated. Transfer to a chafing dish, sprinkle with a bit of fresh minced parsley and serve with toothpicks.

This is an especially easy hors d'oeuvre to prepare for a large crowd. The combination of the sweet chutney with the spicy sausage is wonderful.

Winter

Water Forcing Bulbs (continued)

TRADITIONAL METHOD:

- Set bulb securely in top of vase
- Allow several inches of space under bottom for emerging roots
- Fill the vase/bowl with water until it almost touches the bottom of the bulb

Place in a cool, dark place for rooting.

Place bulbs and their water containers in brown grocery bags in a cool place (50°–55°F)

Make sure water levels remain steady

If roots don't appear, add more water, if mold appears, keep water level lower

Roots will sprout in about 2 weeks

When top shoots show (Crocuses 1", Hyacinths 2") place water forced bulbs in cool light place

It takes about 1 month for bulb to bloom

APPETIZERS

Baked Crab Dip
SERVES 16

1 pound lump crabmeat, picked over carefully
16 ounces cream cheese, softened
1/3 cup mayonnaise
1 tablespoon white wine
1 tablespoon powdered sugar
1/2 teaspoon Dijon mustard
1/4 teaspoon garlic powder
1 teaspoon salt
1/2 teaspoon white pepper
1 tablespoon onion, grated

In a large bowl, combine cream cheese, mayonnaise, wine, sugar, mustard, garlic powder, salt, pepper and onion. Beat until smooth. Gently fold in crabmeat and turn into a 1 1/2-quart casserole. Bake in a 350° oven for 20–30 minutes or until hot and bubbly. Do not overheat. Serve immediately in a chafing dish with Bremner® wafers.

This recipe is always a hit. The subtle seasonings will not mask the delicate flavor of the crabmeat. Be sure to buy lump or back fin meat for the best results.

APPETIZERS

Hot Chile Chicken Dip
SERVES 50

6 tablespoons butter
6 tablespoons flour
3 cups milk
3 cups Monterey Jack cheese, shredded
3 cans artichokes, chopped
2 cans green chile peppers, chopped
2 canned jalapeño peppers, minced
1 bunch green onions, minced
1 tablespoon chili powder
1 tablespoon fresh lime juice
1 teaspoon salt
1/4 teaspoon cayenne pepper
2 teaspoons ground cumin
12 boneless chicken breast halves, cooked and shredded

Melt butter in a 4-quart saucepan and whisk in the flour. Cook 3–4 minutes, stirring constantly. Whisk in the milk and continue to cook and stir until thickened. Remove from heat and stir in cheese, artichokes, peppers, onion, chili powder, lime juice, salt, cayenne and cumin. Stir in chicken and turn into a greased casserole. Bake at 350° for 45 minutes until hot. To serve, place in a chafing dish with tortilla chips to dip.

Winter

Winter

APPETIZERS

Piccadillo Dip
SERVES 10–15

- 1 pound ground beef
- 1 pound country sausage
- 5 cloves garlic, minced
- 2 medium onions, finely chopped
- 28 ounce can diced tomatoes
- 3 canned jalapeños, diced
- ¾ cup chopped pimiento
- 1 cup raisins
- 2 teaspoons salt
- ½ teaspoon black pepper
- 1 teaspoon oregano
- 2 tablespoons chili powder
- 1 teaspoon sugar
- 1 teaspoon ground cumin

Cook and crumble ground beef and sausage in large pot until browned. Drain well, reserving one tablespoon of fat. Cook garlic and onion in reserved fat until translucent. Return cooked meat to pot and add tomatoes, jalapeños, pimientos, raisins, salt, pepper, oregano, chili powder, sugar and cumin. Simmer until thickened, stirring often to keep from sticking. Serve Piccadillo as a filling for epañodos or in a chafing dish with tortilla chips. Piccadillo may also be served over rice as an entree.

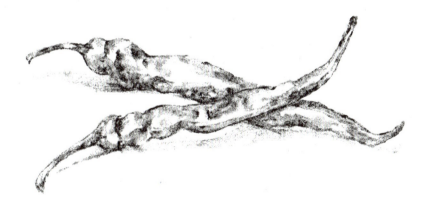

BEVERAGES

Hot Mulled Cider
SERVES 8

    1 medium orange, cut in slices
    2 quarts apple cider
    1/2 cup brown sugar
    1 teaspoon whole allspice
    16 whole cloves
    10 cinnamon sticks
    2 medium oranges, cut in wedges

Combine orange slices, apple cider and brown sugar in a 3-quart saucepan. Make a small bag of allspice and cloves with a piece of cheesecloth. Place in the saucepan with the cinnamon sticks and heat slowly to a boil. Reduce the heat to simmer, stirring occasionally, for 15 minutes. Serve in mugs garnished with an orange wedge and a stick of cinnamon if desired.

Winter

Winter

BEVERAGES

Kate's Eggnog Punch
SERVES 15

12 eggs, separated
1 1/2 cups sugar, divided
2 quarts half and half
1 quart bourbon
1/4 cup dark Jamaican rum

Beat egg whites in a large bowl until frothy. Gradually add 1/2 cup of sugar, beating until stiff but not dry. Set aside.

Beat egg yolks and one cup of sugar in large bowl until thick and lemon colored. Add cream. Fold in egg whites, being sure to totally combine the two mixtures. Gently fold in the bourbon and rum. Refrigerate until ready to use. To serve top each serving with freshly grated nutmeg.

BEVERAGES

Hot Buttered Rum

12 DRINKS

    2 sticks butter
    1/2 teaspoon ground cinnamon
    1/2 teaspoon ground cloves
    1/2 teaspoon ground allspice
    1 pound dark brown sugar
    2 eggs
    18 ounces dark Jamaican rum
    cinnamon sticks for garnish

Melt butter in small saucepan and stir in spices. Place brown sugar in medium mixing bowl and pour butter over sugar. Beat well and cool. Add eggs, one at a time, beating 5 minutes after each addition. Continue beating 10 more minutes until thick and fluffy. Place in plastic or glass container in refrigerator until ready to serve.

Place 2 heaping tablespoons of "butter" in a 12 ounce mug, 1 1/2 ounces of rum and fill with boiling water. Stir with cinnamon stick and serve immediately.

This "butter" will keep several weeks in the refrigerator. If serving for a crowd, keep water hot in a coffee urn, with bowls of "butter" and a bottle of rum to the side.

Winter

Winter

BEVERAGES

Russian Tea Mix
SERVES 20–25

1 jar (1 pound 2 ounces) instant orange beverage
3 cups sugar
1 cup instant unsweetened tea mix
3 (½ ounce) tubs sugar-free lemonade drink mix
2 teaspoons ground cinnamon
1 teaspoon ground cloves
dash salt

Combine all ingredient in food processor and blend until thoroughly mixed. To serve, stir 2 heaping tablespoons of mix into one cup of boiling water. Serve immediately.

For testing purposes I used Tang® orange drink and Crystal Light® lemonade mix.

BEVERAGES

Hot Cocoa Mix
SERVES 36

    2 cups non-dairy coffee creamer
    2 cups sugar
    1 cup good quality cocoa
    1/2 cup instant nonfat milk
    1/4 teaspoon salt

Combine all ingredients in a food processor and blend thoroughly. To serve, place 2 tablespoons of the mix in a mug and add one cup boiling water. Stir until dissolved and top with miniature marshmallows if desired. Store in airtight container.

Winter

267

Winter

Six-Step Snowflakes

Kids of any age enjoy making paper snowflakes. There's no such thing as a wrong design—every snowflake is unique.

1. Take a square piece of paper and fold on the diagonal to make a triangle.

2. Fold the triangle in half again, being careful to match up the corners.

3. Loosely fold the triangle in thirds. Crease when you're sure the sides are even.

4. Now, pick up your scissors and snip straight across the bottom.

5. Next, cut out a pattern of semicircles and triangles around the bottom and sides.

6. Carefully unfold to reveal your one-of-a-kind snowflake.

SOUPS

Lamb and Navy Bean Soup
SERVES 8

2 cups dried navy beans, washed and sorted
2 pounds ground lamb
3 cups water
6 cups chicken stock
3 bay leaves
8 cloves garlic, minced
1 medium onion, minced
16-ounce can diced tomatoes
15-ounce can beef broth
2 tablespoons red wine vinegar
1 teaspoon black pepper, freshly ground
1 tablespoon salt
1 tablespoon fresh rosemary, snipped
1 tablespoon Worcestershire sauce
1 teaspoon Tabasco® sauce

Soak dried beans as directed. Drain, rinse beans and set aside. Brown ground lamb in a skillet until no longer pink. Drain well and set aside. In a heavy 8-quart stockpot, combine beans, 3 cups of water, chicken stock, bay leaves, garlic and onion. Bring to a boil and cook at a low boil until beans are soft, about 45 minutes. When beans are thoroughly cooked, add lamb and remaining ingredients. Reduce to a simmer and cook 1 1/2 hours. Serve in warmed bowls and garnish with freshly grated Parmesan cheese if desired.

SOUPS

Hearty Green Soup
SERVES 6

    2 cans condensed chicken broth, undiluted
    10 ounce box frozen chopped or leaf spinach
    1/4 pound boiled ham, coarsely chopped
    1/4 cup instant mashed potatoes
    1/4 cup thinly sliced pepperoni

Pour broth into a 4-quart saucepan and stir in one cup of water. Add spinach and ham and bring to a boil. Reduce to a simmer and cook 5 minutes, stirring occasionally to separate spinach. Stir in instant potatoes and pepperoni, cooking until soup thickens slightly. Serve immediately.

Serve this soup with a grilled cheese sandwich for a quick and nutritious Sunday night supper.

Winter

SOUPS

Chili

SERVES 12

- 3 pounds ground beef
- 2 medium onions, finely chopped
- 6 cloves garlic, minced
- 3 medium red bell peppers, finely chopped
- 4 fresh jalapeño peppers, seeded and finely chopped
- 1 tablespoon paprika
- 1 tablespoon ground oregano
- 1 tablespoon ground cumin
- 1 teaspoon cayenne pepper
- 1/2 cup chili powder
- 1 tablespoon salt
- 1 8-ounce can tomato sauce
- 1 cup water
- 2 tablespoons masa corn flour, optional

Brown ground beef in 8-quart stock pot. Remove with a slotted spoon and reserve 4 tablespoons of fat. Sauté onions, garlic, bell peppers and jalapeño peppers in fat until translucent. Return ground beef to pot and add seasonings, tomato sauce and water. Bring to a boil and simmer for one hour, stirring often. If needed, additional water may be added to prevent sticking. If chili needs thickening, mix together masa corn flour (or regular wheat flour) with 2 tablespoons of water. Stir into chili and continue to simmer until thickens. Serve in heated bowls with garnishes of sour cream, grated cheddar cheese and wedges of lime.

SOUPS

Tucker's Soup for Supper
SERVES 8

- 1 pound country sausage
- 1 medium onion, chopped
- 1 can chicken broth
- 2 cups water
- 1 pound frozen hashed brown potatoes
- 1 can cream of chicken soup
- 1 can cream of celery soup
- 2 cups milk
- 1/2 cup cheddar cheese, grated

Brown sausage in heavy 4-quart pot. Drain all but one tablespoon of fat and add onions. Cook until translucent. Stir in the broth, water and potatoes. Bring to a boil and reduce heat. Simmer 20 minutes or until potatoes are done. Return the sausage to the pot and add creamed soups and milk. Heat thoroughly, but do not boil. Serve in a large soup bowl, garnishing with the cheese.

This is a hearty supper for any college student. Tucker says she likes to make a big pot at the beginning of the week and freeze part of it in batches for later use.

Winter

SOUPS

Black Bean Soup
SERVES 6

2 cups dried black beans, sorted and soaked overnight
6 cups water
1 sprig fresh oregano
2 sage leaves
2 bay leaves
1 tablespoon olive oil
1 large onion, minced
8 cloves garlic, minced
1 teaspoon salt, divided
1/2 teaspoon black pepper, divided
1/2 teaspoon dried oregano, toasted
3 chipotle peppers, finely minced
1 teaspoon ancho chili powder
1/4 cup dry sherry
1 (8 ounce) can diced tomatoes, undrained
1/2 cup fresh orange juice
1 cup sour cream
1 tablespoon lime juice, freshly squeezed
1 teaspoon dried cilantro
1/4 teaspoon salt
1 large tomato diced
1 tablespoon fresh cilantro minced

SOUPS

Drain beans and place in large soup pot with oregano, sage, and bay leaves. Add cold water to cover. Bring to a boil and reduce to simmer. Cook until beans are soft, usually 45 minutes. Drain beans, reserving liquid. Remove herbs and bay leaves. Set aside to cool slightly.

In a saucepan, heat olive oil and stir in onions, garlic, $1/2$ teaspoon salt, $1/8$ teaspoon pepper and toasted oregano. Sauté until onion is soft. Add chipotle, ancho chili powder and sherry and simmer until liquid is reduced by half. Add the tomatoes and the remaining salt. Continue to simmer 10–15 minutes.

Place beans in the bowl of a food processor and add enough bean liquid to puree to a smooth consistency. Place in a large pot and add additional liquid if necessary. Place sautéed onion mixture in a processor and process until smooth. Stir into the beans and add orange juice. Season to taste with additional salt and pepper. Simmer slowly an additional hour.

In small bowl, combine sour cream, lime juice, dried cilantro and salt. Refrigerate several hours to blend flavors. To serve soup, place in heated bowls and offer diced fresh tomatoes, fresh cilantro, lime slices and sour cream sauce as toppings for soup.

Winter

Ideas for Christmas Gift Baskets

Be creative combine foods and small gifts.

CHILDREN'S BASKETS
Baked but undecorated gingerbread men or sugar cookies. Include the following in the basket: Tubes of decorating icing or one ziplock Royal icing. Decorating sugars, candies, or dried fruits. Jar of cocoa mix and ziplock bag of marshmallows.

BREAKFAST BASKET
Homemade Coffee Cake or sweet rolls, granola, gourmet coffee, smokey country style bacon, maple syrup, pancake mix.

(continued on next page)

SOUPS

Cheddar Cheese Chowder
SERVES 8

3 cups water
4 medium potatoes, diced
1 cup diced celery
1 cup diced carrots
1/2 cup minced onions
1/2 cup butter
1/2 cup flour
4 cups milk
1 pound sharp cheddar cheese, grated
2 teaspoon salt
1/4 teaspoon pepper
hot sauce to taste
2 cups diced baked ham

Combine water, potatoes, celery, carrots and onions in a 6-quart saucepan. Bring to a boil and boil for 10 minutes until vegetables are tender. While vegetables are cooking, melt butter in a separate 4-quart saucepan. Whisk in flour and cook for 2–3 minutes. Slowly whisk in milk and cook over low heat until mixture thickens. Stir in cheese until it melts. Combine vegetables and cheese sauce. Season with salt, pepper and hot sauce. Stir in ham and heat thoroughly, but do not boil. Serve in heated bowls.

SOUPS

Cream of Broccoli and Stilton Soup
SERVES 8

- 4 cups broccoli, chopped
- 1/3 cup celery, chopped
- 1 cup onion, chopped
- 7 tablespoons butter, divided
- 7 cups chicken broth
- 2 1/2 tablespoons flour
- 8 ounces Stilton cheese, trimmed of rind
- 1 1/4 cups half and half
- 1 bunch green onions, minced
- 1/4 teaspoon white pepper

Cook broccoli, celery and onion in 4 tablespoons of butter for 5 minutes. Add chicken stock and simmer covered for 30 minutes. Strain and purée the vegetables. Add back to the liquid. To make a roux, combine 3 tablespoons of butter and 2 1/2 tablespoons of flour in a small skillet. Cook, stirring constantly for 3–5 minutes until just golden. Gradually stir roux into the soup mixture and simmer until it thickens, stirring constantly.

Process the Stilton cheese and the half and half until smooth. Add to the soup and heat slowly. Be careful not to let soup boil. Serve in warmed soup bowls and garnish with minced green onions.

A rich and flavorful soup, that needs only a light citrus fruit salad and crusty French bread.

Winter

Ideas for Christmas Gift Baskets
(continued)

BRUNCH FOR CHRISTMAS MORNING
Ham biscuits, cheese straws, dilly beans, bloody Mary mix, small bottle of vodka.

COME FOR COCKTAILS
Beer cheese, spicey almonds or pecans, gourmet olives, shrimp Louisiane, vodka or gin, martini glasses (Put nuts in glasses).

SPICE BASKET
Rib, chicken and tuna rubs, Henry Bain Steak sauce, Barbeque brush.

Winter

SOUPS

Oyster Stew
SERVES 4

> 2 tablespoons butter
> 1 small onion, finely minced
> 2 cups half and half
> 1 cup milk
> 1 teaspoon salt
> ½ teaspoon white pepper
> 1 pint oysters, shucked

Melt butter in a 2-quart saucepan and sauté onions until they are transparent. Stir in half and half, milk, salt and pepper. Bring just to the point of boiling, stirring frequently. Do not let boil. Drain oysters in colander, reserving liquid. Pick through oysters for any shells and stir into the stew. Continue to cook for 3–5 minutes just to the boiling point. You may add oyster liquid if needed. Taste for seasoning. Serve the Oyster Stew in heated bowls with oyster crackers and freshly ground black pepper if desired.

Oyster stew was a Christmas morning tradition for my husband's family. Oysters are at the height of their season and the stew takes only a few minutes to put together on a very busy morning.

SOUPS

Manhattan Seafood Chowder
SERVES 12

2 tablespoons crab boil seasoning
2 cups water
4 stalks celery, diced
1 large onion, diced
1 small green pepper, diced
1 clove garlic, minced
1/2 cup butter, melted
2 (8 ounce) cans clams, minced and drained
6 ounces crabmeat
1 cup shrimp, shelled, uncooked and chopped
1 cup haddock, cooked and flaked
1 (28 ounce) can diced tomatoes, undrained
1 tablespoon dried basil leaves
1 1/2 teaspoons sugar
2 tablespoons lemon juice, freshly squeezed
1 teaspoon kosher salt
1/2 teaspoon black pepper, freshly ground

Combine crab boil and water in pot and bring to a boil. Remove from heat, cover and set aside for 10 minutes. Strain water into a large Dutch oven. Sauté celery, onion, green pepper and garlic in 1/2 cup of butter until tender. Add to the strained water with the remaining ingredients. Bring to a boil, stirring occasionally, and reduce to a simmer for one hour. Taste for seasoning. Serve chowder in heated bowls with oyster crackers on the side.

Winter

Winter

Seasonal Plant Materials

White Pine
Holly
Leyland Cypress
Scotch Pine
Eleagnus
Witch Hazel
Mahonia
Camellia
Acuba
Magnolia
Boxwood
Andromeda
Rosemary
Winter Berry
Deodar Pine
Daphne
Hellebore
Walking Stick
Lawsons Cypress
Ivy
Nandina
Arum

SOUPS

Marge's Split Pea Soup
SERVES 12

4 cups dried split peas
6 quarts water
1 good size ham bone
1 cup finely chopped onion
2 cups diced celery
1 cup diced carrots
2 medium turnips, diced
2 cloves garlic, minced
2 bay leaves
2 teaspoons sugar
dash cayenne pepper
1/2 teaspoon thyme leaves
1 teaspoon salt
1/2 teaspoon black pepper
1 teaspoon paprika

Combine split peas, water and ham bone in large stock pot and soak for 3–4 hours. Add the remaining ingredients and bring to a boil. Reduce heat to a simmer and cook 1–1 1/2 hours until peas are completely cooked through. Taste for seasoning and remove ham bone. If soup seems too thin, cornmeal may be sprinkled over the top to thicken. Serve soup with a dollop of sour cream and a sprinkle of dill weed.

SOUPS

Carrot and Parsnip Soup with Orange

- 1 large onion, cut into medium dice
- 2 teaspoons ground coriander
- 1 teaspoon ground cumin seed
- 1/2 cup (1 stick) unsalted butter
- 1 cup dry white wine
- 4 carrots, cut into medium dice
- 3 parsnips, cut into medium dice
- 8 cups chicken broth
- 1/2 cup fresh orange juice
- pinch cayenne pepper
- 1 tablespoon sherry vinegar
- salt and pepper to taste
- minced fresh chives or parsley for garnish

Cook the onion, coriander and cumin seed in the butter over moderate heat for 15 minutes. Add the white wine and cook until the wine evaporates, about 15 minutes. Add the carrots and parsnips and cook for 5 minutes. Add the chicken stock and bring to a boil. Reduce the heat to low and simmer until the vegetables are tender, about 35–40 minutes. Remove from the heat and let cool slightly. Transfer the mixture to a blender or food processor and puree in batches until smooth. Return to the pot and add the orange juice, cayenne pepper, and vinegar and mix well. Bring to a boil, reduce the heat, and season with the salt and pepper. Serve hot, garnished with chives or parsley.

Winter

SOUPS

Southwest Chicken and Hominy Stew

2 teaspoon dried oregano, divided
1 cup chopped red onion, divided
3 1/2 cups defatted reduced-sodium chicken stock, divided
1/8 teaspoon salt
1 clove garlic, finely chopped
1 teaspoon chili powder
15 ounce can yellow or white hominy, drained and rinsed
15 ounce can black beans, drained and rinsed
3/4 pound skinless, boneless chicken breasts, cut into 3/4 inch pieces
1 cup shredded green cabbage
1 lime
Tortilla chips
Shredded cheddar cheese

Combine one teaspoon toasted oregano with 1/4 cup onions. Set aside. In a medium saucepan combine remaining onions with 3 tablespoons of chicken stock and salt. Cover and cook until the onions are translucent, about 3 minutes. Add garlic and cook for one minute more. Add remaining teaspoon oregano and chili powder, cook one minute. Add hominy, remaining stock, and chicken. Bring to simmer for another 5 minutes.

Serve in bowls garnished with cabbage, cheese, tortilla chips, squeeze of lime and reserved onion mixture.

SALADS

Warmed Tuscan Bean Salad
SERVES 8

- 1 tablespoon butter
- 1 3/4 cups ham, diced
- 2 cups cannellini beans, drained
- 1/4 cup red bell pepper, diced
- 1/3 cup black olives, sliced
- 1 tablespoon red wine vinegar
- 1 tablespoon Dijon mustard
- 1/4 teaspoon black pepper, freshly ground
- 1 teaspoon kosher salt
- 3 tablespoons boiling water
- 6 tablespoons olive oil
- 2 tablespoons fresh parsley, minced
- 1 head Romaine lettuce, coarsely torn
- 1 medium red onion, thinly sliced

Melt butter in a medium skillet. Toss in the ham and cook 2–3 minutes. Add the cannellini beans, red pepper and olives. Continue cooking an additional 4–5 minutes, stirring constantly until just warmed. Remove from heat.

In a small bowl, combine red wine vinegar, mustard, black pepper and salt. Whisk in boiling water and then gradually whisk in olive oil until it thickens. Stir in the parsley and set aside.

Arrange torn lettuce on each plate and spoon 1/2 cup of bean mixture in middle. Top with a few slices of red onion and spoon dressing on top. Serve immediately.

Winter

SALADS

Cherry Fruit Salad
SERVES 12

16 ounces canned, sour cherries
16 ounces crushed pineapple
1 envelope plain gelatin
3 ounces lemon flavored gelatin
1/2 cup sugar
2 oranges, zest and juice
1 lemon, zest and juice
1/2 cup chopped pecans

Drain juice from cherries and pineapple, reserving 1/4 cup of juice to soften plain gelatin. Add remaining juice, along with orange and lemon juice, to a 2-quart saucepan. Heat just to the boiling point. Remove from heat and stir in softened gelatin, lemon gelatin and sugar until they are completely dissolved.

Add cherries, pineapple, lemon and orange zest and nuts. Pour into a 1 1/2-quart mold and refrigerate until congealed.

A pretty holiday salad that is excellent served with roasted turkey or pork.

Winter

SALADS

Winter Salad
SERVES 8

- 2 tablespoons sugar
- 2 cups of water
- 1 small red onion, thinly sliced
- 4 cups mesclun salad mixture
- 4 grapefruits, peeled and sectioned
- 6 oranges, peeled and sectioned
- 2 bananas, sliced 1/4-inch thick
- 1/4 cup sliced almonds, toasted
- 1 recipe JOHN TUCKER PERCY'S DRESSING (see next page)

Dissolve sugar in 2 cups of water. Add onion slices and cover with ice cubes. Refrigerate for one hour to remove the bite of the onion.

To serve, place 1/2 cup of mesclun greens on each salad plate. Arrange alternating slices of grapefruit and oranges around plate. Place a few slices of banana in the middle. Drain the onions and pat dry. Place 4–5 rings on each salad and scatter almonds on top. Spoon on 1 1/2 tablespoons of dressing and serve immediately.

Winter

SALADS

John Tucker Percy's Dressing
MAKES 2 CUPS

1/4 teaspoon garlic powder
1 small onion, chopped
4 tablespoons lemon juice, freshly squeezed
1 tablespoon red wine vinegar
1 tablespoon kosher salt
1 teaspoon mustard powder
1/2 teaspoon cayenne pepper
1/2 cup vegetable oil
1/2 cup olive oil
1 tablespoon paprika

Process in a blender the first seven ingredients, until smooth. Gradually add vegetable and olive oil until thick and creamy. Stir in paprika and store in a glass pint jar in the refrigerator.

SALADS

Grapefruit Aspic
SERVES 6

- 3 grapefruits, peeled and sectioned
- 1 cup grapefruit juice
- 1 tablespoon plain gelatin
- 2 tablespoons of water
- 1/3 cup sugar
- 1/3 cup water
- 1 tablespoon lemon juice, freshly squeezed
- 1 dash salt
- 1/2 cup mayonnaise
- 1/4 cup GINGER PRESERVES (P. 147) or chopped fresh ginger
- 1 tablespoon honey
- Candied ginger, chopped

Place grapefruit sections in a colander and allow them to drain over a bowl for 15 minutes. Measure juice and add additional grapefruit juice to make one cup.

Stir gelatin into 2 tablespoons of cold water and set aside to soften. Place sugar and 1/3 cup of water into a medium saucepan. Bring to a boil and cook 3 minutes. Remove from heat and stir in gelatin until it is completely dissolved. Add the grapefruit sections, lemon juice, salt, grapefruit juice and sugar. Pour into a lightly greased one-quart mold and chill overnight or until set.

Combine mayonnaise and 1/4 cup of finely chopped GINGER PRESERVES. If you do not have the homemade version use store-bought or combine 2 tablespoons of chopped fresh ginger with one tablespoon of honey. Refrigerate several hours to allow flavors to blend.

To serve, unmold aspic onto a lettuce-lined platter. Serve the ginger mayonnaise in a small bowl on the side, garnishing with chopped candied ginger sprinkled on top.

Winter

ENTREES

Boeuf Au Pot
SERVES 8

- 4 pound chuck roast, cut 3 inches thick
- 1 tablespoon salt
- 1 teaspoon black pepper
- 1 teaspoon nutmeg, freshly ground
- 3 tablespoons vegetable oil
- 1/4 cup brandy
- 1 cup red wine
- 1 1/2 cups beef broth
- 3 tablespoons butter
- 12 carrots, peeled and cut into 2-inch sections
- 18 pearl onions, peeled
- 24 small new potatoes, unpeeled

Rub roast with salt, pepper and nutmeg. In a heavy casserole or cast iron roasting pan, heat oil until sizzling. Brown roast on all sides. Reduce heat. Carefully heat brandy until warm and pour over meat. Light brandy with a long match and allow to burn out. Pour red wine and broth over meat and bring to a boil. Cover and put into a 350° oven for 1 1/2 hours.

Melt butter in a large skillet and sauté carrots and onions for 5 minutes. Remove pot roast and add carrots, onions and potatoes. Cover and return to oven for 1 1/2 hours longer.

To slice roast, lay flat on cutting board and slice in 1/4-inch vertical pieces, being sure to cut against the grain of the meat. Arrange slices on a heated platter. Surround with roasted vegetables and garnish with fresh parsley. Cover with foil, keeping warm until serving.

If desired, gravy may be made with the drippings. Skim off the excess fat and strain. In separate saucepan, melt 4 tablespoons of butter. Whisk in 4 tablespoons of flour and cook 3–4 minutes. Gradually whisk in 2 cups of the drippings and cook until it thickens. Season to taste with salt and pepper.

Use your imagination with this familiar recipe. Additional vegetables may be roasted with the meat, such as whole bulbs of garlic, peeled chunks of turnips or wedges of cabbage. Add the cabbage for the last 30 minutes of cooking. If you are a working or soccer mom, put the roast in a 250° oven and cook 7–8 hours covered. Add the vegetables and raise the temperature to 350° for 1 hour.

ENTREES

Orla's Chicken and Shrimp Spaghetti
SERVES 12

- 1 pound fini linguine
- 4 tablespoons butter
- 4 cloves garlic, minced
- 3 medium onions, chopped
- 3–4 stalks of celery, chopped
- 1 pound fresh mushrooms, sliced
- 4 tablespoons flour
- 1 tablespoon chili powder
- 1 teaspoon sugar
- 1 tablespoon salt
- 1 teaspoon black pepper, freshly ground
- 2 teaspoon Worcestershire sauce
- 2 cups chicken stock
- 2 cups canned tomatoes, diced
- 3 pounds shrimp, peeled and uncooked
- 4 cups cooked and cut up chicken
- 2 cups shredded Gruyere cheese
- ½ cup Parmesan cheese, grated

Break linguini in half and cook according to the directions. Rinse in cold water and set aside.

In a large skillet, melt butter and stir in garlic, onions, celery and mushrooms. Sauté 5–10 minutes until mushrooms are cooked through. Sprinkle flour over the top and stir into onion mixture. Add chili powder, sugar, salt, pepper and Worcestershire. Stir in the chicken stock and undrained tomatoes. Cook mixture until it thickens slightly. Stir in shrimp and cook just until it turns pink. Taste for seasoning and adjust if needed. Remove from heat and stir in chicken and cooked linguini. Grease a large lasagna-size casserole. Add half of the chicken spaghetti and sprinkle Gruyere cheese on top. Add remaining chicken mixture and top entire casserole with the Parmesan cheese. Dot with butter and bake for 45 minutes in a 350° oven. Serve immediately with a fresh green salad and crusty garlic bread.

See MARGARET'S FUNERAL CASSEROLE (P. 38), for the best method of cooking chicken.

Winter

Coloring Sheet Moss Green

To give new life to aged sheet moss, add the following:

1 ounce yellow food coloring

½ ounce green food coloring

1 quart water

Put the above in a spritzer bottle, and shake. As the sheet moss ages and loses color, spritz moss with the above solution.

Note: It is easier to work with the moss if it is damp.

—Betty Jo Hamner

Winter

ENTREES

Sausage and Rice Casserole
SERVES 4

- 1 pound country style sausage
- 1 tablespoon butter
- 1 medium green pepper, chopped
- 1 medium onion, chopped
- 1 10 ounce can cream of mushroom soup
- 1 10 ounce can cream of chicken soup
- 1 cup uncooked rice
- 4 ounces diced pimientos
- 1 cup shredded cheddar cheese

Cook sausage in skillet until no longer pink and cooked through. Drain, reserving one tablespoon of the drippings. Sauté peppers and onions in sausage drippings and one tablespoon of butter for 3–4 minutes. Stir sausage back into mixture and add soups, rice, pimientos and 1/2 cup water. Spoon into a 1 1/2-quart casserole and cover with the shredded cheese. Cover tightly and bake in a 325° oven for 1 1/2 hours. Serve immediately.

Polly's Pot Luck
SERVES 4

- 1 pound ground beef
- 1/2 cup chopped onions
- 3/4 cup uncooked macaroni
- 16 ounces tomato sauce
- 3/4 teaspoon chili powder
- 1 15 ounce can kidney beans
- Salt and pepper to taste
- 1/4 pound grated cheddar cheese

Cook ground beef and onions, add sauce, beans, and seasonings. Cook for 15 minutes.

Cook macaroni until al dente. Mix into beef and beans mixture. Top with cheese.

Cook at 375° for 20 to 30 minutes.

ENTREES

Sea Scallops in Saffron Sauce
SERVES 4

    1 head garlic, unpeeled and separated into cloves
    2 tablespoons olive oil
    2 tablespoons butter
    1 1/3 pounds sea scallops
    1/4 cup shallots, minced
    1/2 cup white wine
    1 cup heavy whipping cream
    1 pinch saffron threads
    1 tablespoon lemon juice, freshly squeezed
    1 teaspoon sugar
    1/2 teaspoon kosher salt
    1/4 teaspoon white pepper
    minced parsley

Drizzle garlic cloves with olive oil and place on a baking sheet in 350° oven for 20–30 minutes until the garlic is soft, but not browned. Cool and mash well. Melt butter in medium skillet and add scallops. Carefully sauté, turning scallops so as not to break them. Cook until no longer transparent. Do no overcook. Remove scallops and drain, reserving juices. Add wine and shallots to pan with juices and bring to a boil. Reduce the liquid by one half and add cream and saffron. Continue to cook until the sauce begins to thicken. Stir in the mashed garlic, lemon juice, sugar, kosher salt and white pepper. Add scallops back to the sauce and heat just until hot. To serve, spoon some of the sauce onto the plate and place 8 scallops on top. Sprinkle with minced parsley and serve immediately.

Winter

ENTREES

Cajun Seafood Gumbo
SERVES 8

- 2 cups onions, chopped
- 1 green pepper, chopped
- 1 1/2 cups celery, chopped
- 2 whole bay leaves
- 1 tablespoon kosher salt
- 1 teaspoon ground white pepper
- 3/4 teaspoon cayenne pepper
- 1 teaspoon black pepper, freshly ground
- 1 teaspoon dried thyme leaves
- 1 teaspoon dried oregano leaves
- 4 cloves garlic, minced
- 1 cup peanut oil
- 1 cup flour
- 8 cups chicken stock
- 1 pound andouille sausage
- 1 pint oysters, shucked
- 1 pound shrimp, uncooked and peeled, cut in 1/2-inch pieces
- 1/2 pound crab meat, picked through for shells
- 2 1/2 cups raw rice
- 1 tablespoon gumbo file

Combine the onions, pepper and celery in a medium bowl. Set aside. In a small bowl, combine the bay leaves, kosher salt, white pepper, cayenne and black pepper, thyme, oregano and garlic. Set aside.

In a 12-inch cast iron skillet, heat the oil until it is smoking hot. Carefully whisk in the flour and continue to cook, stirring constantly, until the flour browns to a dark red color. This will take 10–15 minutes, but be patient. When roux has darkened, add half of the vegetables and cook 1–2 minutes. Add the remaining

ENTREES

vegetables and cook an additional 2 minutes. Stir in the seasoning mixture and cook 1–2 minutes. Remove from the heat.

Heat the chicken stock until it is boiling and stir in a spoonful of vegetables and roux at a time, being careful not to let it spatter. Stir until smooth. Bring gumbo back to a boil and add andouille sausage. Cook gumbo over medium heat for 20 minutes, stirring frequently. While gumbo is simmering, bring 2 quarts of water to a boil. Add rice and boil for 17 minutes until it is done. Drain in a colander and rinse immediately with hot water. Set aside or place serve.

Just before serving, stir the oysters and liquid, shrimp and crab meat into the gumbo. Heat 5–8 minutes or until shrimp is pink and oysters have begun to curl. Spoon one cup of rice into a heated bowl and ladle gumbo over the top. Serve immediately.

This entree may be made well in advance with only a bit of last minute preparation. Here are some suggestions for keeping it easy.

- *Have all vegetables chopped in advance.*
- *Cook rice in advance—held at room temperature or kept warm over simmering water for one hour*
- *Have stock already simmering.*
- *Prepare seafood and keep refrigerated.*
- *Measure and combine seasonings.*
- *Make roux several hours ahead and leave at room temperature.*

Winter

Coaxing Amaryllis

Amaryllis blooms help to chase away the winter blues. Here's how to make sure your bulbs bring an uplifting burst of spring.

- **Buy bulbs in the fall, place in paper bags, and keep in a cool (55°F), dark place until the New Year begins.**
- **Start by selecting a clay pot with a diameter that is only one inch larger than the bulb.**
- **Add a layer of potting soil, center the bulb, and add more. Pat soil firmly around the roots and bulb as you go. The upper half of the bulb should remain above the soil line.**
- **Water sparingly once and place in a warm (60°F) spot out of direct sunlight.**
- **Don't water again until the bud and stalk appear, usually in two weeks to one month.**
- **Once growth begins, water regularly. Rotate the pot every other day to prevent stalk from leaning toward the light.**

ENTREES

Chicken Curry with Seven Boys

SERVES 12

>   10 chicken breasts
>   1/2 cup olive oil
>   3 medium onions, diced
>   6 stalks celery, chopped
>   2 Granny Smith apples, diced
>   1/4 quart reserve stock
>   1/4 cup curry powder
>   1/2 teaspoon black pepper, freshly ground
>   1 teaspoon Tabasco® sauce
>   1 teaspoon ginger
>   1 tablespoon Worcestershire sauce
>   1 tablespoon kosher salt
>   1/4 cup flour
>   1/2 cup water
>   1 1/2 cups heavy whipping cream

Place chicken breasts in large stock pot and cover with cold water. Bring to a slow boil and stir chicken to distribute evenly. When water boils, remove from heat and cover. Allow chicken to remain in water until cool and refrigerate overnight. The next day, remove chicken and strain reserved broth. Pick and shred chicken breasts and set aside.

Heat olive oil in a heavy 8-quart stock pot. Sauté onions, celery and apples until they are tender, 10–15 minutes, stirring often. Add 1 quart of reserved stock, curry powder, black pepper, ginger, Tabasco®, Worcestershire and kosher salt to taste. Bring to a boil and add chicken. Simmer, stirring occasionally, for 30–45 minutes.

In a small bowl, whisk together the flour and 1/2 cup of water until smooth. Gradually stir into curry and cook until it thickens slightly. Remove from heat and allow to cool. Curry may be refrigerated overnight to allow flavors to blend.

Reheat curry slowly, stirring frequently, so as not to scorch. When mixture is hot, stir in cream and continue to heat, but do not allow to boil. Taste for seasoning and if desired add a little more flour and water to thicken as for gravy. Serve curry over cooked rice with any or all of the following boys: shredded coconut, PEACH CHUTNEY (P. 154), chopped peanuts, riced hard cooked egg yolks, riced hard cooked egg whites, crumbled cooked bacon, canned fried onion rings.

The toppings are called "boys," traditionally being served by boys in the far east

ENTREES

Garlic Roasted Chicken
SERVES 6

1 6 pound roasting hen
2 whole garlic bulbs, separated into cloves
olive oil
kosher salt
freshly ground black pepper
fresh thyme or rosemary if desired

Sometimes the simplest of recipes can be the tastiest. This roasted chicken can be served not only to your family but to company as well. Although the baking time is rather long, the preparation is simple. While the hen is cooking, take advantage by fixing the rest of the meal and setting your table.

Rub the hen with olive oil and sprinkle well both inside and out with salt and pepper. Coat the garlic cloves with olive oil and place in cavity of bird. Slip fresh herbs under breast skin and place hen in a roasting pan. Bake in a 350° oven for 2 hours. If chicken browns too quickly, lightly cover with aluminum foil. Test for doneness; temperature should register 160° when placed in the thickest part of the thigh. Allow to sit 15–20 minutes before carving. Don't forget the cloves of garlic inside—once baked the garlic pops out of their skin. It has a mild, nutty taste that is delicious alone and spread on crusty bread. CURRY BUTTER BEANS and a fresh green salad would round out this meal with time to spare.

Winter

Winter

ENTREES

Chinese Glazed Chicken Wings
SERVES 4

20 whole chicken wings
1 2-inch piece of fresh ginger, thinly sliced
5 cloves garlic, thinly sliced
2/3 cup red wine
1/3 cup soy sauce

Fold wing tips under the larger end to form a triangle. Place in a shallow baking or jelly roll pan. Sprinkle evenly with ginger and garlic slices. Combine red wine and soy sauce and pour over chicken. Cover with aluminum foil and bake at 300° for 2 hours. Uncover and turn wings over. Increase temperature to 350° and continue to cook 45–60 minutes until wings are glazed over. Serve immediately as a main entree or as an hors d'oeuvre.

Potting and Cooling Chart for Hardy Bulbs

BULB	POTTING DEPTH	COLD DARK PERIOD	COOL LIGHT PERIOD
Crocus	1 inch deep	10-12 weeks	2-3 weeks
Hyacinth	Tops of bulbs out	12-15 weeks	2-3 weeks
Narcissus (Hardy)	1 inch deep	12-15 weeks	2-4 weeks
Tulip	Tops of bulbs out	14-16 weeks	2-4 weeks
Iris	½ inch deep	12-15 weeks	2-3 weeks
Scilla	1 inch deep	10-12 weeks	2-4 weeks

ENTREES

Pork Tenderloin with Apples and Mustard Glaze
SERVES 6

- 1/2 cup vegetable oil
- 1/3 cup hoisin sauce
- 1/2 cup orange juice
- 1/2 cup cola soda
- 2 tablespoons soy sauce
- 2 pork tenderloins, 1 pound each
- 1/2 cup bourbon or apple juice
- 1/4 cup raisins
- 1 small Granny Smith apple, thinly sliced
- 1 small onion, thinly sliced
- 6 garlic cloves, halved
- 1 tablespoon chopped fresh rosemary
- 1/4 cup maple syrup
- 2 tablespoons brown sugar
- 2 tablespoons Dijon mustard

Combine oil, hoisin, cola, orange juice, and soy sauce, mixing well. Place tenderloins in ziplock bag and marinate 8 hours or overnight

Combine bourbon or apple juice and raisins in small bowl and let stand 45 minutes.

Butterfly tenderloins lengthwise, lay open flat. Alternate apple and onion slices down center of each. Top evenly with raisins, garlic, and rosemary. Place tenderloins in aluminum foil and place in a baking pan. Combine syrup, brown sugar and mustard. Brush half of the mixture over tenderloins. Fold foil closed. Bake 325° for 25 minutes. Pour remaining syrup mixture over tenderloins, close foil and bake another 20-25 minutes or until meat thermometer registers 160°.

Winter

ENTREES

Wild Duck

SERVES 4–8

> 4 wild ducks at room temperature
> 2 apples, quartered and cored
> 1 medium onion, quartered
> 1 cup dry sherry
> 1/2 tsp. black pepper
> 1/2 tsp. salt
> 1/4 pound butter, melted

Pre-heat oven to 400°. Rub duck breasts with melted butter, salt and pepper. Wipe out the cavities and rub with salt and pepper. Place two apple quarters and an onion quarter in the cavity of each duck.

Place ducks in middle of oven and roast for 20 minutes for smaller ducks such as wood ducks, teal, pintail or widgeon. Cook 25–30 minutes for larger ducks such as mallards or black ducks. Just before removing, pour the sherry over the ducks. A sauce can be made from the drippings

Keep in mind that wild ducks are not as mild flavored as domestic duck. They should be medium rare since they tend to have a strong "liver-like" or gamey flavor when well done.

Serve one smaller duck or half of a larger duck per person. Very good with a nice red wine such as a Bordeaux red or a California Cabernet Sauvignon.

ENTREES

Braised Pheasant with Sour Cream and Grapes
SERVES 4

>   ¾ pound bacon
>   3 pheasants, cut into serving pieces
>   2 cups flour
>   6 shallots, diced
>   ½ cup dry vermouth or dry white wine
>   3 tablespoons minced fresh thyme,
>   or 1 tablespoon dried thyme
>   5–7 cups chicken broth
>   1¼ cups sour cream
>   1½ cups seedless white grapes, halved
>   salt and pepper to taste

In a large sauté pan or skillet over medium high heat, cook the bacon until crisp. Remove with a slotted spoon and set aside to drain on paper towels. When cool, chop coarsely. Remove and save all but ⅓ cup fat.

Heat the reserved bacon fat over high heat in the same pan. Dust the pheasant lightly in the flour and cook in the fat in batches, adding more bacon drippings as nesessary. Remove each piece to a large kettle as it turns golden brown. When all the pheasants have been browned and placed in the kettle, lower the heat and add the shallots. Cook until translucent, 1–2 minutes, then degrease the pan with the wine, scraping all the bits of meat stuck to the pan. Add the 5 cups chicken broth and thyme, bring to a boil, reduce the heat to moderate, and cook, covered for 1½ hours. When the meat is tender, remove the pheasant from the kettle with a slotted spoon, reserving the liquid. Let the pheasant cool enough to handle, them remove the meat from the bones and set aside.

Meanwhile, over high heat, reduce the cooking liquid to about 1¾ cups. If there is not that much cooking liquid left, add chicken broth until about 2½ cups and reduce over high heat to about 1¾ cups. Reduce the heat to moderate and add the sour cream a little at a time, whisking all the time to make a smooth sauce. Add the pheasant and mix well, then add and mix the bacon. Taste and adjust the seasoning with salt and pepper. To serve, add the grapes, and place the pheasant on top of or along side of rice.

Winter

ENTREES

Pizza or Focaccia Dough
SERVES 4

3/4 cup water, 110°
3/4 cup milk, 110°
1 tablespoon dry yeast
pinch of sugar
2 tablespoons cornmeal
2 tablespoons rye flour
1 teaspoon kosher salt
1/4 cup olive oil
3 1/2 cups unbleached flour

Mix together water, milk, yeast and sugar in a small bowl. Set aside to proof. In a large mixing bowl, stir together the cornmeal, rye flour, salt and olive oil. Stir in the yeast mixture and add flour one cup at a time, stirring well after each addition. Turn dough out onto a floured board and knead 8–10 minutes until smooth and elastic. Set in an oiled bowl and cover. Place in a warm draft-free spot to rise until double in size, about 1 1/2 hours. Punch down and turn out onto a floured board. Roll dough out in one large 16-inch round or 2 smaller rounds, taking care to roll evenly. Place dough on a wooden peel or pizza pan that has been lightly sprinkled with cornmeal. (Parchment paper also helps to keep dough from sticking to the peel when transferring to a hot stone). Drizzle the dough with olive oil and top with any of the following: thinly sliced tomatoes, fresh slivers of garlic, crumbled goat cheese, mozzarella cheese, sliced mushrooms, snipped fresh herbs and freshly grated Parmesan. Allow the pizza to rest 15–20 minutes and drizzle again with olive oil just before placing in a preheated 450° oven. Always bake the pizza on the lowest rack and if possible use a pizza stone that has been preheated. Bake 15–20 minutes until puffed and lightly browned.

To make focaccia, simply add 1/2 cup mashed potatoes to the dough when you mix it up. Roll out in 2 round shapes to 1/2-inch thickness. Let rise 30 minutes and dimple the top with your thumb. Sprinkle with kosher salt, freshly ground pepper, snipped fresh herbs, grated cheese or other toppings of your choice.

Bake as you would for the pizza. Serve immediately.

ENTREES

A pizza supper can be a fun informal way of entertaining your family and friends. The dough and toppings can be prepared in advance. Gather your guests around your kitchen counter and let them choose the topping combination. Children especially enjoy being included in the fun. These are a few suggestions, but use your imagination to create your own combination.

- quartered artichokes, sliced mushrooms, roasted red peppers, sliced tomatoes and Parmesan cheese
- cooked, cut up chicken, sliced onions, fresh garlic, tomatoes, fresh basil and goat cheese
- fresh spinach lightly dressed with olive oil, Prosciuto cut into strips, fresh garlic, mozzarella and Parmesan cheese

Winter

Winter

ENTREES

Lemon Thyme Stuffed Chicken Breast
SERVES 6

6 boneless, skinless breast halves
1/2 cup cream cheese, softened
4 green onions, finely chopped
2 tablespoons fresh lemon thyme or French thyme
1/4 teaspoon grated lemon
1/2 cup dried bread crumbs
1/2 cup Parmesan cheese, freshly grated
1/3 cup flour
1 teaspoon paprika
1/2 teaspoon salt
1/2 teaspoon black pepper, freshly ground
2 eggs, beaten
2 teaspoons water
2 tablespoons butter, melted

Pound chicken breasts between 2 sheets of plastic wrap, with the flat side of a metal meat mallet until it is 1/4-inch thick. Keep cold in the refrigerator until ready to roll.

In a small bowl, combine the cream cheese, green onions, thyme and grated lemon. In another bowl, combine the breadcrumbs and Parmesan cheese. Sift together the flour, paprika, salt and pepper onto a sheet of wax paper and set aside. Finally beat together the eggs and water in a small bowl.

To make the stuffed chicken, lay one breast on the counter and spread with cream cheese mixture. Roll up tightly, starting with the short side and secure with two toothpicks. Continue rolling until all the chicken is finished. Line up the bowls of dipping ingredients, starting with the flour, then egg and breadcrumbs last. Keeping one hand always in dry ingredients and one in wet, pick up the chicken with the wet hand, drop in the flour. Toss to coat with the dry hand and place in the egg. Lift out with the wet hand and drop in the breadcrumbs. (You get the idea. Just don't mix the hands up) Place the finished chicken breasts on a greased shallow baking dish. Drizzle with melted butter and bake at 350° for 40–45 minutes. Let rest for 10 minutes and remove toothpicks. Each breast may be cut in 1/2 slices and spread slightly on the plate. Garnish with fresh thyme sprigs and twists of sliced lemon.

TOMATO CHUTNEY *makes a delicious accompaniment to this dish.*

ENTREES

Caribbean Chicken Sandwich

SERVES 4

3 tablespoons curry powder
3 tablespoons cumin seed, toasted and ground
2 tablespoons ground allspice
3 tablespoons paprika
2 tablespoons ground ginger
3 tablespoons cayenne pepper
2 tablespoons kosher salt
2 tablespoons black pepper, freshly ground
4 boneless, skinless chicken breast halves
1 small onion, thinly sliced
1 small cucumber, thinly sliced
1 package alfalfa sprouts
4 thick slices sourdough bread
1/4 cup olive oil

Prepare spice rub by combining curry powder, cumin, allspice, paprika, ginger, cayenne, salt and black pepper. Set aside. Place each chicken breast between 2 pieces of plastic wrap and pound to 1/4-inch thickness. Sprinkle both sides with one tablespoon rub mixture, cover and refrigerate at least 2 hours.

Heat grill until medium hot and cook chicken breasts 4–5 minutes per side or until cooked through. Brush one side of sourdough bread with olive oil and grill oiled side until lightly browned.

To assemble sandwiches, place one chicken breast on untoasted side of bread, then add sliced onions, cucumbers and sprouts. Drizzle with additional olive oil and serve immediately. A cup of Black Bean Soup and sweet potato chips complete this delicious and satisfying lunch.

Winter

SIDE DISHES

Shredded Potato Casserole
SERVES 6

4 cups frozen shredded potatoes
2 cups grated sharp cheddar cheese
6 tablespoons butter, divided
1 small onion, finely chopped
2 cups sour cream
1 teaspoon salt
1/4 teaspoon cayenne pepper

Allow potatoes to sit at room temperature for 15–20 minutes before proceeding with recipe. Combine potatoes and cheese in large bowl. Melt 4 tablespoons of butter in a small skillet and sauté onions 2–3 minutes until transparent. Stir into the potatoes along with the sour cream, salt and pepper. Spoon into a greased 2-quart casserole and dot with the remaining 2 tablespoons of butter. Bake uncovered in a 350° oven until puffed and lightly browned. Serve immediately. Casserole may be made in advance and held in the refrigerator up to 36 hours.

SIDE DISHES

Country Snaps With Cucumber Garnish
SERVES 6

    50 ounces canned green beans
    3 teaspoons kosher salt, divided
    4 teaspoons sugar
    1 1/2 teaspoons black pepper, divided
    2 tablespoons bacon grease
    2 medium cucumbers, unpeeled
    1 small onion, thinly sliced
    2 tablespoons cider vinegar
    4 tablespoons seasoned rice vinegar

Drain green beans and place in a 4-quart pot. Add 2 1/2 teaspoons kosher salt, sugar, 1 teaspoon black pepper and bacon grease. Add enough fresh cold water to just come to the top of the beans. Bring to a low boil and cook uncovered until most of the water has boiled out. Do not stir the beans too often or they will break up. When done, cover until ready to reheat or serve immediately.

To make garnish, score cucumbers and slice 1/8-inch thick. Place in a ziplock bag and add onion, cider and rice vinegar, 1/2 teaspoon salt and 1/2 teaspoon black pepper. Place in the refrigerator and allow to marinate at least one hour. This step may be done a day ahead. To serve, place drained snaps in a heated serving dish with the cucumber garnish in a glass bowl beside them.

Winter

Winter

SIDE DISHES

Wild Rice and Mushroom Casserole
SERVES 12

- 8 tablespoons butter
- 4–8 cloves of garlic
- 12 ounces mushrooms, sliced
- 2 cups wild rice
- 1 cup regular rice
- 1 tablespoon salt
- 1/4 cup chopped fresh parsley
- 7–8 cups chicken stock

In large 8-quart stock pot melt the butter and sauté the mushrooms and garlic until cooked through. Stir in the rices, salt, parsley and 7 cups of stock. Bring to a boil and remove from heat. Cover tightly and bake in a 350° oven for one hour. Check after 45 minutes and add more stock if necessary. Continue baking until rice is cooked through. Serve immediately.

SIDE DISHES

Caramelized Onions with Pasta
SERVES 12

    3 large onions, chopped
    6 cloves garlic, minced
    4 tablespoons olive oil
    12 ounces fine linguine
    1 cup Provolone cheese, shredded
    1/2 cup asiago cheese, shredded
    1/2 cup Parmesan cheese, grated
    1/4 cup minced fresh parsley

Sauté onions and garlic in olive oil until golden brown, stirring constantly, about 15–20 minutes. Keep warm. Cook linguine according to directions. Drain and toss while hot with cheeses and onion mixture. Sprinkle with fresh minced parsley and serve immediately.

Winter

Winter

Pomander Balls

The spicy scent of pomanders fill the air with holiday cheer. Start by selecting your fruit such as oranges or lemons, then gather a pencil, ribbon, whole long-stemmed cloves, sturdy toothpicks, and a shallow bowl. Select ¼ cup of each of the following spices: allspice, ground cinnamon, ginger, nutmeg, and powdered oris root. (Consider substituting a few cloves with star anise.)

- Plan your design on the fruit with a pencil
- Punch holes using a sturdy toothpick or nail
- Space holes 1/8-1/4 inch apart.
- Insert cloves in the holes
- Mix spices in a shallow bowl
- Roll fruit in bowl until completely covered
- Dry for 2-3 weeks until hardened
- Tie with a ribbon for hanging or display

SIDE DISHES

Spinach and Artichoke Casserole
SERVES 10

4 (10 ounce) boxes chopped, frozen spinach
11 ounces cream cheese, softened
5 tablespoons butter, melted
1 tablespoon lemon juice, freshly squeezed
1 dash nutmeg
1 teaspoon Goldies Seasoning or seasoned salt
½ teaspoon salt
½ teaspoon black pepper, freshly ground
2 16 ounce cans artichoke hearts
¼ cup Parmesan cheese, grated

Cook spinach according to directions. Drain well and set aside. In a large bowl, combine the cream cheese and butter until smooth. Stir in the lemon juice, nutmeg and seasonings. Taste and adjust if necessary. Drain the artichoke hearts and cut into quarters. Gently stir the spinach and artichokes into the cream cheese mixture. Spoon into a 3-quart casserole and top with the Parmesan cheese. Bake uncovered at 350° for 30 minutes until heated through. Serve immediately.

Goldies Seasoning can be purchased at The Cavalier Store in Lynchburg.

SIDE DISHES

Baked Herb Tomatoes
SERVES 6

- 3 medium tomatoes, slightly green
- 4 tablespoons bacon grease or olive oil
- 1 1/2 teaspoons kosher salt
- 1 teaspoon black pepper, freshly ground
- 1 tablespoon Worcestershire sauce
- 1 1/2 cups fresh bread crumbs, toasted
- 1 1/2 teaspoons dried basil
- 1 1/2 teaspoons dried parsley
- 1/2 teaspoon dried thyme

Cut a thin slice off the top and bottom of the unpeeled tomatoes. Cut each tomato in half and place on a lightly greased shallow baking dish, cut side up. Pierce the cut portion of the tomato several times with a fork. Drizzle one teaspoon of bacon grease or olive oil over each tomato half. Sprinkle with salt, pepper and Worcestershire sauce. Combine the bread crumbs and herbs and mound on top of each tomato. Drizzle with the remaining bacon grease and place uncovered in a 300° oven for one hour or until lightly browned. Serve immediately or hold in a warm oven until ready to serve.

This recipe gives winter tomatoes a taste of the summertime. They may be prepared in advance and then baked at the last minute.

Winter

Salt Dough Ornaments

Christmas, Valentine's, Easter—when the occasion calls for traditional, folk-art inspired ornaments, this technique shines through.

Salt Dough:
2-3 cups unbleached flour
1 cup salt
1 tablespoon vegetable oil
1 cup water
Egg whites, beaten

Supplies:
Pastry board
Rolling pin
Toothpicks
Aluminum foil
Wax paper
Spray varnish

Continued on next page

SIDE DISHES

Meg's Company Beans
SERVES 4

1 pound green beans, washed and stems removed
3 tablespoons olive oil
3 cloves garlic, sliced
½ cup chicken stock
⅛ teaspoon red pepper flakes
¼ teaspoon sugar
1 teaspoon chili oil
1 tablespoon soy sauce
1 tablespoon sesame oil
2 tablespoons green onions, minced
1½ teaspoons cornstarch
1 tablespoon water

Blanch green beans in boiling water for 2–3 minutes. Drain well. Heat olive oil in wok over medium heat. Stir in green beans and garlic. Stir fry 2 minutes and add chicken stock, pepper flakes, sugar, chili oil, soy sauce, sesame oil and green onions. Bring to a boil and then reduce to a simmer. Cook 4 minutes. Combine cornstarch and water in a small bowl. Stir into beans and cook until sauce thickens slightly. Serve immediately.

DESSERTS

Virginia Jefferson's Chocolate Tarts
MAKES 12 MEDIUM TARTS

- 12 baked tart shells
- 1 1/2 cups sugar
- 1 tablespoon flour
- 1/2 teaspoon salt
- 3 tablespoons cornstarch
- 3 cups milk, scalded
- 3 squares unsweetened chocolate, chopped coarsely
- 3 egg yolks, beaten
- 1 tablespoon butter
- 1 1/2 teaspoon vanilla extract

Combine dry ingredients in double boiler. Stir in milk until smooth and add chocolate pieces. Cook over low simmer, stirring constantly, until mixture is thick and coats the spoon. This may take 15 minutes or more, but be patient. It will become very smooth and glossy brown. Add egg yolks, which have been tempered and cook an additional minute. Stir in the butter and vanilla extract. Transfer filling to a storage bowl and place a piece of plastic wrap directly onto the surface to prevent skimming. Refrigerate until chilled. When ready to serve, fill the tart shells with the chocolate filling and garnish with freshly whipped cream and a sprig of mint or a fresh flower. It is best not to fill the tarts until you are ready to serve.

Winter

Salt Dough Ornaments
continued

Start by mixing 2 cups of flour and all of the salt together in a bowl. Make a well in the center and pour in the oil and water. Mix by hand, adding flour as needed until the dough is smooth and elastic. Lift the dough onto a flour-coated pastry board and knead to an even, non-stick consistency. Working with a third of the dough at a time, roll out to 1/4-inch thickness. Cut out basic shapes using cookie cutters or patterns. To assemble layers or add details, brush each side with beaten egg white then gently press together. To make a hole for hanging, snap a toothpick in half and pierce the dough with the wide end; leave the toothpick in place during baking. Transfer ornaments to a foil-lined baking sheet and brush with egg whites. Bake at 325°F for about 30 minutes. Ornaments should be golden brown. Let cool, transfer to wax paper, and spray with varnish. Each side should receive several light coats.

DESSERTS

Brown Sugar Ginger Crisps
MAKES 6 DOZEN

1 cup butter, softened
1 cup brown sugar
1 egg yolk
1 teaspoon vanilla extract
3/4 cup crystallized ginger, finely chopped
1 1/2 cups flour
3/4 teaspoon baking powder
1/2 teaspoon salt
1/2 teaspoon ground ginger

Cream together butter and sugar. Beat in egg yolk, vanilla and crystallized ginger. Sift together flour, baking powder, salt and ground ginger. Stir into butter mixture just until it is incorporated. Line cookie sheets with ungreased parchment paper and drop cookies by the teaspoonful, 2–3 inches apart. Bake in a 350° oven for 10–12 minutes. Let cool for a few minutes on cookie sheet and then remove paper and cookies to a rack. When cool, store in an airtight container up to one week. Cookies may be frozen for 3–4 weeks if wrapped tightly.

DESSERTS

Gum Drop Cookies
MAKES 8 DOZEN

    1 cup margarine
    1 cup brown sugar
    1 cup white sugar
    2 eggs, beaten
    1 tablespoon vanilla extract
    1 1/2 cups flour
    1 teaspoon baking powder
    1/2 teaspoon baking soda
    1/2 teaspoon salt
    1/2 cup shredded coconut
    2 cups quick-cook oats
    1 cup pecans, toasted and chopped
    2 cups gumdrops, chopped (omit black drops)

In a large mixing bowl, combine margarine and both sugars. Beat until fluffy. Add eggs and vanilla, stirring well. In a separate bowl, sift together flour, baking powder, baking soda and salt. Stir into the above mixture until just combined. Add coconut, oats, pecans and gumdrops. Stir well until thoroughly mixed.

Line cookie sheets with greased parchment paper. Drop by teaspoonfull 2 inches apart. Bake at 350° until lightly browned. Remove parchment and cookies immediately to a cooling rack. When totally cooled, carefully remove cookies from paper. Store in tightly-sealed container, up to 2 weeks or up to one month in the freezer.

Use sharp kitchen shears dipped in cold water to cut up the gumdrops. Place cut pieces in a small bowl of sugar, tossing to keep pieces from sticking together.

Winter

DESSERTS

Winnie's Three-Layer Candy
MAKES 6 DOZEN PIECES

1 cup butter, divided
1/4 cup sugar
5 tablespoons cocoa
1 egg, beaten
1 1/4 teaspoons vanilla extract, divided
2 cups graham cracker crumbs
1/2 cup shredded coconut
1/4 cup pecans, toasted and chopped
4 tablespoons milk
3 tablespoons instant vanilla pudding mix
3 cups powdered sugar
3 ounces bittersweet chocolate

Butter a 9 x 9-inch square pan well and set aside. In a small saucepan, melt 1/2 cup butter. Stir in 1/4 cup sugar, cocoa and egg. Cook in a double boiler over simmering water 3 minutes or longer until thickens, stirring constantly. (If mixture separates, pour into a food processor bowl and process for 30–60 seconds until creamy). Remove from heat and stir in one teaspoon of vanilla. Combine graham cracker crumbs, coconut and pecans in bowl. Pour chocolate egg mixture over crumbs and mix well. Press in prepared pan and refrigerate several hours. For second layer, combine 1/4 cup of melted butter, milk, pudding mix, 1/4 teaspoon of vanilla and powdered sugar in small bowl. Beat until smooth and spread over chilled first layer. Refrigerate at least one hour.

In a small saucepan, melt bitter chocolate and 4 tablespoons of butter. Pour over second layer, tipping pan to cover completely. Immediately place a piece of plastic wrap directly onto the chocolate, pressing lightly to smooth top and remove any wrinkles. Placing the plastic wrap on the chocolate will give it a glossy finish. Refrigerate until chocolate hardens and cut in small, 1-inch squares. Store in airtight container in the refrigerator up to 2 weeks or you may freeze them.

Very rich with a dense chocolate flavor. Cut in small pieces as for candy. Keep chilled until ready to serve.

DESSERTS

Danish Pudding Cake
MAKES ONE BUNDT CAKE

 1 cup butter, softened
 2¾ cups sugar
 3 eggs
 3 cups flour
 ½ teaspoon baking soda
 ½ teaspoon salt
 1 cup buttermilk
 1 (7¼ ounce) package chopped and floured dates
 1 cup chopped pecans
 3 tablespoons grated orange rind (divided)
 1¼ cups and 2 tablespoons orange juice (divided)
 2 tablespoon lemon juice (divided)

In a large bowl, cream together butter and 1¾ cups of sugar. Add eggs, one at a time, beating well after each addition. Sift together the flour, baking soda and salt. Stir into cake batter, alternating with the buttermilk and beginning and ending with flour. Stir in the dates, pecans, 2 tablespoons orange rind, 2 tablespoons orange juice and one tablespoon lemon juice just until they are completely incorporated. Spoon into a well-greased and floured bundt pan and bake at 325° for one hour, or until cake tests done.

In small bowl, combine one tablespoon orange rind, one cup sugar, 1¼ cups orange juice and one tablespoon lemon juice. Brush sauce over hot cake while it is still in the pan. Allow to cool on a rack for 15 minutes and turn out onto the rack to completely cool.

Winter

How to Keep Your Christmas Tree Fresh

Make a fresh cut to your Christmas Tree. Mix the following:

1 gallon hot water

2 cups light corn syrup

4 tablespoons Clorox®

4 teaspoons lemon juice or vinegar

Toni Piggott shares this recipe from André Viette:

DESSERTS

Kakkie's Christmas Cookies
MAKES APPROXIMATELY 6 DOZEN

½ cup butter, softened
1 cup sugar
1 tablespoon milk
½ teaspoon vanilla extract
1 egg, beaten
2 cups flour
1 teaspoon baking powder
½ teaspoon nutmeg, freshly ground

In a medium bowl, cream together the butter and sugar for 5 minutes. Stir in the milk, vanilla and egg. Sift together the flour, baking powder and nutmeg. Stir into cookie dough just until incorporated. Divide dough in half and flatten into 2½-inch thick disks. Wrap in plastic film and chill 1–2 hours. Roll each disk on a lightly floured board or pastry cloth to ¼-inch thickness. Cut out with Christmas shaped cutters. Place on cookie sheets lined with parchment paper. Bake at 350° until just lightly browned on the edges, 6–8 minutes. Be careful not to overbake. Remove paper and cookies to a cooling rack immediately. Cookies may be decorated before baking with candies or sugars, however some melting will occur. An alternative method uses white corn syrup, brushed on cooled cookies, and then decorated with the candies or sugars. After the syrup has dried, it acts like glue, disappearing and holding the decorations on.

A lemon variation can be made by substituting the nutmeg with ½ teaspoon of grated lemon and the vanilla extract with ¼ teaspoon almond extract. Glaze the baked cookies with a lemon glaze made from lemon juice and powdered sugar.

DESSERTS

Christmas Gingerbread Boys
MAKES 24 LARGE BOYS

    1/3 cup shortening
    1 cup brown sugar
    1 1/2 cups dark molasses
    2/3 cup cold water
    7 cups flour
    2 teaspoons baking soda
    1 teaspoon salt
    1 teaspoon ground allspice
    1 teaspoon powdered ginger
    1 teaspoon ground cloves
    1 teaspoon ground cinnamon
    1 cup raisins, for decoration

In a large mixing bowl, combine the shortening, brown sugar, molasses and water. In a separate bowl, sift together the dry ingredients. Stir into the molasses mixture until completely incorporated. Divide the dough into three parts and wrap separately in plastic film, flattening into a 1-inch round disk. Chill several hours or overnight.

Roll disks one at a time on a well-floured board to 1/4-inch thickness. Dough may be stiff at first, but keep rolling until it becomes pliable. Turn dough often to prevent sticking, adding a little flour as needed. Cut dough with gingerbread cutter, decorate with raisin eyes, mouth and buttons and bake 13 minutes on parchment lined cookie sheets in a 350° oven. Remove parchment and cookies to a wire rack and cool completely.

Memories of past Christmases will permeate your home when you bake a batch of these cookies. They will keep several weeks if tightly covered.

Winter

DESSERTS

English Trifle
SERVES 8

1 quart strawberries
6 jumbo eggs
1 cup sugar
1 quart whole milk
1 vanilla bean
1 loaf pound cake
1 cup strawberry jam
1/3 cup dry sherry
2 bananas, sliced
1 cup heavy whipping cream, whipped

Wash and slice the strawberries, reserving 6 whole berries for garnishing the top. Set aside.

Beat the eggs and sugar together until they are thick and lemon colored, about 5 minutes. Place milk and the vanilla bean in a heavy 2-quart saucepan and slowly bring to a simmer. Stir 1/2 cup of the hot milk into the beaten eggs and then slowly stir the eggs into the milk. Continue to slowly heat, stirring constantly until the custard begins to thicken and coats the back of a wooden spoon, approximately 180°. Do not overcook or boil as the mixture will curdle. Remove the vanilla bean and split down the middle. Scrape any seeds into the custard and set the bean aside. Pour the custard into a heat-proof bowl and place a piece of plastic film directly on top of the custard. Place in the refrigerator to chill.

Slice the pound cake into 1/4-inch pieces and spread with a thick layer of jam. Top with a second slice of cake to make a sandwich and cut each one into fourths. Line the bottom of a 4-inch high, three-quart crystal bowl with one third of the cake squares. Sprinkle with a little sherry and layer with a third of the banana and strawberry slices. Carefully pour a third of the custard over the fruit and repeat the layers two more times. Dollop the whipped cream on the top of the trifle and garnish with whole strawberries. Refrigerate for several hours before serving. The trifle may be made one day ahead, but no longer.

A beautiful dessert that is a favorite with men. Any combination of fruits and jams may be substituted. Individual desserts may also be made in parfait glasses.

DESSERTS

Cherry Cobbler Jubilee
SERVES 8

> 2 pints of PICKING CHERRIES JUBILEE (P. 155)
>   or 2 (16 ounce) cans sour cherries (reserve juice)
> 18 tablespoons sugar, divided
> 1 1/2 tablespoon cornstarch
> 1 tablespoon lemon juice, freshly squeezed
> 1/2 teaspoon ground cinnamon
> 1/2 teaspoon lemon zest
> 1 pinch ground cloves
> 1 pinch ground nutmeg
> 2 cups flour
> 2 1/2 teaspoons baking powder
> 1 teaspoon salt
> 4 tablespoons butter, divided
> 18 tablespoons cream, divided
> 1/4 cup brandy

Drain cherries and reserve juice. In a small bowl, combine the cherries, one cup of sugar, cornstarch, lemon juice, cinnamon, zest, cloves, nutmeg and 1/4 cup of the reserved juice. Let stand 15 minutes.

While cherries are resting, combine the flour, 2 tablespoons of sugar, baking powder and salt in a medium bowl. Cut in 4 tablespoons of chilled butter until it resembles coarse cornmeal. Make a well in the center and pour in one cup of the cream. Mix quickly just until ingredients are incorporated. Turn out onto a lightly floured board and knead gently one or two times. Roll out the dough to fit across the top of a 2-quart shallow baking dish. Pour the cherries into the bottom of the dish and then cover with the biscuit dough. Pinch dough to adhere to the side and cut steam vents in the top of the dough. Brush with the remaining 2 tablespoons of cream and bake in a preheated 425° oven for 30 minutes until crust is golden brown. Remove from the oven and keep warm until ready to serve.

Slowly heat 4 tablespoons of cherry juice with the brandy, just until hot but do not let boil. Spoon the cobbler into stemmed heavy glass sherberts. Pour one tablespoon of sauce over each and carefully light with a long match. Serve immediately.

Winter

DESSERTS

Caramel Pound Cake
SERVES 16

    3 cups flour
    1 teaspoon baking powder
    1 teaspoon salt
    1/4 teaspoon baking soda
    1 cup butter, softened
    1 cup light brown sugar
    1 cup dark brown sugar
    1 cup white sugar
    4 eggs, beaten
    2 teaspoons vanilla extract
    1 cup buttermilk
    CARAMEL GLAZE (see next page)

Preheat oven to 325°. Grease and flour a 12-cup bundt or tube pan. Combine flour, baking powder, salt and baking soda. Set aside.

In a large bowl beat until smooth the butter and sugars. Add eggs and vanilla. Mix well. Alternately stir in the flour and buttermilk, mixing only until incorporated, beginning and ending with the flour. Pour into the prepared pan and smooth top out evenly. Rap sharply on the counter to break up any trapped air bubbles. Place in the oven and bake 60–75 minutes or until a pick comes out clean when inserted in the center. Remove from oven and cool in pan on rack 10 minutes. Turn out on cooling rack and cool completely before glazing.

DESSERTS

Winter

Caramel Glaze
MAKES 2 CUPS

    1 pound light brown sugar
    ½ cup butter
    5 ounces unsweetened evaporated milk
    ⅛ teaspoon salt
    ½ teaspoon baking powder
    ½ teaspoon vanilla extract

In medium saucepan bring brown sugar, butter, milk and salt to a boil, stirring constantly. Remove from heat and add baking powder and vanilla. Beat vigorously with electric mixer until thick and smooth, about 5–7 minutes. Drizzle immediately over CARAMEL POUND CAKE.

This sauce is also excellent served over vanilla ice cream and topped with fresh sliced peaches.

Winter

Figs in Whiskey

Kathy Muehlemamn shares this fabulous fig recipe from Chef Maurice Coscuella at the La Ripa Alta restaurant in Plaisance, France. It originally appeared in a *New York Times* article written by James Salter.

One package dried figs, Turkish or Greek seem best

2 cups sugar

1 1/2 cups Scotch whiskey.

Boil the figs for 20 minutes in about a quart of water in which the sugar has been dissolved. Allow to cool until tepid. Drain half the remaining water (or a bit more) and add the Scotch. Allow to steep a good while in a covered bowl before serving.

DESSERTS

Fresh Ginger Pound Cake
SERVES 18

> 4 cups cake flour
> 1 teaspoon baking powder
> 1 1/2 teaspoons ground ginger
> 1/4 teaspoon ground mace
> 1/4 teaspoon salt
> 2 1/2 cups butter, softened and divided
> 1 teaspoon orange zest
> 4 cups sugar, divided
> 6 large eggs, room temperature
> 1/2 cup grated fresh ginger
> 3/4 cup milk, room temperature
> 2 oranges, juice and zest
> ½ cups orange flavored liqueur (may use triple sec)

Butter and flour a 10-inch tube pan or 3 loaf pans. In a medium bowl, sift together flour, baking powder, ground ginger, mace and salt. Set aside.

In a large mixing bowl, cream together 2 cups butter and one teaspoon orange zest, gradually adding 3 cups of sugar, until it is light and fluffy. Add eggs, one at a time, beating well after each addition. Stir in the grated ginger. Add the sifted ingredients, alternating with the milk and stirring just until incorporated.

Begin and end with flour. Pour into the prepared pan and bake in a 300° oven for 1 3/4 –2 hours (Baking time is 1 1/4 hours for loaf pans). Test for doneness. Remove from oven and pour glaze over cake while it is hot. Let cool in pan for 15–20 minutes and turn out carefully onto a rack to cool completely before slicing.

Glaze: Combine 8 tablespoons butter, juice and zest of 2 oranges and one cup of sugar in a small saucepan. Bring to a boil and cook 3–4 minutes. Remove from heat and stir in the liqueur.

This moist and tender cake has a spicy ginger flavor that complements many dinner menus. It is well worth the effort that it takes to make it. To ease grating this amount of ginger, peel the root and cut in 1-inch chunks. Place in the bowl of a processor and pulse until finely chopped.

DESSERTS

Rum Cake
SERVES 15

- 1 cup pecans, toasted and chopped
- 1 yellow cake mix
- 1 small instant vanilla pudding mix
- 4 large eggs
- 1/2 cup cold water
- 1/2 cup vegetable oil
- 1 cup dark rum, divided
- 1/2 cup butter, melted
- 1/2 cup water
- 1 cup sugar

Grease and flour a 10-inch bundt pan. Sprinkle the chopped nuts in the bottom. In a medium mixing bowl, combine the cake mix, pudding, eggs, 1/2 cup water and oil. Beat for 2 minutes and add 1/2 cup rum. Mix well and carefully pour over the nuts. Bake in a 325° oven for one hour or until cake tests done. While cake is baking, combine butter, 1/2 cup water and sugar in a small saucepan. Boil for 5 minutes, stirring constantly. Allow to cool and then stir in remaining 1/2 cup rum. Remove cake from oven and allow to cool in pan for 20 minutes. Invert on rack and prick with fork. Slowly drizzle glaze evenly over cake, allowing to soak in. Serve with whipped cream or coffee ice cream if desired.

Winter

DESSERTS

Chocolate Yule Log
SERVES 12

> 4 eggs, separated
> 2/3 cup sugar, divided
> 1 teaspoon vanilla extract
> 1/2 cup flour
> 2 tablespoons cocoa
> 1 teaspoon baking powder
> 1/4 teaspoon salt
> 1 recipe CHOCOLATE MOUSSE (P.45)
> 1 recipe RICH FUDGE FROSTING (see next page)
> MUSHROOM MERINGUES (P. 324)

Grease an 11 x 14 1/2-inch jelly roll pan. Cut parchment paper to fit in the bottom and grease and flour the paper. Set aside. Beat the egg yolks and 1/3 cup of sugar until thick and lemon colored, approximately 5–8 minutes. Stir in the vanilla. Beat the egg whites in a separate bowl until frothy. Gradually add 1/3 cup of sugar and continue to beat until stiff, but not dry. Fold egg whites into egg yolk mixture. Combine dry ingredients and carefully fold into egg mixture. Spread evenly in prepared pan and bake in a 375° oven for 8–10 minutes or until done. While cake is baking, lightly dust a linen towel with a little cocoa. Spread flat on a counter. Immediately turn out cake onto towel when removed from oven. Beginning at 11-inch end, carefully roll cake, lifting and rolling towel with cake. Place on a cooling rack, seam side down, until completely cooled.

To fill and ice cake, unroll and fill with 1/2 recipe of CHOCOLATE MOUSSE. Roll cake back up and place seam side down on a platter. Refrigerate several hours or overnight. Do not make icing until ready to frost the cake. Carefully ice the outside and ends of the yule log. Use the tines of a fork to make a bark like texture. Decorate the platter with fresh cut greens and MUSHROOM MERINGUES if desired. Refrigerate until ready to use, but do not decorate with the meringues until ready to serve.

This festive cake makes a beautiful presentation on any holiday table.

DESSERTS

Rich Fudge Frosting
MAKES 2 CUPS

- 1 cup brown sugar
- 3 tablespoons cocoa
- 3 tablespoons margarine
- 1 tablespoon butter
- 1/4 teaspoon salt
- 1/3 cup milk
- 1 1/2 cups powdered sugar
- 1 teaspoon vanilla extract

Combine first six ingredients in a heavy 3-quart saucepan. Cook over medium heat, stirring constantly, until it comes to a boil. Continue to boil, stirring for 3 minutes. Cool 10–15 minutes. Add powdered sugar and vanilla. Beat on medium speed until smooth and creamy. Spread on two 9-inch cake layers immediately. If icing becomes too stiff to spread, dip knife the hot water as you ice the cake.

A deliciously rich frosting that satisfies the most discriminating chocolate palate.

DESSERTS

Mushroom Meringues
MAKES ONE DOZEN

>2 egg whites
>8 tablespoons superfine sugar
>1 teaspoon vanilla extract
>cocoa powder for dusting

Beat the egg whites until they are stiff, but not dry. Gradually add the sugar, a spoonful at a time, beating well after each addition. Stir in the vanilla. Line a cookie sheet with a sheet of parchment paper. Use a pastry bag fitted with a large round tip. Pipe out 12 1½-inch mounds, to resemble the mushroom caps, smoothing the tops with a wet finger. Fashion 12 "stems" by using a slightly smaller tip, piping to form a 1-inch cylinder. Bake the meringues in a 250° oven for one hour. Turn off the oven and let the meringues remain in the oven for 6 more hours. The meringues should be pale white and crisp.

Remove from the parchment paper and using a bit of fudge frosting or melted chocolate chips, "glue" the stem to the bottom of the cap, spreading the chocolate to the edge. Allow to dry and dust the tops with just a sprinkle of cocoa. Store mushrooms in an airtight tin at room temperature.

DESSERTS

Christmas Cookies For Man's Best Friend
MAKES 110, 3-INCH BONES

    1 tablespoon dry yeast
    1/4 cup warm water
    1 pinch sugar
    3 1/2 cups unbleached flour
    2 cups whole wheat
    1 cup cornmeal or 2 cups cracked wheat
    1 cup rye flour
    1/2 cup nonfat dry milk
    4 teaspoons kelp powder (available at health food stores)
    4 cups beef or chicken broth

Sprinkle dry yeast over warm water and whisk in sugar. Set aside to proof. In large bowl combine all the dry ingredients. Stir in the yeast mixture and 3 cups of broth. Mix with your hands or spoon, adding more broth as necessary to make a smooth and pliable dough. Knead dough lightly. Roll out half of the dough at a time, to 1/4-inch thickness and cut with desired cutters. Place on cookie sheets lined with parchment paper. If desired brush with egg wash before baking. Place in a 300° oven for one hour or until brown and firm. Cool on rack completely before storing.

BREAD

Sopaipillas
SERVES 6

2 cups flour
2 teaspoons baking powder
1/2 teaspoon salt
2 tablespoons margarine, chilled
10 tablespoons warm water
4 cups vegetable oil
1/2 cup sugar
2 tablespoons ground cinnamon

Place flour, baking powder and salt in the bowl of a food processor. Pulse to mix a few times and drop in margarine. Pulse mixture until it resembles coarse cornmeal. Gradually add warm water while machine is running. Mix just until it forms a ball. Turn onto a lightly floured board, rolling in flour to coat and knead a few times. Dough will be very soft and should be handled lightly. Form into a ball, wrap in plastic film and refrigerate 30 minutes.

Heat 2 inches of oil to 400° or until a cube of bread sizzles when dropped into oil. Roll dough on a floured surface to 1/4-inch thickness. Cut in 2 x 2-inch squares and fry in hot oil approximately 2 minutes. Remove to a paper towel to drain. Combine sugar and cinnamon in a small bowl and roll hot Sopaipillas in mixture, coating well. Cool and serve with honey if desired.

Serve these fresh in the morning with a cup of coffee or as dessert after a Mexican supper with a scoop of your favorite ice cream.

BREAD

Ro's Oatmeal Bread

MAKES 2 LOAVES

- 1 cup regular oats
- 2 cups boiling water
- 1 1/2 teaspoons salt
- 1 tablespoon dry yeast
- 1/2 cup warm water, 110°
- 1 teaspoon sugar
- 1/2 cup dark molasses
- 2 tablespoons shortening
- 4 1/2 cups flour

Prepare oats in boiling water and salt as directed. Set aside to cool. In a small bowl, combine the yeast, warm water and sugar, whisking to dissolve. Set in a warm place to proof. Place oatmeal in large bowl and stir in molasses and shortening. Cool slightly and stir in yeast mixture. Gradually add flour, one cup at a time. Turn out onto a floured board and knead 5–6 minutes until smooth. Place in an oiled bowl and let rise until doubled in size. Punch down, knead a few times and divide dough in half. Place each half in a greased 8 x 4 x 2-inch loaf pan. Let rise in a warm, draft-free place 45 minutes to one hour. Preheat oven to 400° and bake for 10 minutes. Reduce heat to 375° and bake 20 minutes or until loaf sounds hollow when tapped. Turn out on a rack and cool completely before slicing. This bread is especially delicious when sliced, buttered and toasted crisp.

A unique and tasty bread. Robust flavor with a chewy crumb.

Winter

BREAD

Cheese Bread with Jalapeño
MAKES ONE LOAF

1 package dry yeast
1 cup warm water, 110°
1/2 teaspoon sugar
1 egg, beaten
2 tablespoons butter, softened
4 1/2 cups flour, divided
1 tablespoon sugar
1 teaspoon salt
1/4 teaspoon garlic powder
4 canned jalapeños, diced
1 cup shredded sharp cheddar cheese
4 ounces diced pimiento, drained
1/4 cup minced onion

In a small bowl, combine yeast, water and sugar. Set aside to proof. In a large bowl stir together the egg, butter and yeast mixture. Combine 3 cups of flour, one tablespoon sugar, salt and garlic powder. Stir into yeast mixture. Beat until smooth and add jalapeños, cheese, pimiento, onion and one cup of flour. Turn out onto a well-floured board and knead 5–10 minutes, incorporating the last 1/2 cup of flour while kneading. Loaf should be smooth and elastic. Allow to rise covered in a warm place about 1 1/2 hours or until doubled in size. Punch down and knead one minute to smooth. Shape in a well-greased loaf pan and let rise until doubled in size. Bake in a 400° oven 40–45 minutes until browned. Turn out onto a cooling rack and tap on bottom to test for doneness. (Loaf should sound hollow when done).

BREAD

Judy's Corn Sticks
MAKES 12 STICKS

- 1 heaping cup finely ground white cornmeal
- 1 teaspoon salt
- 2 teaspoons baking powder
- 1/4 teaspoon baking soda
- 1 teaspoon sugar
- 1 cup water
- 2 tablespoons butter
- 2 tablespoons shortening
- 3/4 cup buttermilk
- 2 whole eggs, beaten

Preheat oven to 450°. Grease corn stick pan well and place in a hot oven to heat. Combine cornmeal, salt, baking powder and baking soda in a medium bowl. In a small saucepan, bring water to a boil. Add butter and shortening and stir until melted. Immediately pour into bowl with cornmeal, stirring until mixed. Add about 1/4 cup of buttermilk stirring well. Stir in eggs and enough buttermilk to make a cake batter consistency, approximately 1/2 cup. Pour immediately into hot pan up to 3/4 full and place in oven. Bake for 20 minutes until golden brown. Turn out onto a cooling rack and serve hot with plenty of butter.

Corn sticks are best when made in an old cast iron mold that has 12 separate compartments. Each one is approximately 3 inches long, 1½ inches wide and 1½ inches deep. If you do not have this particular piece of equipment, a heavy muffin pan will work.

Winter

BREADS

Country Spoon Bread
SERVES 8

- 1 cup finely ground white corn meal
- 1 teaspoon salt
- 1 teaspoon baking powder
- 1 cup milk
- 2 cups milk, scalded
- 2 tablespoons butter
- 3 egg yolks, beaten
- 3 egg whites, beaten stiff

In a 4-quart saucepan, combine cornmeal, salt and baking powder. Stir in one cup of milk until smooth. Stir in the scalded milk and butter, mixing until butter melts. Temper the egg yolks with the hot mixture and then stir into the spoon bread. Place over medium heat and cook slowly until mixture thickens, stirring constantly. Remove from heat and fold in egg whites. Pour into buttered 2-quart souffle casserole. Bake at 375° 30 to 40 minutes until puffed and browned. Serve immediately with lots of butter. If desired, the spoon bread may be made up to the point of baking and held on the counter.

A favorite in Virginia. Although a bit more complicated than some recipes, the light, creamy texture of the bread makes it worth the effort and it can be made a few hours ahead.

BRUNCHES

Creamed Eggs
SERVES 6

- 8 tablespoons butter, divided
- 1 cup celery, chopped
- 1 cup green pepper, chopped
- 1 small onion, chopped
- 1 (16 ounce) can diced tomatoes, undrained
- ½ teaspoon salt
- 1 pinch baking soda
- 6 eggs, hard cooked and peeled
- 4 tablespoons flour
- 2 cups milk
- ½ cup bread crumbs

In a medium skillet, melt 4 tablespoons of butter. Add celery, green pepper and onion. Sauté 5–6 minutes and add tomatoes, salt and baking soda. Bring to a boil and reduce to a simmer, continuing to cook an additional 10 minutes. Taste for seasoning and remove from heat.

Slice eggs in 4–5 slices and set aside. Melt 4 tablespoons of butter in a small saucepan. Whisk in the flour and cook 2–3 minutes. Whisk in the milk and stir constantly until sauce thickens.

Grease a 2-quart casserole and layer half the eggs, sprinkling with salt and pepper if desired, half the vegetables and half the cream sauce. Repeat the layers and top with the bread crumbs. Sprinkle with paprika and bake at 350° for 30 minutes until hot and bubbly.

Winter

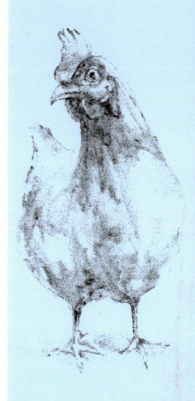

Winter

BRUNCHES

Huevos Rancheros
SERVES 6

1 1/2 pounds ground beef
3 cloves of garlic, crushed
1 small onion, diced
15 ounces tomato sauce
10 ounces tomatoes with green chilies
1 1/2 teaspoons salt
1 tablespoon chili powder
1 teaspoon ground cumin
1/2 teaspoon black pepper, freshly ground
1 teaspoon sugar
1/4 teaspoon cayenne pepper
6 corn tortillas
6 eggs
1 cup cheddar cheese, grated
1 bunch fresh cilantro
6 tablespoons sour cream
1 lime, cut in wedges

Brown ground beef in a 10-inch skillet. Remove with a slotted spoon and set aside. Discard all but one tablespoon of the drippings and stir in the garlic and onion. Sauté a few minutes until soft and return ground beef to the skillet. Stir in the tomato sauce, tomatoes with chilies, salt, chili powder, cumin, black pepper, sugar and cayenne pepper. Simmer on low for 20 minutes, stirring occasionally. While meat is simmering, fry each corn tortilla until crisp and golden brown. Drain on a paper towel.

Make 6 indentations in the meat with the back of a wooden spoon. Carefully break each egg into the indentation and cover the skillet with a tight-fitting lid. Continue to cook on low for 15 minutes, or until the eggs are just set. Top with cheddar cheese and cover to allow the cheese to melt.

To serve, place a crisp tortilla round on each plate. Use a spatula to carefully pick up each egg and the meat under it and place them on the tortilla. Sprinkle the top with the freshly chopped cilantro and garnish with a dollop of sour cream and a lime wedge. Serve immediately.

A spicy way to start the day. Serve these hearty eggs with an assortment of fresh fruit and homemade SOPAIPILLAS if desired.

BRUNCHES

Christmas Morning Buckwheat Cakes
SERVES 6

- 4 cups water, 110°
- 1 tablespoon dry yeast
- 2 tablespoons sugar
- 1 1/2 cups fine ground white cornmeal
- 1 cup flour
- 2 teaspoons salt
- 2 1/2 cups buckwheat flour
- 1/3 teaspoon baking soda
- 1 tablespoon molasses

In a large 1- to 2-gallon crock or pottery pitcher, combine water, yeast and sugar. Whisk until completely dissolved. Stir in the cornmeal, flour, salt and buckwheat flour until smooth. Cover and let sit overnight on the counter. The next morning, combine the baking soda and molasses and stir into the batter. Heat a large skillet until medium hot and brush with vegetable oil. Cook cakes until crisp and golden on both sides. Serve with lots of sweet butter, molasses and maple syrup.

These buckwheat cakes were a Christmas tradition for my family. My mother used a large gallon crock to mix the batter on Christmas Eve. As we excitedly opened presents and delighted over our Santa gifts on Christmas morning, Momma would fry homemade country sausage and cook stacks of these crispy yeast cakes. Sorghum molasses and crocks of sweet butter were the usual accompaniment to this holiday breakfast.

BRUNCHES

Melissa's Sour Cream Coffee Cake
MAKES ONE BUNDT CAKE

> 2 teaspoons cinnamon
> 4 tablespoons brown sugar
> 1 cup chopped pecans
> 1 cup margarine
> 2 cups sugar
> 2 eggs, beaten
> 1 cup sour cream
> 2 cups flour
> 1/4 teaspoon salt
> 1 teaspoon baking powder
> 1/2 teaspoon baking soda
> 1/2 teaspoon vanilla extract

Preheat oven to 350°. Mix together cinnamon, brown sugar and pecans in a small bowl. Set aside. In a large mixing bowl, cream together the margarine and sugar, until light and fluffy. Stir in the eggs and sour cream. Sift together the flour, salt, baking powder and baking soda. Add to creamed mixture, stirring until all ingredients are incorporated. Stir in the vanilla.

Grease and flour a tube pan and sprinkle half of the pecan mixture in the bottom. Spoon half the batter over the pecans and sprinkle the remaining nut mixture over the batter. Spoon on the remaining batter and rap pan sharply on the counter top to remove any air bubbles. Bake for 45 minutes to an hour, or until a straw comes out clean. Allow to rest 10 minutes on a cooling rack before turning out on the rack to cool completely. This recipe freezes very well up to one month.

BRUNCHES

Fresh Blueberry Coffee Cake
MAKES ONE BUNDT CAKE

    4 tablespoons sugar
    1 cup walnuts, coarsely chopped
    1 teaspoon cinnamon
    1 tablespoon grated orange peel
    1 cup butter, softened
    2 cups sugar
    2 eggs
    1 cup sour cream
    2 cups flour
    1 teaspoon baking powder
    1/2 teaspoon baking soda
    1/4 teaspoon salt
    1 cup blueberries, fresh
    1/2 teaspoon vanilla extract

Combine 4 tablespoons of sugar, walnuts, cinnamon and orange peel in a small bowl. Grease and flour a tube pan and set aside. In a large bowl, cream together the butter and sugar. Add the eggs, one at a time, beating well after each addition. Stir in the sour cream. Sift together the flour, baking powder, baking soda and salt. Stir into the batter along with the blueberries and vanilla extract. Spoon half the batter into the prepared pan and sprinkle the nut mixture over top. Spoon in the remaining batter and bake at 350° for one hour. Allow to cool on a rack for 10–15 minutes, before turning out of pan.

Winter

Winter

BRUNCHES

Caramel Sticky Buns
MAKES 24 BUNS

1 tablespoon dry yeast
1/4 cup warm water
1 teaspoon sugar
1 cup scalded milk
1 1/3 cups butter, divided
3/4 cup sugar
2 eggs, well beaten
1 teaspoon salt
4 cups flour, divided
1 teaspoon cinnamon
2/3 cup brown sugar
1/4 cup dark corn syrup
1/2 cup pecans, finely chopped

Proof yeast in a small bowl by combining the yeast, warm water and one teaspoon of sugar. Stir until dissolved and set aside until mixture begins to foam. In a large mixing bowl, combine milk, 1/2 cup butter and 6 tablespoons of sugar. Stir until butter melts. Cool to lukewarm and add eggs, salt and 2 cups of flour. Stir until smooth and add yeast mixture and remaining flour. Combine until well mixed. Turn out onto a floured board and knead a few minutes until smooth and elastic. Dough will be very soft and you will need to keep your hands and board well floured. Place in a greased bowl and cover with a towel. Let rise in a warm, draft-free place until doubled.

BRUNCHES

Punch dough down, knead one minute and roll out to make a 9 x 18-inch rectangle. Spread with ½ cup softened butter, sprinkle with 6 tablespoons of sugar and one teaspoon of cinnamon. Roll up tightly to make an 18-inch roll, pinching edge of roll closed. Cut in ½-inch slices with thread (see note) or a sharp knife.

In a small saucepan, melt ⅓ cup of butter, brown sugar and corn syrup. Stir in the pecans and pour into the bottom of a greased 9 x 13-inch pan. Place sliced rolls on top of syrup mixture, approximately ½-inch apart. Cover and let rise until double. Bake in a preheated 350° oven for 20–25 minutes. Place on a cooling rack in the pan for 5 minutes. Invert onto a cookie sheet lined with parchment paper or foil, allowing the syrup to drip from the bottom of the pan onto the buns. Cool completely.

To easily cut uncooked bread dough, take an 18-inch piece of sewing thread. Wrap it around the dough at the width desired, bringing the ends up above the dough. Cross the two ends, pulling the thread through the dough at the same time. You should have a cleanly sliced bun, with no pulled edges.

Orange Poppy Seed Muffins
MAKES ONE DOZEN

8 tablespoons butter, room temperature
3/4 cup sugar
2 eggs
1/2 cup sour cream
1/4 cup poppy seed
1/4 frozen concentrated orange juice, thawed
1 tablespoon orange rind, grated
1 teaspoon vanilla extract
1 1/4 cups flour
1/2 teaspoon baking powder
1/4 teaspoon baking soda
1 pinch salt

Cream together butter and sugar until light and fluffy. Add eggs, one at a time, beating well after each addition. Stir in sour cream, poppy seeds, orange concentrate, orange rind and vanilla. Sift together the dry ingredients and quickly stir into the batter, just until moistened. Fill the greased and floured muffin cups 2/3 full. Bake in a 350° oven for 20–25 minutes until done. Remove immediately from pan and, when cool, dust with powdered sugar if desired.

Ginger Dipping Sauce
MAKES ½ CUP

- 3 tablespoons soy sauce
- 2 tablespoons seasoned rice wine vinegar
- 1 teaspoon ginger paste (available in Indian markets)
- 1½ tablespoons sesame oil
- 2 tablespoons finely minced green onion
- 2 teaspoons toasted sesame seeds

In a small bowl, combine soy sauce, vinegar and ginger paste, whisking until smooth. Slowly whisk in sesame oil and stir in green onion and sesame seeds. Allow sauce to sit for 30 minutes or more. Serve this sauce with egg rolls, tempura vegetables, seafood or potstickers.

Toast sesame seeds in a dry skillet on top of the stove over medium heat. Stir constantly until they just begin to turn golden. Remove from the heat and allow to cool in the pan. Keep stored in a tightly closed container at room temperature.

All Seasons

All Seasons

Sesame Sauce
SERVES 10

 1 clove garlic, minced
 2 tablespoons sesame oil
 6 tablespoons peanut oil
 2 tablespoons seasoned rice wine vinegar
 1 teaspoon soy sauce
 2 tablespoons freshly squeezed lemon juice
 1/2 cup tofu or bean curd
 1/2 teaspoon salt
 1/4 teaspoon black pepper, freshly ground
 2 tablespoons toasted sesame seeds

Combine all ingredients except sesame seeds in a food processor bowl. Process until smooth, scraping down sides of bowl several times. Transfer to a plastic container and refrigerate up to 2 days. Serve the sauce over steamed fresh vegetables, such as broccoli or asparagus. Sprinkle a few toasted sesame seeds on top as a garnish.

Plum Sauce
MAKES 1 ¾ CUPS

> 1 ½ cups plum jam, warmed slightly
> 1 ½ tablespoons horseradish
> 1 ½ tablespoons Dijon mustard
> 1 ½ teaspoons lemon juice, freshly squeezed

Combine all ingredients, stirring until smooth. Cool and refrigerate until needed. Serve at room temperature with PICNIC CHICKEN STRIPS, egg rolls or fried won tons.

Horseradish Sauce for Tenderloin
MAKES 1 ½ CUPS

> 1 cup sour cream
> ½ jar horseradish or to taste
> ½ teaspoon sugar
> ¼ cup mayonnaise
> 1 teaspoon Dijon mustard
> 1 teaspoon season salt
> 1 tablespoon black pepper, freshly ground

Combine all ingredients in a small bowl, stirring well. Store in the refrigerator up to 2 days.

All Seasons

Cleaning Your Coffeemaker

For many of us, a good hot cup of morning coffee is indispensable to our day! Over time, though, hard-water deposits and oily residue can build up in your coffeemaker, giving your coffee an unpleasant flavor. Here's how you can keep your coffeemaker clean and your coffee tasting fresh and good:

- Once a month, fill the water reservoir with equal parts distilled white vinegar and water.

- Turn the coffeemaker on and let several cups of the vinegar water run through; turn the coffeemaker off and let it sit for an hour.

- Restart the coffeemaker and complete the cycle. Discard the vinegar water and run plain water through the coffeemaker two or three times until the odor of vinegar disappears.

- Place the carafe and filter basket in the top rack of the dishwasher.

All Seasons

Well-Seasoned Iron Skillet

A properly seasoned skillet is hard to find, and one that's been lovingly kept over the years is priceless!

TEN RULES OF SEASONING

WARM cast-iron cookware before peeling off any label.

WASH the skillet in some hot water, making sure to rinse and dry. Use soap this one time only.

MELT 1/8 cup solid vegetable shortening. Apply melted shortening onto the skillet with a soft cloth, completely coating the entire surface.

PREHEAT oven to 350°. Place skillet in oven upside down. Place aluminum foil on rack below to catch drippings. Bake for one hour, then turn oven off and let skillet remain inside until oven cools.

No Fail Béarnaise
MAKES 2 CUPS

- 1/4 cup white wine vinegar
- 1/4 cup vermouth
- 1 tablespoon finely minced onion
- 1 teaspoon tarragon
- 1 teaspoon salt
- 1/2 teaspoon white pepper
- 4 egg yolks, beaten
- 12 tablespoons butter, room temperature

In a small stainless steel saucepan, combine wine vinegar, vermouth, onion, tarragon, salt and pepper. Bring to a boil and cook until reduced by half. Set aside and allow to cool. In a one-quart microwavable bowl, gradually beat butter into egg yolks until smooth. Stir in the cooled onion mixture. Microwave on high one minute, remove and whisk until smooth. Return to microwave and continue to cook at 30 to 60 second intervals, whisking well each time. Bearnaise will become very loose at first, but as it cooks it will begin to thicken. If sauce becomes lumpy, place in a food processor until smooth. If sauce separates from cooking too fast, place in a blender and dribble in a few drops of boiling water until sauce comes back together.

Bearnaise is done in about 4 minutes, depending on the power of your microwave. It should be the consistency of a thick gravy when warm, but as it cools it will become more like the consistency of mayonnaise. Store in a plastic or glass container in the refrigerator. It will keep for 2 weeks in the refrigerator or up to 6 months in the freezer.

Spicy Steak Sauce
MAKES 5 CUPS

    1 1/2 cups Peach Chutney (p. 154), or store-bought brand
    3 cups catsup
    1 1/2 cups steak sauce
    1 1/2 cups chili sauce
    1/2 cup Worcestershire sauce
    1/4 cup Tabasco® sauce

Combine all ingredients and serve with Grilled Chuck Steak or your favorite hamburger hot off the grill with all the other fixings. Sauce may be kept for several weeks in the refrigerator.

Chipotle Mayonnaise
MAKES 1 1/4 CUPS

    1 cup mayonnaise
    2 chipotle peppers in adobo sauce
    1 teaspoon fresh lemon juice
    1/2 teaspoon salt
    1/4 teaspoon garlic, crushed
    2 teaspoons minced fresh cilantro

Finely chop chipotle peppers, leaving any sauce that sticks to the peppers. Combine the remaining ingredients and store in the refrigerator in a glass or plastic container.

A spicy companion for sliced turkey or chicken, or as a dipping sauce for steamed shrimp.

All Seasons

Well-Seasoned Iron Skillet

CARE INSTRUCTIONS

RE-SEASON after cooking beans or any acidic foods such as tomatoes.

DO NOT WASH SKILLET in soap or dishwashing detergent. Use boiling water and bristle brush to clean.

WASH immediately after use, while still hot.

SCOUR any grease buildup with steel-wool pad, sand paper, etc. then re-season.

AFTER washing skillet, dry carefully. Spray lightly with a vegetable oil, wipe dry and store. **NEVER** store skillet with lid on; as cast iron needs air circulation.

DEEP FRY in Dutch ovens at least six times prior to cooking beans of any kind, and re-season after cooking.

—Lodge Manufacturing Co.

All Seasons

Caper Sauce
MAKES 2 1/2 CUPS

2 cups mayonnaise
1 bunch green onions, minced
4–5 ounces capers, finely chopped
1/2 teaspoon kosher salt
1/2 teaspoon cayenne pepper
1/4 teaspoon catsup
pinch dried tarragon
dash Worcestershire sauce
2 tablespoons fresh lemon juice

Combine all ingredients and allow flavors to blend in the refrigerator for one or two hours. Serve with fresh fish or seafood.

Seafood Cocktail Sauce
MAKES 1 1/2 CUPS

1/2 cup mayonnaise
1/3 cup catsup
1 tablespoon Peach Chutney (p. 154),
    or store-bought brand, finely chopped
1/2 teaspoon hot sauce
1 teaspoon brandy
1 teaspoon fresh lemon juice
1/2 cup heavy whipping cream, whipped

In a small bowl, combine mayonnaise, catsup, chutney, hot sauce, brandy and lemon juice. Fold in whipped cream and refrigerate until ready to serve.

Excellent sauce to serve with shrimp, crab or fish. A delicious change from the usual cocktail sauce.

Ginger Sauce
MAKES 2½ CUPS

    1 cup mayonnaise
    1 cup sour cream
    ¼ cup onion, finely chopped
    ¼ cup fresh parsley, minced
    ¼ cup water chestnuts, finely chopped
    2 tablespoons candied ginger, finely chopped
    1 teaspoon ginger paste
    1 tablespoon soy sauce

Combine all ingredients and refrigerate overnight to allow flavors to blend.

This versatile sauce is excellent on fish or seafood. It is also an unusual but tasty sauce to serve with fresh pineapple or raw vegetables. Sprinkle the top of the sauce with additional parsley when serving.

All Seasons

How to Remove Red Wine Stains

The contemplation of a dinner guest spilling his red wine is enough to send shivers down the spine of any hostess. When this happens, here's any easy rescue:

- **Pour lukewarm water over the stain, then sprinkle it with a layer of table salt. Rub, and let the item sit for 5 minutes.**

- **Pull the stained fabric tight over a heat-proof bowl, and secure it in place with a rubber band or twine.**

- **Place the bowl in the sink, and slowly pour boiling water onto the stain from a height of three feet. The heat of the water, combined with the pressure of its falling, will take out the stain.**

All Seasons

Garden Dill Sauce
MAKES 2¾ CUPS

- 1 cup mayonnaise
- 1/2 cup Dijon mustard
- 1/2 cup sour cream
- 2 tablespoons white wine
- 2 tablespoons white wine vinegar
- 1 teaspoon sugar
- 1 teaspoon kosher salt
- 1/4 teaspoon cayenne pepper
- 1 cup fresh dill weed, snipped
- 1 teaspoon grated onion

Combine all ingredients, mixing well. Taste for seasoning and store up to one week in the refrigerator. Serve with fresh vegetables as an hors d'oeuvre or as a sauce with seafood or fresh steamed vegetables.

Hollandaise
MAKES 1 1/2 CUPS

- 4 egg yolks, lightly beaten
- 2 tablespoons lemon juice, freshly squeezed
- 1/2 teaspoon salt
- 1/4 teaspoon cayenne pepper
- 1/2 cup melted butter
- 1/2 cup boiling water

Combine egg yolks, lemon juice, salt and pepper in a blender. Combine butter and boiling water and with blender running, slowly drizzle into egg yolk mixture. Pour Hollandaise into a microwave proof bowl and cook on highest setting in 45 second intervals, whisking well between intervals, until sauce thickens. This process should take no more than 5 minutes, depending on the strength of your microwave. Serve the Hollandaise immediately or refrigerate until ready to use.

Chocolate Fondue Sauce
MAKES ONE PINT

    6 ounces semi-sweet chocolate chips
    2 ounces unsweetened chocolate, coarsely chopped
    1 cup powdered sugar
    2/3 cup half and half
    1/2 cup white corn syrup
    2 tablespoons butter
    1/2 teaspoon salt
    1 tablespoon vanilla extract

Place chocolate chips and unsweetened chocolate in a food processor bowl. In a medium saucepan, combine powdered sugar, half and half, corn syrup, butter and salt. Bring to a boil, watching carefully, and remove from heat. Stir once or twice and pour over chocolate bits in processor. Pulse and then process until smooth. Add vanilla, pulsing to combine. Pour immediately into heat-proof jars and allow to cool. Screw on lids and refrigerate up to one month. To serve sauce warm, heat in a double boiler to prevent scorching.

A wonderful sauce that becomes thick and fudge like when served warm over ice cream. It is also delicious served in a fondue pot with fresh fruit and pieces of pound cake. A must try!

All Seasons

Encouraging Moss Growth

To create the old world look and charm of green moss growth to your terra-cotta pots and statuary more quickly, you can make a "moss cocktail" in the blender by adding the following:

12 ounces of buttermilk or beer

½ teaspoon sugar

A few clumps of moss

Blend and apply the mixture, thickly, onto the damp surface. Mist the surface daily to keep the area moist, and in a few months moss will appear!

All Seasons

Raspberry Sauce
MAKES ONE CUP

10 ounces frozen raspberries, thawed
⅓ cup sugar
1 tablespoon lemon juice, freshly squeezed
1 tablespoon orange flavored liqueur

Process raspberries until puréed and press through a fine sieve to remove the seeds. Stir the sugar, lemon juice and liqueur into the raspberry purée. Place in a glass jar and refrigerate until ready to use.

This sauce can be used over fresh strawberries or as a plate sauce for tarts or cakes.

All Seasons

Mom's Biscuits

    1 ¾ cup flour
    2 teaspoons baking powder
    1 teaspoon sugar
    ½ teaspoon salt
    ½ teaspoon baking soda
    4–5 tablespoons margarine
    ¾ cup buttermilk
    ¼ cup melted butter

Sift together dry ingredients. Cut in margarine. QUICKLY fold in buttermilk. Roll out to about ⅓ inch thick and cut into rounds. Prick the top of dough with a fork. Bake at 450° 8–10 minutes until golden brown. Brush with melted butter while hot.

These are perfect with thinly sliced country ham.

                                            — *Tucker*

All Seasons

FRESH MARKET PRODUCE

	Spring	Summer	Fall	Winter
APPLES				
Mixed Varieties		❂	❂	❂
June apples		❂		
ASPARAGUS	❂			
BLACKBERRIES		❂		
BEANS				
Butter beans, Lima beans		❂	❂	
French filet beans		❂	❂	
Pole beans		❂	❂	
BEETS		❂	❂	
Blueberries		❂		
BROCCOLI	❂	❂	❂	
CABBAGE	❂	❂	❂	
CANTALOUPES		❂	❂	
CAULIFLOWER		❂	❂	
CARROTS		❂	❂	
CHERRIES		❂		
CORN		❂	❂	
CUCUMBERS		❂	❂	
EGGPLANT		❂	❂	
FIGS		❂	❂	
GRAPES		❂	❂	
GREEN BEANS		❂	❂	
GREEN PEPPERS –		❂	❂	
GREENS				
Collards			❂	❂
Mustard			❂	❂
Kale			❂	❂
Turnips			❂	❂
Swiss Chard	❂	❂	❂	
Creasy salad	❂			❂
HERBS				
Basil		❂	❂	
Chives	❂	❂	❂	
Lavender	❂	❂	❂	❂

FRESH MARKET PRODUCE

	Spring	Summer	Fall	Winter
Oregano	❋	❋	❋	
Parsley	❋	❋	❋	
Rosemary	❋	❋	❋	❋
Sage	❋	❋	❋	
Thyme	❋	❋	❋	
LETTUCE				
Mixed varieties	❋	❋	❋	
Arugula	❋		❋	
NECTARINES		❋		
PEACHES		❋		
PEARS			❋	
PEAS				
Blackeye		❋	❋	
Snow Peas	❋	❋		
Sugar snap	❋	❋		
PEPPERS				
Green Peppers		❋	❋	
Red Peppers			❋	
Sweet & Hot Peppers		❋	❋	
PLUMS		❋		
PUMPKINS			❋	
RADISHES	❋	❋	❋	
RASBERRIES (black, red, golden)		❋		
SPINACH	❋		❋	
OKRA		❋	❋	
ONIONS				
Spring onions	❋		❋	
White onions		❋		
SQUASH				
Butternut squash			❋	❋
Yellow crookneck squash		❋	❋	
Zucchini		❋	❋	
STRAWBERRIES	❋	❋		
TOMATOES		❋	❋	
WATERMELONS		❋	❋	

All Seasons

All Seasons

STEPS FOR MAKING A FLOWER ARRANGEMENT

Be Creative & Have Fun!

GATHERING

- Gather flowers early in the morning or late in the afternoon.
- CLEAN YOUR BUCKETS! They should be cleaned after each use with bleach/soap inside and out.
- Remove all leaves or unnecessary foliage that would be underwater in the bucket.
- Re-cut the stem to remove ½ inch to 1 inch of stem. Stems should be cut under running water or "under water" to prevent air pockets from forming in the step.
- As quickly as possible, immerse the stem in water to a depth of at least 1/3 the stems length. Depth of water is important because of evaporation.
- Flowers should condition "harden" 8 to 10 hours before use.

ADDITIONAL STEPS

- Use Floral Food, preservatives
- Place flowers in cool place, outside of wind to condition
- Handle flowers as little as possible.
- To *revive* a wilted, or drooping flower, condition cut stem by immersing in HOT water to a depth of 1/3 or more up the cut end. Tap water, 100 to 110°. This works especially well on roses, gerbera daisies, hellebores, viburnums and lilacs. Leave flower in water 20 minutes to two hours.
- For longevity of flowers, refrigerate or place in cooler. Use a NON-SELF DEFROSTING refrigerator, to lessen water loss.

CHOOSING PLANT MATERIAL

- For a fail-proof combination, choose blooms that are all the same color, but have varied hues.
- Narrow down your choices by clipping flowers that are opposites on the color wheel.

All Seasons

ARRANGING

- THINK OUTSIDE THE BOX FOR UNIQUE CONTAINERS!
- Look around your house for unusual pitchers, serving pieces or antique wooden boxes.
- Protect your containers by lining them with several layers of plastic. Then place floral foil over the plastic prior to adding wet oasis. A plastic bowl insert may also be used.
- NEVER use moss as a liner in a wooden container, as moss tends to drip.
- Soak oasis with punched side down, and allow it to "sink naturally"
- DO NOT SOAK OASIS more than 24 hours prior to making arrangement, to eliminate bacteria build up.
- Push soaked oasis securely into vase and tape to container. Sometimes, chicken wire will be required if using heavier branches/material.
- Leave some space around oasis so water can be added to the container.
- If using oasis, do not extend more than 3 to 4 inches above the top of the container. DO NOT CUT OFF OASIS BELOW THE LIP OF THE CONTAINER!

MAINTENANCE OF FINISHED ARRANGEMENT

- Keep arrangement away from heat and strong light.
- Change water after 3-4 days
- Remove old flowers
- Check water daily, and add as necessary.

IF ALL ELSE FAILS AND YOU WANT A PERFECT ARRANGEMENT

Bobby Shorter suggests the *following!*

1. Soak the oasis thoroughly. (This should take about 3 gin and tonics depending on the size of your glass.)
2. Have a good pair of night vision binoculars.
3. Never cut your own flowers!
4. Know your neighborhood well.
5. Always have a "roady ready".
6. Work in threes…one driver, one gatherer, and one bartender.
7. Remember the three magic words to get you off the hook if you're caught. ("Here, kitty kitty!")
8. Hope the housekeeper knows how to arrange whatever you end up with…if or when you get home!

All Seasons

Supplies For Arranging

Floral Foam, oasis (instant "dots" for faster water absorption)

Chicken wire, green coated variety, to prevent rusting

Knife

Tape, clear and green

Sharp Clippers

"Clean Buckets," jars – should vary in size

Floralife – hydration solution will increase water intake

Toothpicks/Pipecleaners

Water Tubes

Florist picks, hyacinth and bulb stakes

Floral Wire, spool and 12 inch

Scissors

Candle

Plastic "Baggies"

Florist Clay, "Stickum"

Watering Can with Spout

All Seasons

Food Gifts

Why give food gifts?

Personal – gift from the heart – "it's the thought that counts"

Don't have to find a space for it

- Always needed
- Can be creative
- Inexpensive

Types of Containers

- Look for inexpensive
- Yard sales or "second hand" stores
- Plastic bags or containers cover with tissue or plastic wrap, and tie with raffia
- Baskets – spray paint if looking shabby
- Think out of the box…teapot for Russian tea, 2 martini glasses with nuts in cocktail baskets

Storage

- Pickles, jams and some sauces hold in refrigerator.
- Nuts, cheese, spreads, granola – 2 weeks ahead
- Cookies – store each type separately. Use heavy duty freezer bags squeeze out air. Store crisp and soft cookies separately.

Index

A

Aged Standing Rib Roast 188
Agnes's Pound Cake 60
Alcohol
  Bahama Mama 84
  Café Margarita 84
  Caribbean Delight 83
  Chilly Irishman Says Goodnight Moon 85
  Dandelion Wine 19
  Dave's Whiskey Sour 85
  Hot Buttered Rum 265
  Mimosa 18
  Minted Whiskey Sour 17
  Rum Painkiller 83
  The Cocktail Bar 16
  Wine Punch 85
Almond Squares, Cissa's 131
Amaretti Nut Crunch Pie, Kathie's 125
Amaretto Filling 47
Amaryllis, How to Make Bloom Again 256
A New Leaf 54
Apple and Fennel Salad 185
Apple Cake 223
Apple Cider Sauce 190
Apple Crisp, Easy 218
Apricot Kugel 212
Artichokes, Marinated Shrimp and 3
Aspic
  Grapefruit 285
  Tomato 93

B

Baby Back Ribs 112
Baby Back Ribs with Salsa Verde 191
Bahama Mama 84
Baked Bean Pot 119
Baked Crab Dip 260
Baked Herb Pasta 42
Baked Herb Tomatoes 307
Banana Bread, Rhonda's 247
Banana Split Pie 133
Barbequed Chicken 104
Barbeque Rib Sauce, Peach 107
Barbeque Sauce
  for Chicken 111
  Pork 106
  Suck Mountain 102
Bar, Cocktail 16
Beans
  Beans and Greens Soup 176
  Black Beans and Saffron Rice 44
  Black Bean Soup 272
  Country Snaps With Cucumber Garnish 303
  Curry Butter Bean Casserole 211
  Green Bean and Potato Salad 207
  Indian Green Beans 123
  Lamb and Navy Bean Soup 268
  Meg's Company Beans 308
  Mississippi Green Beans 43
  Three Baked Bean Pot 119
Béarnaise, No Fail 344
Becca's Burgers 103
Beef
  Aged Standing Rib Roast 188
  Becca's Burgers 103
  Beef Tenderloin, Grilled 108
  Boeuf Au Pot 286
  Corned Beef and Oven Steamed Vegetables 33
  Grilled Chuck Steak 105
Beer Cheese 165
Beet Borscht 90
Beverages, also see Alcohol
  Hot Cocoa Mix 267
  Lu's Iced Tea 20
  Russian Tea Mix 266
  Wedding Punch 18
Biscuit, Buttermilk 65
Biscuits, Cheese 228
Biscuits, Mom's 351
Bittersweet, Collecting 183
Black Bean and Rice Salad 91
Black Beans and Saffron Rice 44
Black Bean Soup 272
Black Forest Cake 220
Black Russian Yeast Bread 233
Blueberries, Fresh, Freezing 230
Blueberry Muffins, Refrigerated 230
Blueberry Pancakes, David Hugh's 238
Boeuf Au Pot 286
Borscht, Toni's Chilled Beet 90
Braised Pheasant with Sour Cream and Grapes 297
Bran Raisin Muffins 245
Bread
  Black Russian Yeast Bread 233
  Bran Raisin Muffins 245
  Challah 66
  Cheese Biscuits 228
  Cheese Bread with Jalapeño 328
  Christmas Morning Buckwheat Cakes 333
  Cinnamon Raisin 67
  Cornbatter Cakes 240
  Cornmeal Waffles 239
  Country Spoon Bread 330
  David Hugh's Blueberry Pancakes 238
  Four Cheeses Focaccia 62
  Fresh Peach Coffee Cake 248
  Honey Sweet Wheat Bread 232
  Irish Soda Bread 61
  Jalapeño Hush Puppies 229
  Jammin' Muffins 235
  Judy's Corn Sticks 329

Index

Onion Dill Bread 234
Orange Swirl Sweet Rolls 246
Refrigerated Blueberry
    Muffins 230
Rhonda's Banana Bread 247
Risen Muffins 231
Ro's Oatmeal Bread 327
Sally Lunn 63, 64
Sopaipillas 326
Bread and Butter Pickle 139
Broccoli Picnic Salad 95
Brownies with variations 46
Brown Sugar Ginger Crisps 310
Brunswick Stew
  For A Crowd 173
  Virginia's 172
Bruschetta, Tomato 163
Burgers 103
Butter Cream Frosting 56
Butter Layer Cake 126
Buttermilk Biscuit 65
Buttermilk Dressing 27

C

Café Margarita 84
Cajun Seafood Gumbo 290
Cake
  Black Forest Cake 220
  Butter Layer Cake 126
  Caramel Cake 221
  Caramel Pound Cake 318
  Caramel Sticky Buns 336
  Carrot Wedding Cake 50
  Chocolate Buttermilk Cake 56
  Chocolate Mocha Cake 128
  Chocolate Pound Cake 130
  Chocolate Yule Log 322
  Danish Pudding Cake 313
  Fresh Blueberry Coffee Cake 335
  Fresh Ginger Pound Cake 320
  Fresh Peach Cake 129

  Fresh Peach Coffee Cake 248
  Lemon Poppy Seed
    Pound Cake 51
  Melissa's Sour Cream
    Coffee Cake 334
  Mile High Birthday Cake 136
  Orange Poppy Seed Muffins 338
  Pound Cake 60
  Raspberry Almond Cake 127
  Rum Cake 321
  Strawberry Shortcake 58
Canapés
  Cheese Canapé Shells 5
  Sausage Swirl 161
  Smoked Salmon 5
Candied Violets 56
Cannellini and Vegetable Soup 24
Caper Sauce 346
Caponata, Eggplant 6
Caramel Cake 221
Caramel Glaze 319
Caramelized Onions
    with Pasta 305
Caramel Pound Cake 318
Caramel Sticky Buns 336
Caribbean Chicken Sandwich 301
Caribbean Delight 83
Carrot and Parsnip Soup with
    Orange 279
Carrot Wedding Cake 50
Casserole
  Baked Herb Pasta 42
  Catherine's Tomato Casserole 124
  Cheese Fondue Casserole 71
  Chicken Enchiladas 197
  Curry Butter Bean Casserole 211
  Easy Chicken Divan 196
  Margaret's Funeral Casserole 38
  Orla's Chicken and Shrimp 287
  Polly's Pot Luck 288
  Potatoes Au Gratin 205
  Sausage and Rice Casserole 288

  Shredded Potato Casserole 302
  Southwestern Sweet Potato
    Casserole 214
  Spicy Chiles and Grits 209
  Spinach and Artichoke Casserole
    306
  Wild Rice and Mushroom
    Casserole 304
  Yellow Squash Casserole 120
Challah 66
Cheddar Cheese Chowder 274
Cheese
  Beer 165
  Cheddar Cheese Chowder 274
  Cheese Biscuits 228
  Cheese Bread with Jalapeño 328
  Cheese Canapé Shells 5
  Cheese Fondue Casserole 71
  Cheese Straws 252
  Mediterranean Cheese Spread 11
  Mississippi Cheese 251
  Swiss Apple Quiche 236
Cherries Jubilee 155
Cherry Cobbler Jubilee 317
Cherry Fruit Salad 282
Chesapeake Bay Crab Cakes 101
Chicken
  Barbequed Chicken 104
  Brunswick Stew For A Crowd 173
  Caribbean Chicken Sandwich 301
  Chicken Curry with Seven Boys 292
  Chicken Enchiladas 197
  Chicken Salad 110
  Chinese Glazed Chicken
    Wings 294
  Country Chicken Salad 39
  Easy Chicken Divan 196
  Fancy Baked Chicken 37
  Garlic Roasted Chicken 293
  Grilled Tandori Chicken 113
  Hot Chile Chicken Dip 261
  Indian Chicken Spread 4
  Lemon Thyme Stuffed Chicken
    Breast 300

Index

Margaret's Funeral Casserole 38
Mushroom and Chicken Crepes 35
Orla's Chicken and Shrimp
    Spaghetti 287
Picnic Chicken Strips 204
Rosemary Chicken Thighs 195
Southern Fried Chicken 40
Southwest Chicken and Hominy
    Stew 280
Virginia's Brunswick Stew 172
White Chili 171
Chile Chicken Dip, Hot 261
Chiles and Grits, Spicy 209
Chili 270
Chili, White 171
Chilled Beet Borscht, Toni's 90
Chilly Irishman 85
Chinese Glazed Chicken
    Wings 294
Chinese Noodles 115
Chipotle Mayonnaise 345
Chipotle Sauce, Creamy 189
Chloknik 88
Chocolate
    Chocolate Buttermilk Cake with
        Butter Cream Frosting 56
    Chocolate Mocha Cake 128
    Chocolate Mousse 45
    Chocolate Mousse Tarts 49
    Chocolate Pound Cake 130
    Chocolate Yule Log 322
    Greg's Best Chocolate Chip
        Cookies 225
    Hot Cocoa Mix 267
    Rich Fudge Frosting 323
    Virginia Jefferson's Chocolate
        Tarts 309
Chocolate Fondue Sauce 349
Christmas Cookies For Man's Best
    Friend 325
Christmas Gift Baskets,
    Ideas for 274

Christmas Gingerbread Boys 315
Christmas Morning Buckwheat
    Cakes 333
Christmas Pâté 255
Christmas Tree, How to Keep
    Fresh 314
Chuck Steak, Grilled 105
Chutney
    Chutney Sauce 259
    Peach 154
    Tomato 153
Cider, Hot Mulled 263
Cider Sorbet 224
Cinnamon Raisin Bread 67
Cissa's Almond Squares 131
Cleaning Your Coffeemaker 343
Coaxing Amaryllis 291
Cobb Salad 96
Cocktail Bar 16
Coconut, Freshly Grated 223
Coffee Cake
    Fresh Blueberry 335
    Fresh Peach 248
    Melissa's Sour Cream 334
Coffeemaker, Cleaning 343
Coleslaw Dressing 94
Coloring Eggs with Natural
    Dyes 30
Coloring Sheet Moss Green 287
Congealed Cranberry Salad 186
Cookies & Bars
    Brown Sugar Ginger Crisps 310
    Christmas Gingerbread Boys 315
    Cissa's Almond Squares 131
    Date Nut Filled Cookies 227
    Estelle's Oatmeal Lace
        Cookies 215
    Greg's Best Chocolate Chip
        Cookies 225
    Gum Drop Cookies 311
    Irresistible Brownies 46, 47

Kakkie's Christmas Cookies 314
Little Bits 55
Mississippi Mud Squares 226
Raspberry Short Bread 48
Cookie-Sheet Grass 18
Corn
    Corn Chowder 170
    Corn On The Cob 116
    Corn Pudding 117
    Corn Salad 92
    Grilled Chipotle Corn
        on the Cob 121
Cornbatter Cakes 240
Corned Beef and Oven Steamed
    Vegetables 33
Cornmeal Waffles 239
Country Chicken Salad 39
Country Layered Pâté 254
Country Snaps With Cucumber
    Garnish 303
Country Spoon Bread 330
Crab
    Baked Crab Dip 260
    Chesapeake Bay Crab Cakes 101
    Crabmeat Tarts 75
    Crab Mold 164
    Deviled Crab Meat 109
    Jellied Seafood Salad 183
    Open Faced Crab Sandwich 244
    Oriental Crab Salad 82
    Spicy Crab and Artichoke Dip 160
Cranberry Dessert Cheese 219
Cranberry Salad, Congealed 186
Cream Cheese Icing 50
Cream Cheese Tart Shells 75
Creamed Eggs 331
Creamed Mushrooms and
    Peppers 258
Creamed Zucchini Soup 86
Cream of Broccoli and Stilton
    Soup 275
Creamy Chipotle Sauce 189

Index

Creamy Herb Risotto 210
Creamy Vidalia Soup 21
Crepes, Elegant Shrimp 193
Crudités, Vegetable 9
Cucumber Aspic 29
Cucumber Gazpacho 25
Cucumber Relish 141
Cucumbers in Sour Cream Sauce 97
Curried Shrimp Salad 26
Curry Butter Bean Casserole 211
Curry Stuffed Potatoes 122

D

Dandelion Wine 19
Danish Pudding Cake 313
Date Nut Breakfast Muffins 70
Date Nut Filled Cookies 227
David Hugh's Blueberry Pancakes 238
Decorating Eggs the "Natural" Way 68
Deep-Fried Soft Shell Crabs 34
Desserts
  Agnes's Pound Cake 60
  Black Forest Cake 220
  Brown Sugar Ginger Crisps 310
  Butter Layer Cake 126
  Caramel Cake 221
  Caramel Pound Cake 318
  Carrot Wedding Cake 50
  Cherry Cobbler Jubilee 317
  Chocolate Buttermilk Cake 56
  Chocolate Mocha Cake 128
  Chocolate Mousse 45
  Chocolate Mousse Tarts 49
  Chocolate Pound Cake 130
  Chocolate Yule Log 322
  Christmas Gingerbread Boys 315
  Cider Sorbet 224
  Cissa's Almond Squares 131
  Cranberry Dessert Cheese 219
  Danish Pudding Cake 313
  Date Nut Filled Cookies 227
  Easy Apple Crisp 218
  English Trifle 316
  Fresh Apple Cake 223
  Fresh Ginger Pound Cake 320
  Fresh Peach Cake 129
  Frozen Lemon Soufflé 52
  Greg's Best Chocolate Chip Cookies 225
  Gum Drop Cookies 311
  Irresistible Brownies with variations 46
  Kakkie's Christmas Cookies 314
  Kathie's Amaretti Nut Crunch Pie 125
  Lemon Butter 53
  Lemon Poppy Seed Pound Cake 51
  Little Bits 55
  Ma's Strawberry Shortcake 58
  Mile High Birthday Cake 136
  Mississippi Mud Squares 226
  Momma's Banana Split Pie 133
  Mrs. Jones' Fried Pies 216
  Mushroom Meringues 324
  Peach Ice Cream 134
  Pecan Pie 217
  Raspberry Almond Cake 127
  Raspberry Shortbread 48
  Reese's Gateau Ganache 54
  Romanov Fruit Sauce 132
  Rum Cake 321
  Sopaipillas 326
  Strawberry Banana Nut Ice Cream 135
  Toffee Ice Cream Torte 222
  Virginia Jefferson's Chocolate Tarts 309
  Winnie's Three-Layer Candy 312
Deviled Crab Meat 109
Deviled Eggs, Rosalie's 206
Dill Pickles 144
Dill Sauce, Garden 348
Dilly Beans, Pickled 142
Dip
  Fresh Herb 8
  Ginger Dipping Sauce 341
  Hot Chile Chicken 261
  Piccadillo 262
  Spicy Crab and Artichoke 160
Doggie Treats
  Christmas Cookies For Man's Best Friend 325
Dolmades, Greek 79
Doves 200
Dressing
  Buttermilk 27
  Coleslaw 94
  French Vinaigrette Dressing 181
  John Tucker Percy's Dressing 284
  Lemon Dijon Vinaigrete 26
  Lime Vinaigrette 92
  Thanksgiving Dressing for Turkey 213
  Yogurt 80
Dried Flowers, Favorite 107
Duck Breast with Porcini Wine Sauce 36
Duck, Wild 296
Dyes, Natural 31

E

Easy Apple Crisp 218
Edible Flowers 24, 25
Eggnog Punch, Kate's 264
Eggplant Caponata 6
Eggplant Pasta, Grilled 118
Eggplant, Pickled 143
Eggs
  Creamed Eggs 331
  Holden Beach Eggs Benedict 68

Index

Huevos Rancheros 332
Mushroom Quiche 69
Smoked Salmon Hash with Poached Egg 242
Swiss Apple Quiche 236
Eggs Benedict 68
English Trifle 316

F

Fall Foliage, Peak, Preserving 197
Fall Leaves, Collecting 169
Fancy Baked Chicken 37
Figs in Whiskey 320
Figs in Wine Sauce 156
Fish Chowder 177
Flossie's Turkey Pot Pie 203
Flower Arrangements, Steps 354
Focaccia Dough 298
Focaccia, Four Cheeses 62
Fondue Sauce, Chocolate 349
Food Gifts 357
Forcing Branches, Rules for 252
Forcing Bulbs 251
Four Cheeses Focaccia 62
French Vinaigrette Dressing 181
Fresh Apple Cake 223
Fresh Blueberry Coffee Cake 335
Fresh Ginger Pound Cake 320
Fresh Herbs, Refrigerating 97
Fresh Market Produce 352
Fresh Peach Cake 129
Fried Pies, Mrs. Jones' 216
Frosting
  Butter Cream Frosting 56
  Caramel Glaze 319
  Cream Cheese 50
  Rich Fudge Frosting 323
Frozen Lemon Soufflé 52
Fruit Sauce, Romanov 132

Fudge Frosting, Rich 323
Funeral Casserole, Margaret's 38

G

Garden Dill Sauce 348
Garden Quesadillas 77
Garlic Roasted Chicken 293
Garlic Spread, Roasted 159
Garnishes
  Green Onion Fans 207
Gateau Ganache, Reece's 54
Gazpacho 89
Gazpacho, Cucumber 25
Gingerbread Boys 315
Ginger Dipping Sauce 341
Ginger Preserves 147
Ginger Sauce 347
Goat Cheese Quesadillas 78
Granola, Sante Fe 237
Grapefruit Aspic 285
Gravy 198
  Spicy Chicken Milk Gravy 41
Greek Dolmades 79
Green Bean and Potato Salad 207
Green Onion Fans 207
Green Tomato Pickle 140
Greg's Best Chocolate Chip Cookies 225
Grilled Beef Tenderloin 108
Grilled Chipotle Corn on the Cob 121
Grilled Chuck Steak 105
Grilled Eggplant Pasta 118
Grilled Tandori Chicken 113
Grilled Yams 114
Gum Drop Cookies 311

H

Hearty Green Soup 269
Herb Dip, Fresh 8
Holiday Stuffed Mushrooms 253
Hollandaise 348
Honey Sweet Wheat Bread 232
Horseradish Sauce for Tenderloin 343
Hot and Sour Soup 22
Hot Buttered Rum 265
Hot Chile Chicken Dip 261
Hot Cocoa Mix 267
Hot Mulled Cider 263
Huevos Rancheros 332
Hummus Spread 14
Hummus with Roasted Red Pepper 15
Hush Puppies, Jalapeño 229
Hydrangeas, Conditioning 64
Hydrangeas, Drying 85

I

Ice Cream
  Peach Ice Cream 134
  Strawberry Banana Nut Ice Cream 135
Iced Tea, Lu's 20
Indian Chicken Spread 4
Indian Green Beans 123
Indian Salad 184
Irish Soda Bread 61
Iron Skillet, Seasoning 344
Irresistible Brownies with variations 46

Index

J

Jalapeño Hush Puppies 229
Jalapeño Peppers, Pickled 145
Jammin' Muffins 235
Jellied Seafood Salad 183
Jodi's Watermelon Tomato Salad 99
John Tucker Percy's Dressing 284
Judy's Corn Sticks 329
Juice, Tomato 149

K

Kakkie's Christmas Cookies 314
Kate's Eggnog Punch 264
Kathie's Amaretti Nut Crunch Pie 125
Kugel, Apricot 212

L

Lamb
  Lamb and Navy Bean Soup 268
  Lamb Salad with Yogurt Dressing 28
  Lamb Sausage Meatballs 13
  Roasted Leg of Lamb 32
Leaves, Fall, Collecting 169
Leaves, Skeletonizing 177
Lemon Butter 53
Lemon Dijon Vinaigrette 26
Lemon Poppy Seed Pound Cake 51
Lemon Soufflé, Frozen 52
Lemon Thyme Stuffed Chicken Breast 300
Lentil and Mushroom Stew 23
Lime Vinaigrette Dressing 92
Little Bits 55
Lox, Smoked Salmon 169
Lucy-and-Her Shrimp 167

M

Manhattan Seafood Chowder 277
Margarita, Café 84
Marge's Split Pea Soup 278
Marinara Sauce, Summer 151
Marinated Shrimp and Artichokes 3
Marmalade, Tomato 146
May Day Baskets 10
Meatballs in Chutney Sauce 259
Meatballs, Lamb Sausage 13
Mediterranean Cheese Spread 11
Mediterranean Shrimp Pasta 30
Meg's Company Beans 308
Melissa's Sour Cream Coffee Cake 334
Mile High Birthday Cake, Nana's 136
Mimosa 18
Minted Whiskey Sour 17
Mint Filling 47
Mint Mayonnaise 29
Mint Sauce 32
Mississippi Cheese 251
Mississippi Green Beans 43
Mississippi Mud Squares 226
Mom's Biscuits 351
Moss Growth, Encouraging 349
Moss, Coloring Green 287
Muffulettas 187
Muffins
  Bran Raisin 245
  Date Nut 70
  Jammin' 235
  Orange Poppy Seed 338
  Risen 231

Mulligatawny Soup 179
Mushroom Meringues 324
Mushrooms
  Creamed Mushrooms and Peppers 258
  Holiday Stuffed Mushrooms 253
  Lentil and Mushroom Stew 23
  Mushroom and Chicken Crêpes 35
  Mushroom Pâté 162
  Mushroom Quiche 69
  Mushroom Tarts 12

N

New Leaves 54
No Fail Béarnaise 344
Nutty Oriental Slaw 182

O

Oatmeal Bread, Ro's 327
Oatmeal Lace Cookies, Estelle's 215
Onion Dill Bread 234
Open Faced Crab Sandwich 244
Orange Filling 47
Orange Poppy Seed Muffins 338
Orange Swirl Sweet Rolls 246
Oriental Crab Salad 82
Oriental Slaw, Nutty 182
Osage Oranges 174
Oven Fried Oysters 168
Oysters, Oven Fried 168
Oyster Spread, Smoked 256
Oyster Stew 276

Index

P

Pasta
  Baked Herb Pasta 42
  Caramelized Onions with Pasta 305
  Grilled Eggplant Pasta 118
  Mediterranean Shrimp Pasta 30
Pâté
  Christmas 255
  Country Layered 254
  Mushroom 162
Peach and Habanero Salsa 150
Peach Barbeque Rib Sauce 107
Peach Cake 129
Peach Chutney 154
Peach Coffee Cake, Fresh 248
Peaches, Peeling 134
Peach Ice Cream 134
Peach Soup 87
Peanut Butter Filling 47
Pear Salad 180
Pecan Pie 217
Peonies, Prolonging 40
Peppermint Candy Filling 47
Peppers
  Hummus with Roasted Red Pepper 15
  Stuffed Banana Peppers 208
Pesto 152
Pheasant, Braised, with Sour Cream and Grapes 297
Pheasant Breast 202
Piccadillo Dip 262
Pickles
  Bread and Butter Pickle 139
  Dill Pickles 144
  Green Tomato Pickle 140
  Pickled Dilly Beans 142
  Pickled Eggplant 143
  Pickled Jalapeño Peppers 145
Picnic Chicken Strips 204
Pie
  Banana Split Pie 133
  Kathie's Amaretti Nut Crunch Pie 125
  Mrs. Jones' Fried Pies 216
  Pecan Pie 217
  Tomato 76
Pizza or Focaccia Dough 298
Planting a Produce Garden, Five Simple Rules for 58
Plum Sauce 343
Polly's Pot Luck 288
Pomander Balls 306
Pork
  Baby Back Ribs 112
  Pork Chops with Creamy Chipotle Sauce 189
  Pork Roast with Apple Cider Sauce 190
  Pork Tenderloin with Apples and Mustard Glaze 295
  Spicy Baby Back Ribs with Salsa Verde 191
  Virginia's Brunswick Stew 172
Pork Barbeque Sauce 106
Potatoes
  Curry Stuffed Potatoes 122
  Green Bean and Potato Salad 207
  Potatoes Au Gratin 205
  Potato Leek Soup with Truffle Oil 174
  Shredded Potato Casserole 302
  Southwest Sweet Potato Casserole 214
Pot-pourri, Homemade 117
Potting Soil, Mix Your Own 4
Pound Cake
  Agnes's 60
  Caramel 318
  Chocolate 130
  Ginger 320
  Lemon Poppy Seed 51
Preserves
  Ginger 147
  Strawberry 148
  Tomato Marmalade 146
Punch
  Kate's Eggnog Punch 264
  Wedding Punch 18
  Wine Punch 85

Q

Quail 201
Quesadillas, Garden 77
Quesadillas, Goat Cheese 78
Quiche, Mushroom 69
Quiche, Swiss Apple 236

R

Raisin Bread, Cinnamon 67
Raspberry Almond Cake 127
Raspberry Sauce 350
Raspberry Shortbread 48
Red Wine Stain Removal 347
Refrigerated Blueberry Muffins 230
Relish, Cucumber 141
Rhonda's Banana Bread 247
Rice
  Black Bean and Rice Salad 91
  Black Beans and Saffron Rice 44
  Summer Rice Salad 98
Risen Muffins 231
Risotto, Creamy Herb 210
Roast, Aged Standing Rib 188
Roasted Corn Salad 92
Roasted Garlic Spread 159
Roasted Turkey and Gravy 198
Rosalie's Deviled Eggs 206

Index

Rose Hip Wreath 200
Rosemary Chicken Thighs 195
Ro's Oatmeal Bread 327
Rum Cake 321
Rum Painkiller 83
Russian Tea Mix 266

S

Salads
  Apple and Fennel Salad 185
  Black Bean and Rice Salad 91
  Broccoli Picnic Salad 95
  Cherry Fruit Salad 282
  Chicken Salad 110
  Cobb Salad 96
  Coleslaw Dressing 94
  Congealed Cranberry Salad 186
  Creamy Lemon Dijon
    Vinaigrette 26
  Cucumbers in Sour Cream
    Sauce 97
  French Vinaigrette Dressing 181
  Fresh Pear Salad 180
  Grapefruit Aspic 285
  Indian Salad 184
  Jellied Seafood Salad 183
  Jodi's Watermelon Tomato
    Salad 99
  Lamb Salad with Yogurt
    Dressing 28
  Nutty Oriental Slaw 182
  Roasted Corn Salad 92
  Sally's Cucumber Aspic with Mint
    Mayonnaise 29
  Spring Salad with Buttermilk
    Dressing 27
  Summer Rice Salad 98
  Tomato Aspic 93
  Warmed Tuscan Bean Salad 281
  Winter Salad 283
Sally Lunn 63, 64

Salmon
  Salmon Canapes, Smoked 5
  Salmon Moutard 31
  Smoked Salmon Hash with
    Poached Egg 242
Salmon Lox, Smoked 169
Salsa
  Peach and Habanero 150
  Salsa Verde 191
Salt Dough Ornaments 308
Sandwiches
  Becca's Burgers 103
  Caribbean Chicken Sandwich 301
  Muffulettas 187
  Open Faced Crab Sandwich 244
Sante Fe Granola 237
Sauce
  Apple Cider Sauce 190
  Chipotle Mayonnaise 345
  Chutney Sauce 259
  Creamy Chipotle Sauce 189
  Ginger Dipping Sauce 341
  Horseradish Sauce for
    Tenderloin 343
  Inglewood Road Barbeque
    Sauce 111
  Louise's Mint Sauce 32
  Marinara 151
  No Fail Béarnaise 344
  Peach Barbeque Rib Sauce 107
  Plum Sauce 343
  Porcini Wine Sauce 36
  Pork Barbeque Sauce 106
  Salsa Verde 191
  Sesame Sauce 342
  Sour Cream Sauce 97
  Spicy Steak Sauce 345
  Suck Mountain Barbeque
    Sauce 102
Sausage
  Lamb Sausage Meatballs 13
  Sausage and Rice Casserole 288
  Sausage Swirl Canapés 161
Seafood Cocktail Sauce 346

Seafood/Fish
  Cajun Seafood Gumbo 290
  Chesapeake Bay Crab Cakes 101
  Crabmeat Tarts 75
  Crab Mold 164
  Deep-Fried Soft Shell Crabs 34
  Deviled Crab Meat 109
  Elegant Shrimp Crêpes 193
  Jellied Seafood Salad 183
  Lucy-and-Her Shrimp 167
  Manhattan Seafood
    Chowder 277
  Open Faced Crab Sandwich 244
  Oriental Crab Salad 82
  Orla's Chicken and Shrimp
    Spaghetti 287
  Oven Fried Oysters 168
  Oyster Stew 276
  Sea Scallops in Saffron Sauce 289
  Shrimp and Cannellini Beans 100
  Shrimp and Cilantro Rollups 81
  Shrimp Bisque 178
  Shrimp Mousse 257
  Smoked Oyster Spread 256
  Smoked Salmon Hash with
    Poached Egg 242
  Smoked Salmon Lox 169
  Smoked Trout Spread 166
  Southwest Seared Tuna 192
  Spring Shad Roe 72
  Westport Fish Chowder 177
Seasonal Plant Materials
  Spring 6
  Summer 80
  Fall 181
  Winter 278
Seeds, Drying and Storing 237
Sesame Sauce 342
Shad Roe 72
Shortbread, Raspberry 48
Shredded Potato Casserole 302
Shrimp
  Curried Shrimp Salad 26
  Elegant Shrimp Crepes 193

Index

Jellied Seafood Salad 183
Lucy-and-Her Shrimp 167
Orla's Chicken and Shrimp Spaghetti 287
Shrimp and artichokes, marinated 3
Shrimp and Cannellini Beans 100
Shrimp and Cilantro Rollups 81
Shrimp Bisque 178
Shrimp Mousse 257
Shrimp Pasta 30

Side Dishes
  Apricot Kugel 212
  Baked Herb Tomatoes 307
  Caramelized Onions with Pasta 305
  Catherine's Tomato Casserole 124
  Chinese Noodles 115
  Corn On The Cob 116
  Country Snaps With Cucumber Garnish 303
  Creamy Herb Risotto 210
  Curry Butter Bean Casserole 211
  Curry Stuffed Potatoes 122
  Green Bean and Potato Salad 207
  Grilled Chipotle Corn on the Cob 121
  Grilled Eggplant Pasta 118
  Grilled Yams 114
  Indian Green Beans 123
  Meg's Company Beans 308
  Potatoes Au Gratin 205
  Rosalie's Deviled Eggs 206
  Shredded Potato Casserole 302
  Southwestern Sweet Potato Casserole 214
  Spicy Chiles and Grits 209
  Spinach and Artichoke Casserole 306
  Stuffed Banana Peppers 208
  Thanksgiving Dressing for Turkey 213
  Three Baked Bean Pot 119

Uncle William's Corn Pudding 117
Wild Rice and Mushroom Casserole 304
Yellow Squash Casserole 120
Slaw, Nutty Oriental 182
Smoked Oyster Spread 256
Smoked Salmon Canapes 5
Smoked Salmon Hash with Poached Egg 242
Smoked Salmon Lox 169
Smoked Trout Spread 166
Snowflakes, Six-Step 268
Soda Bread, Irish 61
Soft Shell Crabs 34
Sopaipillas 326
Sorbet, Cider 224
Soufflé, Frozen Lemon 52

Soup
  Beans and Greens Soup 176
  Black Bean Soup 272
  Brunswick Stew For A Crowd 173
  Cannellini and Vegetable Soup 24
  Carrot and Parsnip Soup with Orange 279
  Cheddar Cheese Chowder 274
  Chili 270
  Chloknik 88
  Corn Chowder 170
  Creamed Zucchini Soup 86
  Cream of Broccoli and Stilton Soup 275
  Creamy Vidalia Soup 21
  Cucumber Gazpacho 25
  Fresh Peach Soup 87
  Gazpacho 89
  Hearty Green Soup 269
  Hot and Sour Soup 22
  Lamb and Navy Bean Soup 268
  Lentil and Mushroom Stew 23
  Manhattan Seafood Chowder 277
  Marge's Split Pea Soup 278

  Mulligatawny Soup 179
  Oyster Stew 276
  Potato Leek Soup with Truffle Oil 174
  Shrimp Bisque 178
  Southwest Chicken and Hominy Stew 280
  Sweet Potato and Jalapeño Soup 175
  Toni's Chilled Beet Borscht 90
  Tucker's Soup for Supper 271
  Virginia's Brunswick Stew 172
  Westport Fish Chowder 177
  White Chili 171

Southern Fried Chicken 40
Southwest Chicken and Hominy Stew 280
Southwestern Sweet Potato Casserole 214
Southwest Seared Tuna 192
Spicy Baby Back Ribs with Salsa Verde 191
Spicy Chicken Milk Gravy 41
Spicy Chiles and Grits 209
Spicy Crab and Artichoke Dip 160
Spicy Steak Sauce 345
Spinach and Artichoke Casserole 306
Spinach Phyllo Triangles 7
Split Pea Soup, Marge's 278

Spreads
  Roasted Garlic 159
  Smoked Trout 166

Spring Salad with Buttermilk Dressing 27
Squash Casserole, Yellow 120
Strawberry Banana Nut Ice Cream 135
Strawberry Preserves 148
Strawberry Shortcake 58
Stuffed Banana Peppers 208

Index

Suck Mountain Barbeque Sauce 102
Summer Rice Salad 98
Sunday night supper, A favorite 92
Supplies for arranging 356
Sweet Potato and Jalapeño Soup 175
Sweet Potato Casserole, Southwestern 214
Sweet Rolls, Orange Swirl 246
Swiss Apple Quiche 236

T

Tarts, Chocolate Mousse 49
Tart Shells, Cream Cheese 75
Tea, Lu's Iced 20
Tea Mix, Russian 266
Thanksgiving Dressing for Turkey 213
Toffee Ice Cream Torte 222
Tomato
  Baked Herb Tomatoes 307
  Bruschetta 163
  Tomato Aspic 93
  Tomato Casserole 124
  Tomato Chutney 153
  Tomato Juice 149
  Tomato Marmalade 146
  Tomato Pies 76
  Watermelon Tomato Salad 99
Tomatoes, Ripening 149
Tomatoes, Sliced Summer 95
Trifle, English 316
Truffle Oil 174
Tucker's Soup for Supper 271
Tuna, Southwest Seared 192
Turkey
  Mulligatawny Soup 179
  Roasted Turkey and Gravy 198
  Turkey Pot Pie, Flossie's 203
Turkey, Brining 198

V

Vegetable Crudites 9
Venison 199
Vidalia Soup, Creamy 21
Vinaigrette Dressing, French 181
Virginia Jefferson's Chocolate Tarts 309
Virginia's Brunswick Stew 172

W

Waffles, Cornmeal 239
Warmed Tuscan Bean Salad 281
Water Forcing Bulbs 258
Watermelon Tomato Salad 99
Wedding Cake, Carrot 50
Wedding Punch 18
Westport Fish Chowder 177
Whiskey Sour 85
Whiskey Sour, Minted 17
White Chili 171
Whitening Yellowed Linens 123
Wild Duck 296
Wild Rice and Mushroom Casserole 304
Wine Punch 85
Winnie's Three-Layer Candy 312
Winter Salad 283

Y

Yams, Grilled 114
Yellow Squash Casserole 120
Yogurt Dressing 28, 80

Z

Zucchini Soup 86

367

NOTES